Writing:
The Nature, Development, and Teaching of Written Communication

Volume 2
Writing:
Process, Development and Communication

Edited by

CARL H. FREDERIKSEN
McGill University

JOSEPH F. DOMINIC
National Institute of Education

LEA LAWRENCE ERLBAUM ASSOCIATES, PUBLISHERS
1981   Hillsdale, New Jersey

Lawrence Erlbaum Associates, Inc., Publishers
365 Broadway
Hillsdale, New Jersey 07642

Library of Congress Cataloging in Publication Data
Main entry under title:
Writing: the nature, development, and teaching of
written communication.

Bibliography: p.
Includes index.
Contents: v. 1. Variation in writing, functional and
linguistic-cultural differences / edited by M. F. Whiteman.—v. 2. Writing, process, development, and communication / edited by C. H. Frederiksen, J. F. Dominic.
1. Writing. 2. Communication. 3. Language and
languages—Variation. 4. Literacy. 5. Rhetoric.
I. Whiteman, Marcia Farr. II. Frederiksen, Carl H.
P211.W72   001.54'3   81-15310

ISBN 0-89859-101-5 (v. 1)   AACR2
ISBN 0-89859-158-9 (v. 2)

Printed in the United States of America

Contents

Preface

The theme of these two volumes, broadly defined, might best be phrased as two questions: How can we learn more about writing? and How can we learn more about the interaction between teaching to write and learning to write?

The papers in these two volumes were originally prepared in draft form for the National Institute of Education's first Conference on Writing in June, 1977. This conference was held in collaboration with SWRL Education Research and Development Laboratory in Los Alamitos, California. The primary intent in conceptualizing and implementing this conference was to encourage multidisciplinary inquiry into writing. The intent was based on the belief that only a broadly based research effort would ultimately result in improving the learning and teaching of writing. The papers consequently represent a variety of views toward writing research and instruction; these views come from such disciplines as anthropology, linguistics (particularly sociolinguistics and psycholinguistics), psychology (particularly cognitive, developmental and educational psychology), English education, English literature and rhetoric.

We believe that to this date these volumes are unique in such a breadth of viewpoints, and hope that they will be useful in promoting multidisciplinary work on writing. The ultimate goal of such work is to better inform both educators and policy makers about the nature of writing and its importance in our society. Thus the intended audiences for these two volumes are researchers, teachers (and those who are both researchers and teachers), as well as both local and national policy makers, and others interested in writing.

Each of these two volumes focuses on different aspects of writing. Using a metaphor from photography, it is as though writing is viewed through a wide angle lens in volume one, and through a telescopic lens in volume two. Volume one explores writing in its many social and cultural variations: the papers in part one show different genres of writing serving various purposes in diverse contexts. The papers in part two explore the effects of oral language differences on the learning and teaching of writing. Writing, then, is seen in volume one in its many forms rather than in its more universal aspects.

Volume two, in contrast, centers on the more universal aspects of writing as an activity of an individual. The papers investigate writing as a cognitive, linguistic and communicative process, and discuss the ways in which such processes develop, and can be nurtured.

We would like to acknowledge several persons who helped make the publication of these two volumes a reality. While editorial responsibility for the individual volumes was divided among us, Marcia Farr Whiteman took overall responsibility for bringing to completion the publication of both volumes. Thomas Sticht, Lawrence Frase and Susan Chipman contributed to the initial planning and conceptualization of the conference. The SWRL staff provided an ideal environment for the exchange of ideas and invaluable support in the preparation of draft materials for the conference. Beatrice Cooper and Diana Thomas typed manuscript revisions under difficult pressures, and Patrick Malizio worked quickly and thoroughly to produce the subject index for each volume. And, finally, Reynaldo Macias gave timely advice and essential administrative support to the project. We are grateful to all of these individuals.

Carl H. Frederiksen
McGill University
Joseph F. Dominic
National Institute of Education

Marcia Farr Whiteman
National Institute of Education

Introduction: Perspectives on the Activity of Writing

Carl H. Frederiksen and Joseph F. Dominic

A major goal of research on writing is to help schools and teachers increase their effectiveness in providing writing instruction. One approach to this goal has been to study not only the mental processes involved in different kinds of writing activity, but also the influences upon them. Consequently, researchers have been studying how the cognitive requirements for producing and revising extended text are constrained by such influences as the *purpose* for writing, the *setting* in which it occurs, the *time* taken for writing, *requirements* for writing, and the *imagined audience* for the writing. This enterprise has benefitted from the participation of researchers with different academic training and experience. Since the relatedness of different research efforts is not always evident, we use this introductory chapter to suggest a framework that integrates several perspectives on writing as an activity.

The chapter by Emig presents a pedagogical rationale for focussing investigations of writing on the processes themselves. Emig challenges many of the stereotypic attitudes and beliefs that have long been associated with the teaching of writing. In doing so, she uses the term "magical thinking" to describe the beliefs of instructors who narrowly regard student learning as the direct outcome of their teaching. In contrast, she suggests that research and theory in linguistics and psychology can provide a basis for viewing children's writing as reflecting the multiple processes they use as they adapt to the increasing cognitive and linguistic demands of writing. She concludes that learning to write is essentially an extension of language development, and that a realistic conception of how writing processes develop in children must replace "magical thinking" in writing instruction.

The chapters in this volume contribute to such a conception as they explore many different aspects of writing processes and influences on them. The chapters also represent diverse viewpoints, theoretical assumptions and methods for studying writing. As research within several disciplines begins to contribute to a comprehensive understanding of writing processes, there is a need for better communication among researchers. For such communication to occur researchers must have a clear understanding of one another's terminology, theoretical orientation, and research methods. This volume is intended to contribute to such interdisciplinary communication by presenting a broad range of research approaches to writing.

In the present chapter we try to organize the research approaches of the various chapters around four perspectives on writing. These emphasize different aspects of writing processes and influences on them; yet, all are concerned centrally with understanding writing processes. The four perspectives view writing as:

1. a cognitive activity
2. a particular form of language and language use
3. a communicative process
4. a contextualized, purposive activity

After discussing how the research presented in the various chapters of this volume pertains to each perspective, we will turn to the question of how these perspectives might serve to organize a theory of writing and writing development. We want to begin by characterizing these four perspectives briefly.

As a *cognitive activity* writing involves the use of specific kinds of knowledge that a writer has and is able to discover in constructing meanings and expressing them in writing. Underlying and enabling this use of knowledge are a variety of cognitive processes, including: discovering or generating an intended propositional meaning; selecting aspects of an intended meaning to be expressed; choosing language forms that encode this meaning explicitly and, simultaneously, guide the writer/reader through different levels of comprehension; reviewing what has been written, and often revising to change and improve meaning and its expression. These processes reflect not only a writer's knowledge, thinking strategies and skills, but also are influenced by general limitations on a writer's processing capacities and performance.

Writing processes are also influenced by what a writer knows about *language forms* and principles for both their selection and use in different contexts, and for different communicative purposes. Writing shares much of this knowledge with oral language, but includes language conventions that are specific to written language at the sub-sentence levels of spelling, punctuation, morphology (of written words) and lexicon; at the level of sentence syntax; and at the discourse level. If written language can be said to have its own identifiable code, a person's success in learning to write depends in part on his or her mastery of the code's resources.

Another aspect of writing involves how writers imagine the *communicative* functions of their written messages. The degree to which a writer is aware of the need to adjust the content and expression of a message to its potential reception can influence a whole range of composing processes. Writers' efforts to anticipate their messages' processing demands are reflected in the rhetorical choices they make at every stage of the composing process. Learning to write involves students in anticipating the possible effects of their messages and in using such knowledge to guide their composing.

How writers perceive the *context* of their writing, that is, the *situations* in which they write and their *purposes* for doing so also influence the processes in which they engage when writing. Since most people learn to write in school, the situations and goals of much student writing are closely associated with instructional writing tasks. Depending on how and to what extent these tasks are structured, student writing will vary in its goals and functions. Situations may be relatively non-specific, emphasizing private, individually-defined goals, or they may be highly structured, identifying specific goals for the writer and approaches for accomplishing those goals. In non-school settings the contexts in which individuals write also vary in their degree of structure and specificity. These contexts might involve specific functions of written language that are defined within a writer's social and cultural group. These contexts might also have a more global function associated generally with written language use. Since the functions of written language are both continuous with and different from those of oral language, young writers, especially, have to adjust to certain fundamental differences between oral and written language. While the nature and general significance of this adjustment are open to question, the description of changes in contexts of language use that accompany the adjustment to literacy is a challenging research problem, with broad implications for our conception of writing activity and instruction.

We will now consider how the chapters in this volume contribute to an understanding of writing from the four perspectives that we have identified. We will also discuss how these perspectives might be interrelated, with a view toward building a descriptive explanation of key issues in understanding writing as an activity. We hope that the framework we develop is both accurate in its portrayal of individual contributors' viewpoints, and useful in identifying relationships among issues raised in different chapters.

WRITING AS A COGNITIVE ACT

Attempts to analyze the complex interactive processes associated with writing confront two important problems:

1. to identify component processes in writing;
2. to explain how component processes interact (they do not necessarily occur in rigid sequence, from planning to language production, to reviewing, and finally, to revising).

A major consideration in trying to understand the cognitive processes writers use and their interaction is the influence on these processes of the particular *cognitive resources* and *characteristics* that writers bring to the task. These resources include writers' knowledge, their already-established strategies and procedures for constructing a meaning and expressing it, and general characteristics of their cognitive systems, such as processing capacity, and both the automaticity and efficiency of component processes. Several of the contributors to this volume have considered these aspects in various ways, and we will try to show how they do so.

Cognitive Processes of the Writer

The chapters by Flower and Hayes and by Nold both identify a number of component processes in writing. They begin with the following segmentation of writing activity: *pre-writing* or *planning,* during which the writer plans, organizes and discovers information; *articulating/ translating/ transcribing,* when the writer puts ideas into words; and, *post-writing/ reviewing/ revising,* when the writer evaluates and modifies the text. Beyond these rather gross categories of mental processes associated with writing, the crucial requirement for cognitive research is to develop convincing sources of evidence on which to base detailed descriptions of processes that writers use.

Flower and Hayes have tried to do this for the *planning* aspects of composing, by studying the protocols of novice writers thinking aloud into a tape recorder as they write. While it is possible that this technique influences the processes used by their writers, Flower and Hayes obtain detailed records of what their subjects think about as they plan. This information is developed into a classification system with examples that illustrate the plans. The researchers were able, generally, to distinguish *plans for generating ideas* (e.g., producing information about a topic, posing problems or generating a structure for ideas, such as a summary); *plans for expressing ideas as text* (e.g., for selecting ideas to be used, for organizing information into sequential, topically-related text, planning for a reader, and using prototypic text structures to frame production. Flower and Hayes also provide examples of how *plans* might interact, either to facilitate composing or to hinder it.

The chapter by Nold focuses on reviewing and revising processes in writing. It also attempts to connect cognitive processes in translating and revising to several characteristics of language by a theoretical analysis of those processes. Beginning with a basic assumption that writing is a "solution to a complex communication problem," Nold presents a model that describes major component processes in writing, and then concentrates on their *processing demands,* particularly those related to *transcribing* and *revising.* She identifies two kinds of constraints that influence transcribing: *global plans* (that reflect a writer's conception of *meaning, audience* and *persona*) and *local plans* (that reflect a writer's knowledge about language, such as syntax, vocabulary and orthography). Her discussion highlights an interesting aspect of text production, namely, the interplay it requires between a writer's *global* structure of discourse and *local* production of sentences. Nold also identifies specific constraints on the transcribing process, such as *word choice, selection of propositions* and the *syntax* required to produce them, and management of *reference,* as well as other cohesive features. Her analysis recognizes different kinds of language knowledge associated with these processes, as well as the writer's need to form a conception of *the reader,* of the writer's *persona* and the *discourse content.*

Nold discusses *revising,* not as a subprocess that is similar to planning, transcribing and reviewing, but as a *retranscribing* of text *already produced.* Thus, she suggests that revising involves very different processes from those of reviewing. She then illustrates certain limitations associated with faulty assumptions about revising processes. This she does by discussing a study of revision carried out by the National Assessment of Educational Progress and some of its questionable assumptions about revising. Nold suggests that those assumptions might have been more accurately framed as follows: that revision is more than a *one-time process* that occurs at the end of a writing session; that difficulty of task *does* affect the revising process; and that *the text* should not be the *only* source of evidence used to analyze revising behaviors. Unlike translating processes that are most difficult to study directly, revising tasks appear to offer a potentially informative environment in which to study their component processes.

Cognitive System Constraints on Writing Processes

Like Nold, Scardamalia asks how characteristics of a writer's cognitive system could influence component processes in writing. Both chapters raise a very important problem for children, namely, that writing requires them to use so many interdependent skills. Given our limited capacities for processing information, we tend to adopt strategies that reduce the processing demands of writing. One way that we do this is by developing regularized (routinized) subprocesses, such as standard phrasing and methods of organization. Scardamalia argues that children construe writing tasks in different ways and that these reflect their capacity to coordinate several units of information simultaneously. She also discusses her finding that beginning writers do not plan or review. In this context she cites Flavell's assumption that planning and reviewing processes are late in developing, because for young children writing tasks are difficult enough without them.

Scardamalia classifies different writing tasks by level, according to the number of ideas that must be coordinated or integrated. She was able to categorize what the children in her study wrote on the basis of its complexity, as well as the maximum number of ideas coordinated. Her study takes an important step toward determining how developmental limits on capacity constrain written production. At this time, though, it is uncertain whether we can appropriately think of children's writing as limited by *general cognitive characteristics* (such as capacity) which increase with age, or rather as reflecting children's increasing *knowledge* of language structures and efficiency in using them. To answer this question will require more detailed analysis of specific discourse characteristics of children's writing.

Writers' Knowledge

In research on text *comprehension* much attention has been given to how readers use their prior knowledge in understanding text. In *writing,* however, little attention has been given to how writers use their knowledge to construct intended meanings. In this volume the chapter by Flower and Hayes describes research aimed at trying to understand the *plans* that writers use for *operating* on knowledge. This particular use of plans, however, is dealt with in general procedural terms, with little reference to the structures of knowledge being expressed. The chapter by Young discusses the problems of selecting and organizing knowledge in more specific terms that reflect the interaction of content knowledge with processes of discovery in composing. He discusses certain kinds of scientific or analytical writing, for example, to illustrate how writers can discover and resolve problems related to text content. Citing Von Frisch's description of how bees perceive color, Young explains how Von Frisch's discovery of inconsistencies in his own knowledge led to the discovery of the essential problems he was confronting. This illustration reinforces Young's argument that writers can use highly systematic procedures for acquiring knowledge as they write. That is, they enhance their *comprehension* of a subject even as they write about it. Further research in this area might be especially productive if it involved contrasting such specific descriptions of knowledge use in different kinds of writing tasks or among persons at different levels of writing development.

Writers' Strategies and Procedures

In addition to their knowledge inventories and multiple strategies for using them, writers also approach composing problems with a repertory of stereotypic procedures and strategies that they can employ routinely. For instance, they might have routine planning procedures, such as making certain kinds of outlines, or routine procedures for expressing relationships among items. It might be the case that experienced writers develop a large repertory of routine procedures and strategies that enable a great variety of expression with little effort. In this context an important issue is whether routine procedures and strategies enable such variety by reducing the complexity of the composing process. Presumably, there is some balance between writers' use of procedures that have general applicability and their need to employ those that are appropriate to specific writing situations or genres.

Several questions arise that illustrate how complex the many relationships are among composing procedures. What are the specific composing procedures that writers acquire? How are these procedures used? How does the use of highly automatic procedures affect other aspects of the writer's planning and writing? These issues are discussed in Read's chapter on the probable relationships among writing and reading. Claiming that the two are not related *inversely,* Read focuses on children's spelling. He documents how children can shift in surprising ways from invented, non-standard spelling to standard spelling. Children's invented spellings are shown to be highly organized, but not routinized, procedures. However interesting this shift is in itself, of greater interest is the inconsistency in some children who read printed words in standard spelling with ease but invent spellings ingeniously when they write the same words. Children at early ages seem to acquire different *procedures* for recognizing and producing printed words. Furthermore, the lack of correlation of levels of children's reading and writing performance might reflect, in part, differences in the automaticity of component processes at the *word* level. Read's study also exemplifies an approach that can be used to study the acquisition and use of procedures for producing higher-level units of written language.

WRITING AS A FORM OF LANGUAGE

Research on writing-as-activity must confront two large questions about language structure and use. First, what *knowledge of language structures and their use* must writers acquire, and how does this knowledge of what Shuy calls different language systems in writing develop? Second, what are the *linguistic characteristics* of the writing children and adults produce at different levels of writing development? Partial answers to these questions might enable more focused studies of how writers use their knowledge of language. Such answers could also contribute greatly to a normative description of writing development. In the following discussion we refer to those aspects of chapters that deal with these questions.

The Linguistic Knowledge of Writers

Shuy's chapter focuses on the knowledge of language systems that developing writers need to acquire. He approaches this topic in two ways: first, by identifying different levels of knowledge about language that are involved in writing, and second, by examining how these might have differential rates of development. Drawing on hypothetical learning models from the fields of second language learning and reading development, Shuy identifies five language systems relevant to writing: *spelling and punctuation, morphology, lexicon, syntax,* and *written discourse.* He suggests that learning to write in one's native tongue involves early development of spelling, punctuation and morphology, while syntactic development occurs later as children master the syntax associated particularly with written expression. Shuy suggests that the most important area of writing development is likely to be that which occurs at the level of written discourse. He emphasizes the origins of discourse units in oral conversational language and then presents a developmental characterization of what linguistic knowledge writers need at the discourse level. To characterize language knowledge at the discourse level it will be necessary to draw on a number of areas of linguistic inquiry including: semantics; pragmatics; analyses of conversational discourse, and of discourse cohesion (e.g., anaphoric referring devices, conjunction and lexical cohesion), organization (e.g., foregrounding, sequencing) and propositional structure; and sociolinguistic study of language variation (genres, registers and dialects). These areas illustrate the richness that is possible in characterizations of writers' language development and of writing instruction.

Characteristics of Children's Writing

One empirical approach to children's written language development is to focus on characterizing the linguistic features of their writing. Having thorough linguistic accounts of language differences in children's writing at different levels of writing development (or expertise as writers) would permit sharpened inquiry into their language knowledge and use. The chapter by Gundlach reflects his interest in both the writing of children and the cognitive processes that underlie the use of language forms. He reviews studies of characteristics of children's writing that reveal how they use elements of at least three different language systems: *orthography, syntax,* and *discourse.* At the orthographic level, Gundlach, like Read, concludes that there is a shift from idiosyncratic rules to standard orthography. He raises the question: does early writing reflect lack of knowledge of English orthography, or failure to use this linguistic knowledge (a process explanation)? He concludes that both *linguistic* and *cognitive* factors enter into the explanation. Moreover, this principle is reflected in children's use of other language systems as well.

As children develop capacities for writing discourse, they also tend to write sentences that are longer and more complex; however, the complexity of the written syntax varies considerably. One possible explanation for this is that the dominance of oral language produces a *crossover effect* as children shift from producing more complex sentences in oral language to more complex syntax in writing. How changes in children's syntactic knowledge influence this shift is uncertain, but there does appear to be change in the ease with which children are able to use syntactic structures in writing discourse. From recent research at the discourse level, a clearer picture is beginning to emerge of how children acquire their knowledge of discourse-level language systems. That is, they produce discourse of increasing length and complexity together with increasing structural variation. Additional work in this area needs to focus on what children learn about discourse-level language structures, how their knowledge develops, and what cognitive processes govern their use of these structures.

Use of Linguistic Knowledge in the Composing Process

The chapter by Bartlett and Scribner reports on a study of how children use a particular kind of discourse-level knowledge, namely, knowledge of referring devices, and their resourcefulness in doing so. The study combines three kinds of analyses:

1. a system for classifying linguistic referring devices based on *usage* (introductory or phoric), *linguistic form* (e.g., a definite noun or pronoun), *wording* (e.g., new or repeated words), and *location of referent* (in prior text, following text or extralinguistic situation);
2. an analysis of the component processes evident in the ways children construct referring expressions such as *assessing location of a referent* and *selecting a referring device* to indicate the domain of search to the reader; and
3. an investigation of *different discourse contexts.*

One way of viewing the connection between the study of writing as language and as cognitive process is to focus on the nature of *cognitive demands* on the writer, i.e., the requirements writing tasks and language use impose on the writer. But comprehensive analysis of the cognitive demands of writing hinges on the ability to identify accurately the complex relationship between the writer's linguistic resources and the various processing requirements of composing. Furthermore, all cognitive demands associated with producing written language are constrained by context, as well as by the specific writing task, purpose or problem. Bartlett and Scribner have tried to illustrate this by showing how the use of referring expressions in text require particular cognitive processes and strategies that are context-specific.

The article by Gundlach draws on the work of Vygotsky in suggesting that the cognitive demands of writing are similar to those required by other symbol-making activities. He notes that writing might be similar to (i.e., *continuous with*) symbolic activities in pretend play, drawing and storytelling, and dissimilar to (i.e., *discontinuous with*) conversational language that shares common language systems, but that differs in its social interactional support for sustained language production. While writing undoubtedly develops out of both kinds of activities and involves features of both, the contrast illustrates cognitive considerations that necessarily enter into any description of writing development as language development.

WRITING AS A COMMUNICATIVE PROCESS

In the last two sections we have discussed briefly how writers' cognitive processes and characteristics can enable and constrain their use of knowledge and procedures when composing. Another focus of these sections is how writers use linguistic knowledge and how that knowledge seems to be reflected in the characteristics of their written texts. In both of these approaches the papers that we cite also acknowledge as important topics the *context* or *situation* for writing and the *audience* addressed. But the papers do not address these topics directly. The last two perspectives on writing that we will consider, then, are *communication* and *context*. In this section we discuss how the particular chapters analyze different demands on writing activity that are attributable to its communicative functions.

Writing tends to occur within a communicative framework that involves the writer, the message, the shaping of the *message* to accord with how the writer perceives its reception, sometimes a real *audience,* and sometimes a response to the message. Writers communicate effectively when they construct their intended messages in ways that enable efficient and accurate comprehension. Within this rhetorical framework several basic questions can be asked about the writer's communicative awareness and how this constrains writing processes:

1. How do writers' conceptions of particular communicative demands influence the rhetorical and linguistic choices they make in signalling their intended message?
2. How do writers use linguistic devices to insure that their text enables appropriate inferences by the reader?
3. What are the characteristics of written messages that result in their communicative effects on the reader?

The chapters that we discuss in the following section deal with these issues directly and indirectly.

Communicative Decisions in Writing

The field of rhetoric has produced considerable theory about the characteristics of communicative decision-making. In the chapter by Lloyd-Jones, for example, rhetoric is characterized as "...the study of effective choices among linguistic and discursive alternatives." Lloyd-Jones explains how the different levels of choices that writers have to make involve decisions about what forms of language to use, with options ranging from lexicon to dialects, styles and discourse forms. He suggests that two overlapping notions govern these kinds of decisions by writers: *policy* and *purpose*. Policy is described as a person's different sets of value systems which include principles that guide thought, habits of thought, and motives for communicating. Purpose, as Lloyd-Jones points out, is "more conscious and situation-specific than the general policy." *Purpose* can incorporate different aspects of the writer's *policy* with respect to the topic being written about.

It is the interaction of policy with purpose that enables the writer to establish a *voice-role* within a particular text. As Lloyd-Jones suggests, *voice,* though an elusive construct, is generally reflected in those features of discourse that signal the writer's relationship to both topic and intended audience. The relationships among *policy, purpose* and *voice* constitute an important research focus if we are to pursue basic inquiry into the rhetorical features of written discourse. Cognitive research in this area could make contributions to the theory already established by the field of rhetoric.

Underlying the writer's ability to implement individual *policies* in written communication are the cognitive processes that are reflected in the writer's rhetorical and linguistic choices. Green and Morgan explore this process of choosing language forms to express specific intentions. Their discussion works toward explaining how levels of *communicative competence* are reflected in young writers' ability to estimate the levels of inference required to read what they write. This ability, they suggest, involves an awareness of differences between oral and written communication and, specifically:

1. *channel differences,* such as stress, intonation, gesture and facial expression;
2. *communicative differences,* such as the absence of pragmatic features that are present in oral communication (e.g., the speaker's knowledge of what a listener does and does not know);
3. *permanence* of the message in written communication;
4. the requirement that a writer *compensate* for a reader's unavailability for immediate feedback, by anticipating the reader's comprehension problems, prior knowledge and likely inferences.

These illustrate the rather full extent to which writers' conceptions of how readers might comprehend their writing could constrain different phases of the writing process.

Choice of Linguistic Devices

A recurring problem for the writer is how to select and use language devices that will enable the reader to comprehend the message. Green and Morgan observe that certain of these devices are selected as a matter of convention in particular communicative settings (e.g., dialect, register, and discourse types or genres). Writers also choose other language devices to express their intentions. Examples are anaphoric (i.e., referring) devices, conversational implicatures (i.e., the logical and pragmatic relations between sentences), devices to signal topical organization and purpose, and explicitness (to establish unambiguous contexts for interpretation). Lloyd-Jones' notion of how the writer's *policy* might govern these kinds of decisions suggests a direction for research that would study the writer's choice-making strategies in terms of how these derive from an awareness of context, purpose, and the communicative demands of the writer-audience relationship.

Communicative Effectiveness

The chapters by Hirsch and Harrington and by Frase discuss the results of different research projects aimed at understanding and describing how different qualities of writing elicit judgments from adult readers about a text's general effectiveness. Hirsch and Harrington have been studying how lexical and grammatical alterations in writing influence judgments about its *inherent communicative effectiveness.* Valid judgments of effective writing, in their view, depend on the stability of a text's meaning for different intended audiences, as well as its communicative efficiency. Thus it is important to determine how judgments about the quality of written text depend on its ability to convey the writer's intended meaning to a generally competent group of readers. This research is designed around expert revision of original student writing so that it is *semantically equivalent* to but more *readable* than the original. Relative reading times are established for the separate texts to assess their inherent communicative effectiveness.

Still in an exploratory stage, this work is providing some useful insight into revising processes and their consequences for readers. One recent finding of considerable importance is the impact of culture-based knowledge on the reader's ability to comprehend written information efficiently. Another productive aspect of Hirsch and Harrington's work is the use of expert-novice contrasts, a technique that has yielded promising results in research on problem-solving. The contrastive framework they have devised might provide opportunities for analyzing differences in decisions that expert and novice writers make when trying to convey similar meaning.

Frase reports on several small-scale studies that were designed to elicit the features of good writing in technical documents. The research, like that of Hirsch & Harrington, used experimental approaches to study how different features of text design altered raters' judgments about a text's communicative effectiveness. Unlike Hirsch and Harrington's work, much of this research concentrated on readers' reactions and judgments at the *sentence level*. The technique used by Frase was to change the appearance of text on the page by enumerating structural components and by segmenting units of meaning. To facilitate meaning he shortened sentences and clarified wording and referents.

Frase's research encountered some typical problems with rater reliability for judgments about text quality. Best results seem to have occurred when raters were able to make *comparisons* between specific sentences. Ratings of single texts were not satisfactory. Studies 1 and 2, however, did produce results that illustrate how subjective ratings of a text's effectiveness can be used to identify features that are important to its comprehension. Overall, the work described by Frase and by Hirsch and Harrington provides a useful framework for applying the construct of *communicative effectiveness* in judgments about text.

WRITING AS A CONTEXTUAL ACTIVITY

The final perspective on writing-as-activity to be taken up in this chapter is that of *context*. The context or *situation* in which a person writes can exert a strong influence on writing processes. The writer's perception and interpretation of the situation can influence the purpose for writing as well as the writer's awareness of what function the writing will serve. A particular situation can also influence how writers perceive relevant information, how they construct meaning, and how they determine the distance they want the written *voice* to have from the topic, the message and the audience. Situations can be very specific, as when in school there are structured pre-writing tasks that create the specific writing environment for students. In other classroom situations, for example, where students write solely for response by other students, there is a social context that strongly defines the functions of the writing as well. In still other instances, particularly with expressive or more personalized writing, students define their own contexts as they write.

Research in oral language use has provided some evidence for the psychological reality of *situations*. For example, there is abundant evidence that language usage varies systematically in objectively different task situations. Much of this research, however, only addresses indirectly questions about the psychological nature of contextual effects. Other kinds of research have focused more directly on how contexts influence processes in language production. For example, analyses of discourse produced under different situations (such as task-oriented dialogues) have shown that situations may be represented explicitly in the conversational discourse people produce. While research in writing has not focused directly on how context influences writing processes, work such as that reported by Flower and Hayes could lead to a powerful and direct method for studying how different situations affect writers' decisions. To be studied effectively, though, situations would have to be viewed in relation to the *purposes* writers adopt as they compose, the *problems* that they think they solve as they write, and the *functions* they imagine their writing would serve.

With the exception of the chapters by Flower and Hayes, and Young, references to context, purpose and function are very general in this volume. Also, these references are not the result of directly focused research. *Purpose* and *function,* for example, are dealt with theoretically in Lloyd-Jones' discussion of choice-making. Greene and Morgan also deal with these aspects as specific functions associated with different language registers. Where individual chapters discuss variations in *context,* they do so either by noting specific contexts in which writing is done, or by emphasizing a very general contrast between private, solitary, *decontextualized* uses of writing and *social* uses.

In very different ways, the chapters by Healy and by Olson and Torrance focus on context, purpose and functions of written language. These two chapters, as well as those by Scribner and Cole and Cook-Gumperz and Gumperz in Volume I, deal variously with three kinds of questions about writing as a contextualized activity:

1. How can we define the different functions of writing?
2. What relationships are there between the contexts of writing and its various functions?
3. How do context and function in writing situations constrain the writer's cognitive processes?

There is considerable disagreement among researchers over the possible answers to these questions. There are, in fact, contrasting positions on each issue, and these derive largely from perceived differences between the processes of oral and written language.

Functions of Written Language

Olson and Torrance approach the question of functions of writing by contrasting written and oral language. Their theoretical framework derives from historical and cultural arguments, and is essentially *developmental;* that is, children become fully literate as they confront and master the requirements of written communication. These *new* requirements are a direct result of (1) *a realignment of functions* in written language, and (2) a shift to *autonomous text.* Olson and Torrance explain their assumptions about how oral and written language differ in function, context and cognitive consequences for different children. With respect to language functions, they maintain that oral language combines many different functions, including interpersonal and ideational functions. These become differentiated and specialized for written language, as it comes to have the exclusive function of maintaining *logical relations within and between sentences.* These ideational functions appear to develop later than interpersonal functions of language, which the beginning writer has to learn to subordinate and realign to communicate successfully. To do so requires placing the recipient at some communicative and social distance from the writer. In addition to the realignment of functions that writing demands, Olson and Torrance view the autonomous nature of written language as an important difference between speaking and writing. The relative permanence of the document differentiates *what was said* from *what was meant,* as well as the speaker from the listener/reader. For children, recognizing this difference is the first step to developing written literacy. The next step, according to the authors, is the more difficult, which is to write sentences that carry intended meaning. The difficulty for the young writer involves the effort required to *conventionalize lexical and syntactic meaning.*

Scribner and Cole (Vol. 1), however, suggest that these kinds of distinctions are most useful when applied to a restricted model of the writing process, namely, the literate essay and essayist technique as a prototype for written language. Their ethnographic study of the Vai culture in Africa led to the identification of various functions served by writing done in different contexts. They were able to document the regular use of three different written languages (Vai script, Arabic and English), each serving a function different from the others. While studies of writing anywhere in North America probably would not yield such dramatic differences, a more refined picture of the different functions of writing would provide a more solid basis for investigating the cognitive requirements of written language.

The chapter by Healy provides an instructional perspective on different functions of writing in school and the consequences for student writers. She reports on a project designed to have seventh grade students encounter writing situations that would enable a variety of functions for the written products. The students used writing in several different academic subjects mainly in the expressive mode. That is, they wrote to explore different uses of information, to acquire new knowledge about the problem being explored, and to express ideas in a variety of written formats. The students also responded to one another's writing. Thus, the writing was intended to serve a variety of active learning functions and to stimulate many different kinds of inquiry and discovery. Though this was not a controlled study, careful observation by the teachers produced claims that the students had a more positive attitude toward writing, that they had less difficulty writing for different audiences, and that they revised more purposefully.

Contexts of Writing

Contexts are explicitly connected to functions of written language in virtually all discussions of language function in this volume, but in different ways. Olson and Torrance, for example, describe how school contexts function to gradually establish written text as *disconnected* from the immediate contexts of students' lives. They argue that written language in school becomes autonomous, as its meaning becomes independent of the social contexts familiar to students in their oral language uses. Cook-Gumperz and Gumperz (Vol. 1) tend to share the view that *decontextualization* of meaning is a dominant aspect of literate cultures.

On the other hand, the project described by Healy was an effort to see what happens to student writing when it is not done for the teacher, but primarily for the writer and peers. Students wrote regularly, exploring subject areas in social studies, mathematics and English. Students wrote as a way of informing themselves and their peers about the different ways that knowledge can be discovered and applied through writing. Because the contexts for writing were determined largely by the students, the writing had more immediacy and served personally useful goals.

Scribner and Cole (Vol. 1) also emphasized the importance of context in establishing different functions and uses of written language. Their study of Vai literacies demonstrated that different writing systems had become specialized both in functions and contexts of use. The results of that study suggest the need for research on the variety of contexts that influence writing activity in different arenas of American life. Such research might also contribute theory for writing instruction. The difference between Olson and Nickerson's explanation of writing as a decontextualized activity and Scribner and Cole's theories about the importance of context is related to how restricted or inclusive a view of written language one adopts. The literate-essay-as-prototype is certainly one dominant type of writing, especially in secondary and postsecondary education. Its distinct characteristics might be consistent with its often decontextualized functions. However, if one adopts a broad view of written language, it is the multifunctionality of written language that impresses. If research is to contribute eventually to writing instruction, it seems important that both of these perspectives be studied.

Cognitive Consequences of Written Language

Another aspect of Olson and Torrance's perspective is that the transition to autonomous written text entails a fundamental developmental shift in children. Their early *pragmatic interpretation* of language is controlled by the immediate knowledge their communicative situation presents to them. At a later stage of development their interpretations are restricted to sentence meanings and confined to the *information explicitly represented* in text and its logically connected propositions. The shift from speech to writing is viewed as an important transition in terms of children's readiness for abstract, formal, logical thought and reasoning.

Scribner and Cole refer to this transition as a *great divide* in human modes of thought. They trace its historical roots (as do Olson and Torrance) to the invention of alphabetic writing systems, the printing press, and writing as a mode of inquiry. Observing that historical processes have no *necessary* implications for psychological processes, Scribner and Cole also examine the psychological literature on the cognitive consequences of language, literacy and schooling. They conclude, from their study of Vai literates, that psychological effects of literacy are very specific to the kinds of written language uses encountered by writers. Their argument suggests the need to look rather specifically at different functions and contexts of writing, as these influence both cognitive skills and knowledge development. The ability to adequately describe what writers do when they write in specific situations, how they think about and establish purposes when writing, how purposes guide composing and revising, and what knowledge and skills generalize to other speaking and writing situations—all would contribute, not only to a more adequate view of writing as a contextualized activity, but also to our knowledge of the cognitive consequences of becoming literate.

TOWARD A FRAMEWORK FOR UNDERSTANDING WRITING

The previous discussion is an attempt to characterize the range of issues that relate to the notion of writing as an *activity*. We have been necessarily restrictive in our approach to the individual chapters in this volume so as to present a more focussed discussion about the psychological aspects of writing. To reflect the kinds of interdependencies possible among them, we think it is important to view the four perspectives—*cognitive, linguistic, communicative* and *contextual*—as emphasizing different kinds of *influences* or *constraints* on writing processes. Here we use the term constraint in the technical sense of conditions that influence or modify the operation of a process. For example, in writing the topic sentence of a paragraph, writers must select meanings to communicate and written language forms to express those meanings. In doing so, the meanings they select are influenced by (i.e., constrained by) their knowledge of particular topics, their knowledge of specific language forms, their assumptions about the reader's knowledge, and their understanding of the context that establishes their writing's function. All of these constraints bear upon the choice of what to say first and how to express it.

There is one additional type of constraint on the writer's processes that received little attention in these chapters. This class of constraints can be referred to as *textual*. As the words, phrases and sentences get written, they likewise can constrain what the writer may say next. An alternative label for this kind of constraint might be a *coherence* constraint, since it derives from the need to be relevant and to produce text that exhibits coherent development of a topic. Textual constraints can operate at all levels of language, from lexical choice to discourse structure. Of the chapters in this volume, that of Bartlett and Scribner deals most directly with how writers respond to the requirements imposed by coherence constraints. Specifically, they discuss the construction of referential relations between sentences in text. Textual constraints are also alluded to by Nold in her discussion of the interplay between a writer's global structure (i.e., the structure of an intended meaning) and local sentence production, which is subject to the constraints of local discourse context.

The need to produce sentences that simultaneously satisfy textual coherence constraints and convey intended meanings accurately makes writing a very demanding task, even when the writer has already framed the content of a message. Research on writing processes needs to focus some of its efforts on how writers develop the capacities to adjust to their own texts' limiting aspects as they write. For this reason, we include *textual constraints* in this framework, as a fifth type of constraint on writing processes. The following figure shows how the five constraints on writing processes are part of a framework for viewing writing as a cognitive activity.

The box in the center of Figure 1 represents the current cognitive processes of the writer. The arrows indicate constraining influences of various types that can affect how writers structure their writing. The constraints listed at the right of Figure 1 all reflect characteristics of the writer's knowledge and the

4. programs that find their physical expressions and codes not only in human habits and speech sounds but also in writing and in other forms of *recorded* speech. These provide the fourth level of coding, also peculiar to man, enabling some of the information for living to be recorded outside of any living creature (Young, 1978, p. 10).

Interesting support for this claim comes from the recent studies by Dr. William Condon of Boston of infants videotaped in a maternity ward: Condon found the seemingly random first movements of neonates, even within the first twelve to twenty-four hours of life, in fact, synchronized with the syllabic breaks in the adult speech around them (Condon & Sander, 1974, pp. 99–101).

Vygotsky makes the further case that the gesture is developmentally a requisite to the development of written language. In *A Prehistory of Written Language* (1934, trans. 1978), Vygotsky claims that the gesture is "the initial visual sign that contains the child's future writing as an acorn contains a future oak" (Vygotsky, 1934, p. 107). Gestures are writing in air, and written signs frequently are simply gestures that have been fixed (Vygotsky, *ibid.*). Early on, children shuttle between actual gestures and scribbles on paper that supplement this *gestural representation*. In fact, Vygotsky regards the child's first marks on paper developmentally as recorded gestures rather than as drawing in the true sense of the word. One thinks as well, of course, of Piaget, who posits that sensori-motor activity is the source of schemes that transform into subsequent modes of representation.

These marks on the paper go through a series of evolutionary change, from undifferentiated marks through indicatory signs and symbolizing marks and scribbles to the drawing of little figures and pictures to the moment when the child realizes that *one can draw not only things but speech*. This recognition makes possible the transformation of writing from a first-order symbolic act, to a second-order symbolic act, from the *mnemotechnic* stage to the stage where one can deal with disembodied signs and symbols—to the stage, that is, of symbolic maturity.

Children's games represent the second realm that *links gestures and written language*. In play children use objects in their representational gestures: a piece of wood can serve as a baby, or a wand, for example:

> ... therefore, children's symbolic play can be understood as a very complex system of *speech* through gestures that communicate and indicate the meaning of playthings. It is only on the basis of these indicatory gestures that playthings themselves gradually acquire their meaning—just as drawing, while initially supported by gesture, becomes an independent sign (Vygotsky, 1934, p. 108).

He concludes:

... symbolic representation in play is essentially a particular form of speech at an earlier stage, one which leads directly to written language (Vygotsky, p. 111).

These two transformations can be represented by the following sketch:

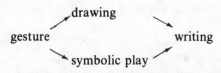

Vygotsky's statements about the requisites of symbolic play to the development of writing in the life of the child are corroborated and extended by studies that examine the roots in childhood of gifted and creative performances in adults, particularly studies by Gardner (1973) and Singer (1973).

Jerome Singer draws from his research into the fantasy lives of children five predisposing conditions to *fantasy play:*

1. An opportunity for privacy and for practice in a relatively protected setting where the external environment is reasonably redundant so that greater attention can be focused on internal activity. Naturally, such a situation exists also at the time of preparation for sleep and during sleep itself.

2. Availability of a variety of materials in the form of stories told, books, and playthings which increase the likelihood that the material presented to the child in the course of the reprocessing activity or in the course of a set toward elaboration of this material will be interesting and sufficiently novel so that the child will experience positive affect while playing make-believe games.

3. Freedom from interference by peers or adults who make demands for immediate motor or perceptual reactions....

4. The availability of adult models or older peers who encourage make-believe activity and provide examples of how this is done or provide basic story material which can be incorporated in privacy into the child's limited schemata.

5. Cultural acceptance of privacy and make-believe activities as a reasonably worthwhile form of play (Singer, 1973).

In *From Two or Five,* the Russian poet Kornei Chukovsky charmingly illustrates his hypothesis that between the ages of two and five all children are linguistic geniuses. Chukovsky confined his examples to the oral utterances of children. But in his recent study of metaphoric development in children (Chukovsky, 1963). Howard Gardner extends the ages and range of art forms for the manifestation of creative genius in children. Gardner's conclusions:

Perhaps the chief mystery confronting the student of artistic development is the relationship between the mature adult practitioner - the skilled poet, the painting master, the virtuoso instrumentalist or composer - and the young child playing with words, humming and inventing melodies, effortlessly producing sketches and paintings while engaging in many other activities that have only a tenuous relationship to the arts. Clearly there are important differences in skill, acquaintance with the artistic tradition, sensitivity to nuance between the child and the adult participants in the artistic process. But a more fundamental question for the psychologist is whether the school-child must pass through further, qualitatively different stages in order to become an artist (as it has been argued that he must pass through qualitatively different stages en route to becoming a practicing scientist). On this question I have arrived at an unexpected conclusion: the child of 7 or 8 has, in most respects, become a participant in the artistic process and he need not pass through any further qualitative reorganization... (Gardner, 1973, p. 213).

What are the possible implications of these research findings for the presentation of writing in schools?

1. Although writing is natural, it is activated by enabling environments;
2. These environments have the following characteristics: they are safe, structured, private, unobtrusive, and literate;
3. Adults in these environments have two special roles: they are fellow practitioners, and they are providers of possible content and experiences;
4. Children need frequent opportunities to practice writing, many of these playful.

Currently, these conditions have no prominence in our schools; indeed, to honor them would require nothing less than a paradigm shift in the ways we present not only writing but also other major cognitive processes as well. Shifting paradigms is no easy task: in fact, developmentally, there is probably no more complex cognitive process. As Gruber points out in a remarkable essay comparing children and scientists—notably, Darwin—making a paradigm shift, such a shift requires not only cognitive change but the courage to make the change. To give up one paradigm about the nature of learning and teaching for another requires that teachers undergo a particularly powerful conversion.

> ...A large change in thought really involves abandoning a paradigm-in other words, abandoning a whole way of thought: a group of ideas, methods, sources of evidence, relationships with colleagues, and so on. Since this change cannot take place instantaneously, every change made in an individual's way of thought moves him away from his own past.
>
> At all times, the changes one is both undergoing and producing are opposed by ongoing vital systems, systems that are personal and idiosyncratic; one's way of perceiving, one's concept of law, one's understanding of the received knowledge of the day. This conflict between the old person and the new one emerging may limit the rate at which one can move (Gruber, 1973).

Before specifying what in my opinion such a conversion requires, how can the two paradigms be characterized? What, first, are the tenets of the magical thinking paradigm about writing that currently dominates the schools? Here is its credo:

1. Writing is predominantly taught rather than learned;
2. Children must be taught to write atomistically, from parts to wholes. The commonplace is that children must be taught to write sentences, before they can be allowed to write paragraphs, before they can be permitted to attempt *whole* pieces of discourse;
3. There is essentially one process of writing that serves all writers for all their aims, modes, intents, and audiences;
4. That process is linear: all planning precedes all writing (often described in the paradigm as transcribing), as all writing precedes all revising;
5. The process of writing is also almost exclusively conscious: as evidence, a full plan or outline can be drawn up and adhered to for any piece of writing: the outline also assumes that writing is transcribing, since it can be so totally pre-figured; thought exists prior to its linguistic formulation;
6. Perhaps because writing is conscious, it can be done swiftly and on order;
7. There is no community or collaboration in writing: it is exclusively a silent and solitary activity.

What, in contrast, are the findings from the developmental research into writing?

1. Writing is predominantly learned rather than taught.
2. Writers of all ages as frequently work from wholes to parts as from parts to wholes: in writing, there is a complex interplay between focal and global concerns: from an interest in what word should come next, to the shape of the total piece.
3. There is no monolithic process of writing: there are processes of writing that differ because of aim, intent, mode, and audience, although there are shared features in the ways we write, there are as well individual, even idiosyncratic, features in our processes of writing.
4. The processes of writing do not proceed in a linear sequence: rather, they are recursive—we not only plan, then write, then revise; but we also revise, then plan, then write.
5. Writing is as often a pre-conscious or unconscious roaming as it is a planned and conscious rendering of information and events.
6. The rhythms of writing are uneven—more, erratic. The pace of writing can be very slow, particularly if the writing represents significant learning. Writing is also slow since it involves what Vygotsky calls *elaborating the web of meaning,* supplying the specific and explicit links

to render lexical, syntactic, semantic, and rhetorical pieces into organic wholes.

7. The processes of writing can be enhanced by working in, and with a group of other writers, perhaps especially a teacher, who give vital response, including advice.

What constitutes a conversion experience for those who present writing in schools, from the magical thinking paradigm to a developmental view? Obviously, since the shift is so great, so dramatic (and, at times, traumatic), the evidence and the experiences must be extremely powerful and, indeed, they must be developmental.

To undergo such a conversion, teachers of writing, our research strongly suggests, must:

a. write themselves in many modes, poetic and imaginative, as well as transactional and extensive, and introspect upon their own histories and processes as writers;

b. observe directly, through such media as videotape, female and male writers of many ages and backgrounds engaging in the processes of writing; and speculate systematically with other teacher-writers about these observations and their implications for presenting writing in schools;[26]

c. ascertain attitudes, constructs, and paradigms of those learning to write because the evidence grows stronger that, as with any learning process, set affects, perhaps even determines, both process and performance;

d. assess growth in writing against its developmental dimensions, with perhaps the most important accomplishment a growing ability to distinguish between a mistake and what can be termed a developmental error (New Jersey Writing Project, 1979).

To examine each of these in turn:

a. What is most powerful and persuasive, developmentally, of course, is direct, active, personal experience since only personal experience can transform into personal knowledge. And for teachers especially, personal knowledge of any process to be presented to learners is not an option: it is a requisite. Persons who don't themselves write cannot sensitively, even sensibly, help others learn to write.

Teachers of writing, then, must themselves write, frequently and widely. And they must introspect upon their writing, since without reflection there has been no experience, as philosophers from Socrates to Dewey point out.

b. To inform themselves about how they at once are like, and different from, their students, teachers of writing need to take an intensive look at actual students working through extended and systematic observation; interviews with the students, peers, former teachers, and parents—in other words, by the preparation of writing of at least two thorough case-studies. (Since the emerging research on writers of all ages suggests sex differences, I would recommend studying at least one of each sex).

Models for case studies are available from many sources—from literary biographies to clinical analyses (see Redinger, 1975, and Bettelheim, 1961). Within the specific research on the composing processes, there are available in doctoral dissertations many exemplars: for young children, Graves (1973) and Sawkins (1971); for children nine to thirteen, Hale (1971) and Carducci (1979); and for college, Rogers (1978); Stokes and Heard (1975).

c. Teachers' own experiences as writers will provide the kinds of developmental issues they will want to examine in these case studies; but it is likely that they will formulate variants on some of the following questions:

> What are the attitudes toward literacy and the educational background of the family?
> When, and under what circumstances, did the child begin to write, and to read?
> If the child remembers these experiences, what description does she give? With what feeling tones?
> If the learner currently has difficulty writing, can the learner or someone else identify specific times and circumstances when difficulties began?
> What does the learner think writing is for? What are its functions?
> Does the learner write equally well in all modes? unevenly? In which modes, well; in which, less well or badly?
> How can his process(es) of writing be characterized? total length? length of given portions? amount and quality of pre-writing including planning? amount and kind of revising, recursive and final? Is the writer self-critical, capable of reflection?
> What are the attitudes, constructs, and paradigms the student has about school, about English and the language arts, about writing?

Recent research suggests that, the older the writer, the more likely that such cumulative clusters of belief will affect the processes of writing and their outcomes (Pianko, 1978).

d. How can teachers learn to assess growth in students' abilities to write, with its concomitant question: how can we teach ourselves to discern the difference between mistakes and what can be termed developmental errors?

We can only make accurate assessments of growth if we have accurate characterizations of writing persons, processes, and outcomes; and thus far what we have are pastels or sketches for the whole or, Wyeth-like, drawings of a few tight particulars, not a fully delineated model of the developmental dimensions of writing.

A few persons have attempted to provide wide views. Perhaps because he has delineated one of the most compelling developmental sequences for modes, James Moffett has, in my opinion, also developed some major strategies for evaluating growth in writing. These appear as Chapter 22 in the second edition of *A Student-Centered Language Arts Curriculum,* with Betty Jane Wagner. John Holt's *How Children Fail* (1964) and *How Children Learn* (1967) remain useful, readable general introductions to developmental issues.

Crucial to a developmental view of assessment is to learn to distinguish between mistakes and developmental errors. Developmental errors contrast readily with mistakes in that developmental errors forward learning while mistakes impede it. Developmental errors have two characteristics that mistakes do not: 1) they are generally bold, chance-taking; 2) and they are rational, intelligent.

While the making of mistakes mark a retreat into the familiar, and often are the result of fear and anxiety, developmental errors represent a student's venturing out and taking chances as a writer, from trying a new spelling, or tying together two sentences with a fresh transition, to a first step into a mode previously unexplored.

A second characteristic of developmental errors is that they are rational and logical; unfortunately, they often happen also to be wrong. In *Errors and Expectations,* our most thorough account of errors among a given segment of writers called BW writers (Basic Writers), Mina Shaughnessy notes the *most damaging aspect* of the BW's experiences with writing:

> they have lost all confidence in the very faculties that serve all language learners: their ability to distinguish between essential and redundant features of a language left them logical but wrong; their abilities to draw analogies between what they knew of language when they began school and what they learned produced mistakes; and such was the quality of their instruction that no one saw the intelligence of their mistakes or thought to harness that intelligence in the service of learning. (Shaughnessy, 1977, pp. 10–11)

Examples of invalid analogies include the over-regularizing of lexical, grammatical, or rhetorical features, as well as more globally, the illogicality of proceeding as if writing were talk written down, a belief some students hold perhaps because some of their teachers have told them it is so.

Assessing growth in writing is a far larger, more complex, more individual, and more interesting matter than testing. Too many testing programs, particularly those devised and given by state and national agencies, public and private, use evidence divorced from the linguistic and human histories of the students involved, and evidence divorced from the only sensible developmental requirement: writing samples in a range of modes that have, like the students themselves, histories and futures.

Presenting writing developmentally in schools will require major transformations: transformations from the traditional school paradigm that promulgates magical thinking; and consequently, transformations of teacher learning and development. It is quite as demanding—perhaps, more demanding—than the ways of teaching writing traditionally, requiring no less than that adults admit that the only way they can help others learn to write is that they themselves become learners and writers.

REFERENCES

Bettelheim, B. *Paul & Mary: Two case histories of truants from life.* New York: Doubleday, Anchor, 1961.

Cazden, C. B. Problems for education: language as curriculum content and learning environment, In Language as a human problem. *Daedalus* (Summer, 1973), CII, 3, 135.

Chomsky, N. *Language and mind.* New York: Harcourt Brace Jovanovich, 1972.

Chukovsky, K. *From two to five.* M. Morton (Ed. & Tr.), Berkeley, California: University of California Press, 1963.

Condon, W., & Sander, L. Neonate movement is synchronized with adult speech: Interactional participation and language acquisition. *Science,* 183 (4120), 1974, 99–101.

Duckworth, E. The having of wonderful ideas, In M. Schwebel & J. Raph (Eds.), *Piaget in the Classroom.* New York: Basic Books, 21–22, 1973.

Feldenkrais, M. *Body and mature behavior,* New York: International Universities Press, 1949, 132. Ken Macrorie brought this reference to my attention.

Gardner, H. *The Arts & Human development: a psychological study of the aristic process.* New York: Wiley, 1973.

Gruber, H. Courage and cognitive growth in children and scientists. In M.Schuebel & J. Raph (Eds.), *Piaget in the Classroom.* New York: Basic Books, 1973, 74.

Lennenberg, E. *Biological foundations of language.* New York: Wiley, 1967.

Pianko, S. A description of the composing processes of college freshman writers. *Research in the teaching of English,* (February 1979), XIII, 1, 5–22.

Polanyi, M. *Personal Knowledge: Towards a post-critical philosophy.* Chicago: University of Chicago Press, 1958.

Redinger, R.V. *George Eliot: The emergent self.* New York: Knopf, 1975.

Report of the New Jersey writing project to the National Review Dissemination Panel, Washington, D.C.: (May 1979).

Schwebel, M. & Raph, J. "Before and beyond the three R's". In M.Schwebel and J. Raph (Eds.), *Piaget in the Classroom.* New York: Basic Books, 1973, 21–22.

Shaughnessy, M. *Errors and expectations: a guide for the teacher of basic writing.* New York: Oxford University Press, 1977, 10–11.

Vygotsky, L. The prehistory of written language: (1934). In S. Scribner *et al.* (Eds.), *Mind in society: The development of higher psychological processes.* Cambridge, Mass.: Harvard University Press, 1978, pp. 105–111.

Young, J. Z. *Programs of the brain.* New York: Oxford University Press, 1978, 10.

2 National Assessments of Writing Ability

Rexford Brown

What do we actually know about the alleged *writing crisis* that has emerged in this country during the 1970's? Attempts to generalize about the quality of written communication in America are frustrated by our continuing lack of systematic inquiry. There is opinion from students and teachers alike about the decline in writing ability. Many students—particularly those entering colleges and universities, have complained that they could not meet the standards for college writing. Some teachers agree with these students; some do not. Some say writing has always been bad, and it is getting worse; some say it has always been mediocre, and it is getting better; many have serious conflict of interest problems and lack confidence in their abilities to judge accomplishment in their students' writing.

Many parents who complain about writing quality with a *back-to-basics* cry urge us back to grammar and middle class usage, not writing. The test makers have drawn us closer to so-called objective evidence of declines in writing achievement, but not convincingly. Few have tested actual writing nationally on samples that are not self-selecting; and, of those test-makers, few have been at it long enough to turn up definitive trends. What do we really know from tests of writing? We know that to varying degrees, *verbal* or *English* or *language* scores have declined since the mid 1960's on such tests as the SAT, ACT, MSAT, etc. Taken by large numbers of students nationally or at the state level, these multiple choice tests center around usage, punctuation, vocabularly, spelling and organization items, i.e., those aspects of writing most readily tested in machine-scorable ways and most often stressed in the traditional English curriculum. Results of various other tests, such as the

PSAT (Preliminary Scholastic Aptitude Test) or the ITED (Iowa Test of Educational Development) test for expression show little or no change.

The news about test score declines seems to have preceded the public clamor about writing competence so that the two phenomena—one observed by testers, the other by college students and teachers—have now become entangled in our minds as if they were one and the same phenomenon. They may well be related, as so many aspects of cultural changes are related but they need not reinforce each other. The tests tell us that incoming freshmen have lower scores, and the composition teachers tell us freshmen cannot write as well as they used to. These two independent observations are based on two different kinds of evidence, neither of which can be fully supported as concrete evidence about writing—the first, because *writing* was not tested; the second, because this so-called evidence is hearsay. The most we can say about the verbal test score declines is that language use is changing (which is not surprising) away from a standard that is implicit in existing multiple-choice aptitude and achievement tests.

The quality of actual writing by students does not appear to be changing radically. In 1957, the California Association of Teachers of English established a scale for evaluation of high school student essays using a representative sample of papers from throughout that state. When the quality scale was established, they asked a panel of experts to speculate about the writing futures of those who wrote the best and the average papers. Here is what the panel said in 1957:

> First, although some of the *best* writing of seniors in California high schools is of good quality, most of it is definitely mediocre in terms of the criteria established by the Subcommittee. Second, *average* writing, taken as a whole, does not represent satisfactory achievement for seniors in high school composition, when *satisfactory* is thought of in relation to probable success in college writing courses.[1]

More specifically, the panel said that one-fourth of the best writers and two thirds of the average writers would probably have to take remedial writing courses in college. These percentages sound very much like those one hears today in 1977.

One major source of testing evidence about writing is The National Assessment of Educational Progress findings in two national writing assessments (1969-70 and 1973-74). Based not upon vocabularly, spelling, usage tests, or the like, NAEP writing results rest upon analysis of actual writing by 9-, 13- and 17-year-olds throughout the country. The writing is

---

[1]California Association of Teachers of English, *A Scale for Evaluation of High School Student Essays;* Urbana, Illinois; 1960.

done under Assessment conditions—somewhat freer and less threatening than standardized testing conditions, but constrained nevertheless; so it is of limited length and of a particular nature. It is produced in response to a wide variety of directives for writing in persuasive, explanatory, descriptive and expressive modes, and in a variety of rhetorical registers. This comprehensiveness is at once the strength of the Assessment data base and its weakness. The weakness lies in the difficulty of comparing some of the results to others in a way that would permit even medium level generalization. Several NAEP statistics illustrate the variability of the findings:

> Fifty-Four percent of America's 9-year-olds write competent thank you notes of a certain kind; 56 percent write competent expressive essays of a certain kind; and 90 percent write acceptable get well cards. 11 percent seem able to organize a report competently; 10 percent appear able to elaborate upon an imaginary role with consistent point of view; 14 percent respond to music with a minimally integrated piece of writing, and 14 percent appear able to order a kite through the mail in a way that might insure receiving it.
>
> Results for 13-year-olds are equally mixed and must be equally qualified: seventy-five percent appear able to write a certain kind of letter correcting a misunderstanding; 61 percent appear able to write an acceptable letter to an organization and 34 percent can respond to music with a somewhat integrated expressive piece of writing. On other expressive, persuasive and descriptive writing tasks, the proportion of competent papers was about one in three.
>
> Seventeen-year-olds write somewhat better than 13-year-olds, but the unevenness of results—ranging from 5 percent who appear able to write a good job application letter to 54 percent who are able to role play imaginatively—defy compression. The most that we can say about all these figures is that the more sophisticated the writing assignment, the fewer the students who can do it well.[2]

From these figures, it is not possible to devise a global index of writing abilities. The criteria for competence in each task vary with the nature of the task. Though there might be a way to put the hundreds of thousands of NAEP essays onto a single scale, it has not been done yet. Until it is, we have only atomized statements about particular aspects of writing to offer. They are suggestive, of course. And as someone who has absorbed them and read, in

---

[2]The data in the preceding three paragraphs are taken from three separate NAEP studies:

Explanatory and Persuasive Letter Writing: Selected Results from the second National Assessment of Writing, Denver: NAEP, 1977.

Expressive Writing: Selected Results from the Second National Assessment of Writing, Denver: NAEP, 1976.

Writing Mechanics, 1969–1974: A Capsule Description of Changes in Writing Mechanics, Denver: NAEP, 1975.

addition, thousands of essays from national samples, I suggest that *about 50–55 percent* of 17-year-olds in America write *competently,* when they write.

Fortunately, there is another kind of NAEP information about writing achievement that, although modest in its scope, is more suggestive. In 1975 essays written by students in 1969 were mixed with those written on the same topic in 1973–74, and these were scored holistically by experienced English teachers. The scorers had no way of knowing which year a particular paper was written, so they applied the same quality criteria to all of them. When they were done, we found that they perceived, in their holistic judgments, a difference in the quality of the writing in the two different years. Specifically, at ages 17 and 13, the more recently written descriptive essays were, as a group, inferior to those written in 1969. The mean holistic score for the recent papers was a fifth of a point lower at age 17 and a third of a point at age 13— statistically significant shifts over a very short period of time. Nine-year-olds were writing somewhat better.

Since holistic scorers do not express specific reasons for their judgments, we went back to the papers to analyze differences in quality from another point of view. Each paper was coded with respect to such factors as number of words, sentences, paragraphs, number of compound sentences, complex sentences, run-ons, fragments, and types of errors, such as spelling, phonetic misspelling and word choice. The papers were then keypunched and computer analyzed to provide us with a means of comparing specific features. We found that at age 17 the more recent papers contained, as a group, more run-on sentences, more awkwardness, and more incoherent paragraphs than the 1969 papers. At age 13 the essays were shorter, the vocabulary, simpler, the amount of embedding, on the decrease; wordiness within the sentence was on the increase, especially among males. These factors were probably influential in leading the holistic scorers to prefer the 1969 papers; however, no regression weights were obtained to support this view.

It appears, from this information and from the statements of students and teachers themselves around the country, that there might be a problem with coherence, with the readability of the things people are writing. There does not appear to be a problem with usage—that is, whether people should or should not say *ain't,* whether they should say *lay* instead of *lie, who* instead of *whom,* and so on. The writing problem does not seem to involve a massive flaunting of the conventions of standard written English; nor does it involve spelling much, either. Many people cannot spell particularly well these days when you give them words to spell; but when they write, they tend to use words they can spell (for obvious reasons), so the percentage of misspelled words in their essays is not very great. The problem does not seem to involve punctuation, either. The vast majority of writers use perfectly the few punctuation marks they employ: the comma, the period and the question mark. They have no trouble with the dash, the semi-colon or the colon because they do not use them; and my guess is that if they did, we could reasonably expect more incoherence because they would be trying difficult constructions. Granted, a paper containing misspellings, barbarisms and grammatical errors could be a difficult paper to read and could well be incoherent. But these things are not necessarily causes of incoherence; they are not problem areas as far as our essay analysis could tell, and they happen to be the aspects of writing most often and thoroughly taught in our schools. The problem includes, but goes beyond, aspects of writing that can be addressed by a traditional grammar and usage-oriented approach to instruction.

The task of trying to establish what is known about writing in America has led me to the following conclusion: there is very little accurate, unbiased, concrete information about writing achievement in America. What little there is suggests that language use is changing; that there is a decline in whatever skills *verbal* tests assess; that skill in actual writing varies widely with the nature of and sophistication required by the writing task; and that skill in writing descriptive essays is less widely distributed than it used to be among 17- and 13-year-olds. The *evidence* of a test score decline, the *feeling* expressed by faculty that there is a decline in the writing skill of incoming freshmen at many universities, and the *indications* of declines from NAEP— all taken together—contribute strongly to an *impression* that learning to write is becoming more difficult for students. But none of this suggests radical change or rapid deterioration.

THE NEED FOR BETTER INFORMATION

Many people are turning to holistic scoring in an attempt to gather more information about students' writing ability. Large numbers of essays can be reliably scored with the holistic method, and these scores are often accurate predictors of future writing success. Also, teachers can be trained to agree on the overall quality of student papers. But what do holistic scores mean? All anyone knows after a holistic scoring is that paper A is higher on the scale than paper B; but, since the criteria for quality are not absolute, no one knows why. Furthermore, it is possible that all of the papers at the top of the scale are horribly written. They may be better than the rest, but still may be unacceptable to most teachers of composition, as was the case with the California scale.

Not only is this traditional kind of holistic scoring incapable of establishing proficiency in any concrete sense, it is a very unsatisfactory system for the evaluation of growth. If a student's first paper is rated 5 at a September scoring session and her 20th paper is rated 6 in a May session, we know nothing, because experience has shown that holistic scorings cannot be replicated reliably. We know more about growth if both papers are included in the same scoring session and the second paper comes out higher on the scale; but we still do not know why it is better or how good it is in an absolute sense.

No matter how reliable holistic scoring is as a way of rank-ordering papers, it is inadequate as a measuring tool in itself, because it is relativistic and is not tied to any absolute definition of quality. There are modifications of holistic scoring that employ rubrics of various kinds, and these are more useful. One of the most promising of these is the NAEP *Primary Traits* system, which rests upon elementary rhetorical theory. It assumes that a carefully defined writing task is a statement of certain rhetorical imperatives; that successful completion of the task entails understanding of and responsiveness to those imperatives; and that degrees of success are definable in concrete terms. We have found the tasks hard, but not impossible to define, the scoring guides complicated, but teachable, and the actual scoring reliable. Most important, we have found the results reportable in terms that have curricular implications.

For many teachers, holistic scoring, as employed in large scale assessments of writing, is not very useful. Nevertheless, because they need evaluation systems, they have used various kinds of *objective,* multiple-choice tests of writing ability. Such tests are cheaper and easier to score; but they, too, suffer from some glaring weaknesses. Their primary function is to rank order people on a scale. This leaves us again with no absolute knowledge about writing ability and a slight sense of embarrassment when we tell people we will test their writing ability by not requiring them to write a single word. We are told that these tests "correlate" with writing ability and often predict academic success; but the number of cars or television sets or bathrooms in one's home also correlates with his writing ability, as does parents' education and financial success. Correlation however, is not causation. Existing objective tests of *writing* test only reading, proofreading, editing, logical and guessing skills. They cannot distinguish between proofreading errors and process errors, reading problems and scribal stutter, failure to consider audience or lack of interest in materials manufactured by someone else. Like holistic essay scoring, multiple-choice testing of writing is seldom diagnostic in any useful way. And since capacity to recognize problems in other people's writing does not insure capacity to avoid them in one's own writing—especially first draft writing—we can never be sure what the final scores on such tests mean, let alone the subscores.

There are even more insidious aspects to multiple-choice writing tests. They require a passive, reactive mental state when actual writing requires and fosters a sense of human agency, an active state. They are also necessarily incomplete, leading the student and perhaps even the teacher to believe that those aspects of writing most easily tested—sentence structure, word meaning, spelling, punctuation and outlining—are the most important to teach and learn. Finally, since the approach of many such tests is to emphasize differences between standard and nonstandard usages, writing courses all too often become, unintentionally, cultural programming laboratories.

From the fund of knowledge accumulated in the last fifteen years and this special climate we should be able to develop a number of evaluation systems that define proficiency in concrete terms, are sensitive to degrees of growth toward that proficiency, require people both to write essays and test their editing skills, are valid, reliable, cheap and—most importantly—are coordinated with the long-range research effort we need to more fully understand and develop strategies for improving the process of composition.

What follows are some suggestions for improving tests of writing:

1. Evaluate writing done under various conditions, not just under test conditions.

2. Base essay evaluations on papers reflecting several modes of discourse, because quality differs for each one and people are not equally proficient in all of them.

3. If we want to evaluate an essay for certain characteristics, then the directions for the assignment must specify those characteristics. This is not a trivial matter: it is extremely difficult to write assignments that define precisely the rhetorical imperatives that will either be met or missed by the students. If we want them to try to elaborate upon a role expressively while maintaining control of point of view and tense, then we have to set the task up in such a way that they must do so.

4. Use computers for tasks that are heavily quantitative, e.g., numerations of words per T-unit, of words per clause, of adjective clauses, of noun clauses, and so on—information about embedding which suggests indices of syntactic maturity.

5. Try to relate quantitative information to qualitative judgments. The computer might provide evidence to support negative and positive holistic judgments.

6. Relate quantitative information to various criterion-scoring systems. The six factors that seem to affect judgment most are ideas, mechanics, organization, vocabulary, what Paul Diedrich calls "flavor," and handwriting. Each can be evaluated independently.

7. Define coherence in specific syntactical, propositional or transformational terms; code papers accordingly and establish a concrete coherence scale.

8. Include in any instrument questions about writing attitudes, prewriting activities and rewriting activities and then look at results in the light of that information.

9. Use basic sentence combining exercises and relate results on such exercises to actual writing performance.

10. Include a battery of objective items that will at least remind students that they should edit.

The third national assessment of writing, currently being analyzed, included many of these features. In addition, it included materials from 1969, enabling us to examine trends spanning a decade. But however inclusive it is, it will not supply all the information we need at the necessary levels of detail. For that, we need a coordinated effort involving writers, teachers, linguists, ethnographers, rhetoricians, philosophers, and educational psychologists.

3 Plans That Guide the Composing Process

Linda Flower and John R. Hayes

Writing is among the most complex of human mental activities. The private nature of the composing process, together with its complexity, challenges the imagination and ingenuity of anyone who would answer the basic question: What happens when people write? This paper attempts to answer a part of that question by viewing writing as a problem-solving process. Writers, like other problem solvers, attack the problem of composing by using a variety of procedures that make thought efficient. Planning, because it can reduce a vast problem to manageable size, is one of the most powerful of what Simon and Newell (1972) refer to as heuristic procedures.

The research we discuss here examines records of the behavior of writers during the act of writing, examining first the kinds of plans college student writers make, and second, the ways in which plans interact. The method used to study the composing process is the *thinking out loud* technique that has been used frequently to study human problem-solving. (Simon & Newell, 1972) In this method, subjects are asked to think out loud as they compose, producing a verbal record of their thought processes. In the act of composing, the writers we studied appeared to rely on a variety of functionally distinct kinds of plans. Two of the most interesting sets we found are plans for generating ideas and plans for producing a written product. Sometimes these two kinds of plans appear to interact smoothly so that thinking leads easily to a written text. In other instances they appear to come into conflict, resulting in a more complicated composing process. The ways in which writers coordinate their different plans appear to affect the efficiency of their composing processes and the effectiveness of their final products.

We start with a basic premise: Writing is problem solving, and can be analyzed from a psychological point of view of problem-solving processes. (Flower & Hayes, 1977) Myths of inspiration to the contrary, writers do not simply receive ideas but, even as they gaze out of the window, they draw on a set of mental operations or *heuristics*. These mental procedures, such as memory search, planning, and defining goals and subgoals, have been found to occur when people solve problems as diverse as deciding on a chess move or doing a painting (Simon & Newell, 1972). To see how writing is a problem-solving activity, imagine that you have just been asked to write a letter of recommendation. Focusing on this task, you must first create an internal representation of the problem. You must define your goals and strategies for achieving these goals. Then, as you write, you must assess your progress toward the goals, and, with disturbing frequency, redefine the goals.

Many problems that we face are *well defined* in the sense that they provide us very little choice as to goals or to the processes we must use to reach those goals. Home work problems in science courses are often of this sort. In contrast, *ill defined* problems, such as the tasks of directing a film or writing an essay, require us to be very active in defining goals or procedures for reaching the goals. To solve such problems people regularly draw on heuristic procedures or strategies (Hayes, 1978). Perhaps the simplest problem-solving procedure one may use in ill-defined problems is the *generate and test* strategy (e.g., pick a puzzle piece and see if it fits). This trial and error strategy reflects our inveterate tendency as problem solvers to jump to a quick solution, often before we thoroughly understand the problem. If we are lucky, this strategy enables us to avoid a need for analysis and planning. A writer's version of *generate and test* might consist of starting that letter of recommendation by generating a trial sentence, then seeing if it is satisfactory by applying a battery of tests for grammar, syntax, rhythm, tone, truth, etc. However, given all of the things one could say about a particular student or colleague and all of the possible linguistic choices for saying it, the *generate and test* strategy turns out to be a remarkably inefficient procedure, though not an entirely uncommon one.

In solving problems of any complexity, human beings typically narrow the field of possible solutions by means of heuristic procedures for working through the problem (Simon & Newell, 1972). A heuristic procedure, unlike a long division rule, will not assure a *correct* solution. It is simply a method that has a high probability of working. Good writers have a repertory of powerful heuristics which might include *brainstorming, planning,* or *simulating a reader's response* techniques. Weak writers may lack these techniques or use them ineffectively; or they may use other techniques which are less effective or even counterproductive. The problem we have set for ourselves is to describe the heuristic procedures writers use during the act of composing. We will not, a priori, decide which procedures are most efficient but rather attempt to describe the procedures writers actually use. By examining how these procedures interact, we can begin to see which ones are most efficient or effective, and which ones are sources of difficulty to writers.

In order to study what writers do as they write, we have used a method called *protocol analysis,* an observational method frequently used in problem-solving research (Simon & Newell, 1972). A *protocol* is a transcript of the writer's tape-recorded speech when he is asked to *think aloud* as he composes. Our subjects either have a real writing assignment from some other source, or they are given writing assignments with substantial content and a realistic audience, such as writing a fellowship application for summer support. In this paper, all of the quoted examples are taken directly from composing protocols of college students under these conditions.

For the purpose of analysis it is useful to break the composing process up into three kinds of activities (Hayes & Flower, 1980):

1. *planning,* in which the writer sets goals, and plans the content of a paper;
2. *translating,* in which plans and knowledge are expressed in a written text;
3. and *reviewing,* in which the results of planning and translating are tested.

In this paper we will investigate writers' planning procedures with two questions in mind: What kinds of plans do our writers characteristically make? And how do these plans interact with one another? We hope that the conclusion we reach from studying this set of student writers will give us insight into composing processes in other situations and open the way for additional research.

PLANS AND THE COMPOSING PROCESS

What is a plan, and why are plans such powerful heuristics? First of all, because plans break a problem down into sub-problems, they enable us to make large, unwieldy situations manageable (Miller, Galanter & Pribram, 1960). Second, good plans are *operational;* that is, they specify a sequence of procedures for solving the problem. The college student who tells himself to *write an excellent paper* has a poor plan which not only fails to specify such procedures, but which may stop the solution process by intimidation. Thus, a good writer may make his plan operational by saying, "I'll write an excellent paper (let's say on dandelions) by reading a botany book, studying the plants myself in the back yard, synthesizing my discoveries, and then deciding what are the most important or interesting things my readers would want to know." The issue here is not just a distinction between abstract and concrete goals, but one of making plans that help one act intelligently. A third major strength of plans is that they enable one to set priorities and decide on an order in which to do things. Plans answer the *what next?* question from the perspective of a final goal. Because of the tendency of any complicated problem to lead one down endless *garden paths,* plans enable one to return to a top-level goal. For example, in composing they may remind us not to spend twenty minutes choosing a syntactic form when we are still trying to figure out what we need to say.

Writers are faced with two principle problems: a knowledge problem and a communication problem. On the one hand they must produce an organized set of ideas for a paper by selecting and arranging a manageable number of concepts and relations from a vast body of knowledge. On the other hand, they must fit what they know to the needs of another person, a reader, and to the constraints of formal prose (Flower & Hayes, 1980). Both of these are demanding problems. To illustrate, let us put the matter more concretely. Suppose you have just been asked to write a twenty-page autobiography. Not only must you select and organize concepts which make sense out of your life, but you must fit these facts to the goals you wish to accomplish with the reader. A document written for a parent, child, or spouse, or for self-examination might be substantially different from one for a job application or security clearance from the FBI.

During the act of composing, writers rely on a variety of specialized kinds of plans. We will discuss three: plans for generating ideas, plans for producing a paper, and plans which guide the act of composing itself.

Figure 1 shows the plans we identified in the composing protocols of our subjects. Although we consider the procedural plans which guide composing

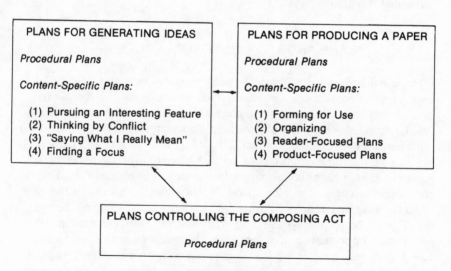

FIG. 1. Plans Writers Use in Composing

to be a separate type of plan, we have chosen to discuss them within the context of idea-generating and paper-producing plans.

Plans for Generating Ideas

Procedural Plans. Some writers have a repertory of relatively content-free methods which they use in generating ideas. For example, when a writer tells herself, "I'm just going to jot things down as they occur to me;" "I won't organize now;" "I'll worry about the spelling later;" or "I should make an outline," she is giving herself a set of procedural directions for how to go about the *process* of writing, regardless of what she has to say. The chief advantage of these procedural plans is that they provide a continuing structure for the composing process. For example, a plan to *brainstorm* or to *outline* creates a high level goal to which the writer can return when ideas stop *flowing* or when writing takes an unproductive turn. The protocol below demonstrates the *end of the line* experience writers frequently undergo when a train of thought has been completed, but they do not have a procedural plan for continuing. The writer in this protocol had been working for about a half hour:

> So, I don't really know what I've done. I mean, I kinda talked about how I was convinced a little bit, but I don't know that I really did it too precisely. And I don't know if this is really the best; it seemed like an okay one—it kinda led somewhere. . . . I'm trying to get myself going again. I'm in a mire. I don't know, I just stalled out, you know; my mind just pooped out after it had all those ideas. The reason I can't generate anything at this point, I was just kinda following things along, you know.

"Just kinda following things along" can be a workable plan, but it leaves many writers in the lurch when the thought plays itself out, and the writer has no plan for how to go about renewing the generating process.

Another advantage of these "how-to" plans is that they enable a writer to establish priorities which keep her focused on high-level goals, such as developing a broad set of ideas. Without such plans, the generating process may be constantly diverted as the writer stops to perfect a phrase or worry about how to get from one sentence to the next. Using procedural plans demands a degree of detachment from the immediate act of composing. The ability to employ such plans may be related to the ability to maintain a consistent topic throughout a stretch of writing. It certainly affects a writer's ability to deal with forms of *writer's block* and the *out-of-ideas* feeling that signals the end of a train of thought. We will return to this problem when we examine how writers switch from one plan to another.

Procedural plans constitute a distinct class of plans for generating ideas because they require a writer to make content-free decisions about how to control her idea-generating activities. However, most idea-generating plans are content-specific, acting on the information immediatley available to the writer. In general, a plan for generating ideas is an instruction a writer gives herself to either: 1) search for topic-related information in memory or external sources; or 2) operate on available information to produce new ideas. We have identified four content-specific plans for generating ideas exhibited by our student writers.

Pursuing an Interesting Feature.   One of the most frequent content-specific generating plans our writers used is the plan of simply *pursuing an interesting feature*. The feature may be a word, or idea, or event. Initially, the writer may have no clear idea where a generating process centered on this feature might lead. But in the process of pursuing it, the writer will usually develop more explicit sub-plans for exploring the feature and turn to various generating techniques, such as searching memory, drawing inferences, reasoning from examples, or matching current evidence to prior knowledge. The feature then becomes a springboard to more complex processes.

Thinking by Conflict.   Another content-specific generating plan which we identified in the protocols of our subjects is the *thinking by conflict* plan. In some cases, this plan appears to be quite specific, the writer asking himself to find a contradiction, to raise an objection, or to pose questions. In other cases, it seems to be a much more global plan in which writers seek out conflicts in their own thinking, or between their ideas or intuitions and commonly held notions. An example of this technique is the procedure of constructing parallel columns of pros and cons as an aid in deciding what to include in an essay. This plan which appeared most frequently at the beginning of protocols, seems to offer writers a way to define their own ideas, or what *is* true, by attacking what seems inadequate or untrue.

Saying What I Really Mean.   A third category of content-specific generating plans is one we have called WIRMI, an acronym for "What I Really Mean Is. . . . " WIRMI is a plan writers appear to use when they want to abstract or reduce a complex body of information to its essential features. Sometimes in the midst of generating ideas writers will cue themselves quite directly to try to select or condense out of train of thought, what it is they really mean, e.g., "So, what I really know is, is. . . . " or I'm thinking that what I'm getting at is, um. . . . " At other times the WIRMI attempt is more implicit, e.g., "Well, basically, what I wanted to talk about is. . . . " Part of the evidence that writers plan this operation, is that they occasionally tell themselves to attempt a WIRMI or sum up their thinking, but find themselves unable to do so.

Finding a Focus.   A fourth idea generating plan was one which writers rarely carried out successfully: the plan to find a focus for the paper. Everyone knows it is easier to write once you have a focus for what you wish to say. Our subjects usually wished for and made a plan to find a focus when they found themselves confused or in trouble.

> I took notes and I have notes in my book, but it's ... they're just not. . . . I just can't get them organized. The . . . I talked about that before. I had a problem with how I was going to focus, what focus I was going to use.
>
> I'm still really having the problem of . . . as to how I'm going to focus this paper. This is ridiculous. This is only a three page paper. I shouldn't be that upset about it. Well, that's probably why I am upset about it, because I have to make sure that what I say, since it's so short, makes sense, because I don't have any time to *B.S.* in the first two pages.

Although it is hard to know what *focus* actually meant to the writers we studied, it seemed to be equated at times with the fully articulated thesis statement which textbooks often advise a writer to formulate before beginning to write. Yet, as these protocols show, writers typically *don't* start with a thesis or well-focused body of ideas. Instead they start with a body of knowlege and set of goals, and they *create* their focus by such complex actions as drawing inferences, creating relationships, or abstracting large bodies of ideas down to *what I really mean.* If a writer believed that the *appropriate focus* was to be found by searching memory, or searching a book, his plan to find a focus might well fail.

Creating a focus is one of the crucial acts that can bridge the gap between generating ideas and turning them into a paper; it is also a task with which many writers have trouble. Our protocols suggest two possibilities that might account for this difficulty. One is that the plan to *find a focus* is not an operational plan. It doesn't tell the writer that in order to create focus one must first explore a variety of ideas, examine alternatives, look for connections, try to generate concepts, and so on. Such a plan does not account for the thinking process a writer must go through to achieve a focus. Further, it is possible that the writer's faith that he can discover a ready-made, appropriate focus may actually interfere with idea generation by directing him to search in memory for what he must create. If a writer's image of the composing process is misdirected or inaccurate, his writing strategies will be counter productive. For example, we have observed a writer abandon a very productive line of idea generation because she thought that *brainstorming* was not an appropriate part of the writing process.

Plans for Producing a Paper

Just as the writers we observed employed idea-generating plans to build up a knowledge network relevant to their assignments, we found they also employed plans for transforming that vast network of ideas into a written paper. A written text, unlike the knowledge network from which it is derived, is subject to two important classes of constraints: the *writer's purpose* (how he intends to use that knowledge) and the *conventional forms of written expression*. A piece of writing is not just a transcription of *what the writer knows*. Writing a paper, even an autobiography written for the purpose of self-examination, is a goal directed activity that demands enormous selectivity. Furthermore, it requires one to express a large interconnected network of information by building a linear sequence of sentences with specific foreward and backward references. Writing is not the same thing as *thinking about* or even *talking about* one's topic. Producing a paper requires satisfying a new set of constraints associated with written language, which in turn demands a particular set of decisions and plans.

We have identified a number of plans for producing a paper in our subjects' protocols. Writers use procedural plans not only for generating ideas but also for translating those ideas into language and for guiding editing processes. For example, by forming editing plans, e.g., "I'll have to revise that," or "Find out how to spell that," the writer can delay the solution of low level editing problems and thus prevent them from interrupting ongoing composing processes. Procedural plans, such as *make an outline,* are also contingency plans that enable a writer to keep composing when a less specific plan (e.g., "I'll just start to write") fails.

In the example below, the writer began with a very promising plan. He had discovered what he thought to be a major topic in his rough outline and had even planned to develop it with a short subordinate discussion ("We'll mention computers and so on."). So he cheerfully instructed himself:

> Well let's try that and see how it works. Alright, there's an organization...uh ...let's try and write something...Now that always requires a fresh piece of paper...This is page 4 that I'm starting on now, and let's see...Oh no, we need more organizing....What do we need to do?....I think...that the thing to do is to start with...[and he returns to his topic].

When the *try-and-write something* strategy didn't work, the writer's procedural repertory was called in with a back-up plan to bail the writer out ("We need to do more organizing."), and he began a renewed effort to define his topic and goals. Here the writer's procedural plans provided him with practical techniques that could help him organize his thinking and eventually create the *focus* he needed. We will now consider several content-specific plans for producing a paper that we observed in our writers' protocols.

Forming for Use

Switching from generating ideas to producing a paper requires the writer to step back and consider how he can use his knowledge to solve the problem of actually writing the paper. In some instances the switch is dramatic. A writer caught in the labyrinth of idea generation, pursuing fleeting nuances of his own thought, will suddenly stop and with a rather ruthless pragmatism ask, "Now, should I bring all that in"? One major group of plans for constructing a paper is concerned with exactly this question; *what to use* (out of all the available language and ideas already generated) and *how to use it.* We refer to these plans as *forming for use.*

In the following example the writer just generates her idea as part of an extended analysis of the topic. "As I was saying before that, (unless I would mention and I probably should mention that this is what I'm going to do) that most poems that fall into the convention of erotic poetry are dramatic monologues." The writer then returned to a reexamination of the topic for seven more lines until she appeared to step back and consider it afresh as a possible candidate for a point in her paper: "So that could be another thing: the fact that the style of the poem is a dramatic monologue." In one sense the writer's comment is simply bringing closure to a train of thought. But the perspective has changed: her idea has been pulled from its context and reshaped to become one of a list of points to be made in the final text.

In some cases writers make elaborate plans for how to use an idea and how it will affect a reader. Here a writer breaks into a half-completed argument with this plan: "ummm, and one might not in parentheses, every time I . . . I see Dave Mills . . . he says . . well, [here, the writer records a joke.]. And I think it's alright to say that because Dave Mills is, indeed, a good friend. Or, at least I think he is . . . But, that's not necessary, could be cut out if we want it very straightforward. Alright." This writer's plan not only considered what material he would use (the anecdote about Dave Mills) but how he would use it (as a joke), how it would affect the tone of his paper and the response of his audience, and finally, how he would handle it typographically to indicate its interpolated status. This example is particularly good at illustrating how writers integrate the multiple decisions which composing demands, from decisions about reader response and self-image, to organization, to sentence generation, down to visual representation in a text.

Organizing. A second major group of plans for producing a paper is concerned with *organizing the writer's ideas* in terms of sequence and their significance. Here we found writers, apparently overwhelmed with the ideas they had produced, firmly instructing themselves to *find a focus,* or to *write a second draft from some angle.* One writer was ruefully certain that *other* writers had a definite plan for constructing a paper and adopted an organizing plan that involved first establishing a definite focus:

Why can't I do that? Why can all these other people do that? They just pick out their little topic sentence and then they write their paper. If I just stuck to the topic sentence, maybe, and I just let the topic sentence govern all my thoughts and let that dictate what I was gonna talk about.

Beyond these global plans for finding a focus, our writers planned the organization of the paper at a number of levels. Comments such as, "I don't know whether this will go at the middle or end," show the writer planning alternative overall organizations even as he is writing a particular part of the paper.

Reader-Based Plans.   In examining the plans our writers employed for producing a paper, some plans appeared to be based on an awareness of an imagined reader and involved a strategy for communicating with the reader, while other plans appeared to be based on a concern with the formal nature of the finished product. Although this distinction was rarely clearcut, our writers did show a strong tendency to prefer either reader-based or product-based plans.

Reader-focused plans occur when writers spend a great deal of time considering who their audience is and developing plans or strategies based on what the reader might assume, object to, or need to know. In our observations, this planning did not seem to be accomplished by a mere, initial audience analysis; instead, it appeared to be a recurring concern of these writers. To some extent, these plans could be more accurately described as audience *tests* or *role playing.* Thus, a writer will generate a few sentences, then stop and remark, "that wouldn't communicate anything to anybody," or "that's not convincing." However, these writers also generated a number of plans for communicative objectives they wanted to achieve with their imagined reader. In the following example, a writer is working on an earlier plan to deal with objections his audience might have to the value of various memory techniques (the subject of his paper). This reader-based goal has a marked effect on his generation of ideas because it leads him to generate two quite different perspectives on his subject (e.g., he could either argue that the techniques are useful or that they are not widely useful, but demonstrate an important principle.)

One of the problems in writing this essay... will be to expand on, either to expand on that usefulness and make it seem more plausible..uh..let's see,...Problem..to make uses more general and acceptable and, uh..or alternatively, if that's not the solution to the problem, alternate approach is to say...so those applications really aren't important...aren't important. What really is important is the instructional value...not the right word,...of the demonstration of encoding the principle behind the technique.

This protocol shows two things. First, the concern for the reader is operating at a number of levels, governing not only the ideas and focus of the paper, but decisions about word choice and the general impression the prose creates. Second, planning for a reader is an intimate part of idea generation, one which leads the writer to go back and explore the topic itself. Perhaps the most interesting fact about reader-based plans is not that some people make them and use them to direct many aspects of their composing process, but that some writers do not. It seems almost axiomatic that if writing is a communicating process, the writer needs to recognize the other side of the equation, the reader. And if writing is a problem-solving process, a writer needs some goal, such as a reader, toward which to plan.

Product-Based Plans.   We might, if we have read enough student papers on a bad day, be tempted to say that for some, writing is simply a printout of the writer's mental state at the moment of composition—a stream of consciousness given readable form. However, for some writers there seems to be another alternative to no plans or to plans based on a reader. That alternative is to generate plans based on the features of the final written product. Product-based plans occur when the composing process is governed by a concern for the form of the finished product. The composing process of the writer we saw earlier was governed by the form a literary *explication de text* should take. Sometimes ideas are seen as potential paragraphs waiting to be written: "Here's an interesting point. I think I'll probably write a paragraph on this." The influence of the product on the composing process appears to become more critical when writers feel confused about their topic, but under pressure to produce something. In the following example, Roger had tried a series of abortive plans to generate ideas and find a focus for the paper. When these failed, he decided to try to compose first a sentence and then an outline as a way to give direction to his bogged-down thinking process.

I can't read this stuff and understand, you know, so. [This appears to be the signal for a new plan.] Well I'm just trying to see, I'm trying to see if I could compose some kind of sentence that would give me a kind of a . . . but maybe I'm too early for a sentence now. Maybe I just need to, . . . maybe what I could, is I could outline this topic. Because it's just small enough to fit into this paper, you know . . . In a way it could be interesting to think about a lot, in other ways and in other times, but in just this one instance here, you know, maybe I might need two instances . . . it might be enough for this paper.

See, I could put down in an outline. I could start the outline Roman Numeral I: Becoming Convinced. *A* implies that I wasn't convinced to start out with. *B* implies a process. Now *A* implies other things, see. If I just go down to 1 sub *A* and I say A1....Specifically, see, but... I don't really know what I'm doing with this *A, B* stuff. I guess I'll just try and do it and see if it helps me by just putting things in lines.

This passage illustrates a number of important strategies. To begin with, Roger is clearly making distinctions between what he knows or might like to think about *in other ways and in other times,* and what he actually wants to produce for this particular paper. Momentarily discouraged by his difficulty with the topic, he has switched (as writers often do) from a generating plan to a composing plan. He attempts to produce a paper. In doing so, he gives us a clear example of a composing plan based on the writer's image of a final product (or outline, in this case) rather than on a reader/writer strategy or an expression of what the writer *really means.* The great advantage of the product plan, of course, is that it offers a much clearer and simpler basis for making decisions and relating ideas. A plan which tells you to make a three-point outline and write sentences is much less intimidating than a plan which asks you to *understand* and then *convince* someone else. But of course, simpler is not always better.

Roger's first plan for constructing the paper was to write a sentence, but when that failed, he tried to let an outline dictate his process, in somewhat the way a paint-by-numbers set directs the process of producing a piece of *art.* The outline seems to offer a series of slots to fill in; having an *A* implies that he should discover some subpoints to fill in the blanks. As the outlining effort continued, it threatened to take over with a plethora of subpoints and ideas with labels that never appeared again:

OK the initial phrase..., yea, I'm gonna call that Ip— Initial phrase that bothered me or initial bothersome phrase. Okay, then I'm gonna put [a quote from his source]. Basically, I want somebody to write this for me. The goal your mind has dreamed of, your mind, mind mind, mind mind. Now, that's another thing about Medieval thought that you get to know, and that's and that's... this is A1. so this is A1—I don't even know what I'm doing at this point.

As the writer says later, "this is very incoherent on a page too, which is unfortunate."

In the long run, the outlining plan, based on the formal properties of a completed outline or finished paper, was no help to the confused writer. Outlining, however, did seem to work when he used it as a loosely structured, visual record of his thinking process. As he says, "I usually can do alright once I can get some kind of outline, because then I can mess around with the form of the outline, because I'm not too fussy about what kind of form an outline has and what kind of form a paper has and where you... where you end up with, as long as it's interesting getting there, you know." While one of Roger's troubles may lie in his standards for a good paper, another lies in his plans for how to compose it.

Product-based plans often appeared to be peculiarly ineffective for our subjects. When the form of the final product (that tightly structured series of well-formed sentences and ideas) was translated into a plan for getting that product, the result appeared to interfere with the normal generating process that occurs during writing. For example, because a finished paper is conventionally a series of sentences with close logical and syntactic links, some writers assumed that they should *generate their ideas* in a correctly ordered, closely reasoned manner, as well as in well-formed and elaborately linked sentences. On the occasions in which they were able to do this, they reported that their ideas were *flowing*. When their thoughts did not *flow out* in a final form, these writers became frustrated and frequently abandoned the results of apparently fruitful but unstructured brainstorming. They appeared not to recognize the potential value of what they had said.

Product plans can affect not only the quality of a writer's thinking process, but also its efficiency. Because papers often begin with an introduction which gives an integrated overview of a subject, a product-based plan tells a writer to start by composing such an overview which is often extremely difficult to write at the beginning. Thus, this product plan can lead to difficulty in getting started. The writing process, like any creative process, is rarely straightforward or direct. A writer's conclusions, his main ideas, even his focus, are often the product of searching, trial and error, and inference. Thus, our protocols show that writers rarely start with the topic headings an outline demands; these too are concepts the writer generates in the process of writing. The composing process of a typical writer appears to be erratic, jumping from high-level plans down to fragments of a sentence destined for the final draft, and up again to a series of inferences leading to the creation of a new category or major issue. Even the writer's definition of a *topic* may change during the composing process.

Often creative thinking proceeds best by a process of assembling topics and arguments in an unordered fashion, and then developing a form to suit the material. This process could easily be disrupted by focussing on form too early. Thus a product-based plan may thwart the dynamics of the normal generating process by placing unnecessarily rigid constraints in the early stages of the composing process. Because our protocols suggest that the use of product plans may be one of the major problems that plague writers, we will return to this topic when we discuss conflicts among plans.

Interaction Among Plans

In the preceding pages we have argued that writers appear to generate two relatively distinct kinds of plans as they write (1) plans for generating ideas, and (2) plans for using those ideas to produce a paper. If writing is not a straightforward, holistic process of *saying what you know,* but is composed of two kinds of planning which may cooperate or compete, then we will want to know how the processes interact. In the following section we will look at three sorts of interaction: switching from one plan to another, mapping from one plan to another, and conflict among plans.

Switching Plans.   The writers we observed not only generated and kept track of a variety of alternative plans; they also frequently *switched* plans. The most predictable and major switches came when a writer had completed a line of reasoning or run into difficulty. In some cases, writers ran out of ideas because they didn't have adequate procedural plans (e.g., "jot down more random questions I have"). In such situations, writers frequently switched to trying to compose a series of sentences. Such clear-cut divisions between plans for generating ideas and for producing a written product seem to be most characteristic of the early stages of the writing process. The following example illustrates a writer switching from one plan to another. In writing an application for a fellowship, her generating plan had been to describe how writers like herself work. Notice how she abruptly switches from this activity to planning ways she might use her rather rambling thoughts in a finished paper.

> I'm thinking about what Wendy was talking about um. . . . taking a character and dropping it into all these kinds of situations. And I'm thinking now that whatever comes out on this page is certainly not going to be suitable for anybody to see and God forbid if they, they wanted to give me a scholarship that they'd probably run me out of the school if they saw it. Taking a character and dropping it into several different situations.
>
> . . . .
>
> I'm thinking now how can I use that in my essay, um . . . [and the writer returns to the topic.]

It often appears as if the writer were testing her body of generated ideas to see if it would fit into a possible plan for constructing a paper. Her conclusion was generally *no,* and she then quickly switched back to generating additional ideas.

Mapping Plans Onto One Another.   Although switching between plans occurs frequently, a complete account of plans in the composing process would have to account for how the processes of generating ideas and producing a text become integrated. One way in which this happens is through a process of mapping in which one plan is superimposed upon another or dictates the formation of the second, so that a single plan can accomplish both tasks.

comment, "I'm just listing things. This is a rip." Judging from the rest of the protocol, Pat simply threw that entire body of ideas away. It didn't look like a paper. Later, when asked to evaluate the generating she had done in the hour, her vigorous criticisms of herself showed an image of idea-generation based on the rules of paper production: coherence, focus, no listing, no repetition, no wandering from point to point. And yet, these are some of the acitivities which are essential to thoughtful and creative generation. Here the writer's plan for constructing a paper was narrowing her intellectual options and stifling the very process she needed to undertake *before* she began to produce a *text*.

The issue of conflicts among plans is not that some plans are good and others, bad. Rather it involves powerful plans in appropriate places. Thus, our protocols suggest that premature outlining—when you try to outline ideas you don't yet know—is a relatively weak procedure for generating fresh ideas. On the other hand, outlining can be quite powerful as a method of giving structure to a large network of ideas already generated. A writer whose initial plan was to jot down random ideas would obviously want to switch tactics when he wished to construct a coherent paper.

IMPLICATIONS FOR INSTRUCTION

We have attempted in our research to be descriptive rather than prescriptive. We would like to approach the topic of writing instruction in a similar fashion by summarizing some of the critical aspects of the composing process we have observed in student writers, and examining some likely implications for instruction.

Writing as a Thinking Process.   The most important outcome of our research has been the opportunity to view writing as a complex problem-solving process. This viewpoint provides a useful orientation to writing instruction. It could enable teachers to intervene at points in the writing process that could do writers the most good—as they are actually engaged in the act of writing. Thus, teachers could help writers to *write,* not just learn to *repair the damage.* By recognizing writing as the difficult thinking problem that it is, we can more accurately define both the problems and the skills a writer has. Although we have achieved a preliminary identification of many of the plans and difficulties college student writers have, we have not yet determined the answers to a number of interesting questions: What are the most basic or fundamental planning strategies needed for expository writing? What is the relationship of these strategies to the plans used in other forms of writing? How do the plans of good writers differ from those of less proficient writers? How do plans develop as writers progress from basic competency to fluency with varied forms of written expression? Is it possible to diagnose the problems of a weak writer in terms of inefficient or inappropriate planning strategies?

The first premise of a problem-solving approach is that there is no single "correct" way to write. There are only alternative approaches to the endless series of problems and decisions writers must confront as they work through the process of composing. Some of these alternative approaches, however,have a better chance of producing a good solution than others. The ultimate goal of a process approach to writing, then, is not to prescribe a proper process, but instead, to give writers increased awareness of alternatives as they work through the problem of writing.

Writer's Awareness of the Process.   When writers' plans conflict, this is a very real, *practical* problem. For example, an initial plan to generate ideas can be thwarted by a sub-plan to produce useable sentences which *flow*. However, this conflict is really symptomatic of a larger problem, for writers' plans reflect the assumptions they hold about the writing process and about how it should work. When plans fail to map easily onto one another and writers give up in frustration, or stop productive idea generation because it doesn't look like a finished paper, we can see how writers' faulty or inadequate understanding of the writing process actually prevents them from doing what they could do. It is not that they lack the skills to write, but that they do not know how or when to use them.

If writers' awareness of the process is important, then this raises the question of how they become aware of this process. The most pertinent example here is the distinction between generating ideas and constructing a paper. These processes make different demands on writers. To do each well, writers at times recognize and maintain the distinction between different processes and their demands (e.g., "I'll worry about organizing later."). At the same time, writers also must try to integrate different plans in order to turn general knowledge into a particular written exposition of that knowledge. This means knowing *how to write,* not just what good writing looks like. One implication is clear: the anthologized essay which purports to teach writing doesn't give students a hint of the intellectual process the writer went through to produce it—the methods and the decisions as well as the false starts and frustrations. In fact, the perfected essay may itself suggest a model of the process as clean, logical, and straightforward which the student, to his disadvantage, tries to emulate.

Writing Without Plans.   If juggling plans can be difficult, working without plans can be more difficult still. In many of the students we observed, the absence of simple procedural plans seemed connected to frustration and confusion. When *trains of thought* inevitably came to an end, writers differed in their ability to invoke alternative procedures (reread, jot down more random thoughts, take a walk and incubate, polish later), and thus restart the composing process. Procedural plans are not mysterious or difficult, but they do require a certain self-consciousness about the thinking/working process of writing and an awareness of the useful techniques writers use.

An even more interesting phenomenon our observations revealed was that some writers appeared to be making no self-conscious plans for their reader. This means that there were writers who not only neglected to mention or discuss their audience but who also failed to think in terms of making a conclusion or a point, or to imagine the criticism, confusion, or agreement they might stimulate by saying x, y, or z. These writers seemed to lack clear plans for communicating with or affecting a reader. This may also account for some of their difficulty in writing. If a writer is not treating writing as a *communication* process, if the imagined reader has dropped out of his decision process, he has made the choice of what to say easier but his chance of successful communication more remote, because he has lost a goal against which to test his progress.

Finally, there was in our sample of student writers a small group whose writing behavior was seemingly inconsistent with our conjecture that working without a high-level plan is difficult. These writers appeared to be working with a very simple plan: write whatever comes to mind. When one writer paused for an instant and was asked what he was thinking, his response was, I'm thinking what to say next." And he then proceeded to write it. For these writers, the composing process was smooth, unbroken act of verbalizing their thoughts. It is probably significant that in college work outside of this study these students tended to write papers with an anecdotal, stream of consciousness structure. In the absence of plans—plans for the reader, plans for constructing a paper, plans for stepping back and saying what you really mean, drawing conclusions, or locating a conflict—the composing process for these writers was a comfortable train of associations in which one idea naturally led to another, but the beginning and the end never met. This apparently comfortable blending of idea generation, organization and production in these writers' prose reminded us once again of the extreme variations in mental activity which produces writing. Through our observations we have come to appreciate even more the large demands which learning to write places on teachers and learners.

REFERENCES

Flower, L. and J. R. Hayes. "The dynamics of composing: Making plans and juggling constraints." In *Cognitive Processes in Writing: An Interdisciplinary Approach.* Eds. Lee Gregg and Erwin Steinberg. Hillsdale, New Jersey: Lawrence Erlbaum, 1980.

Flower, L. and J. R. Hayes "Problem-solving strategies and the writing process," *College English,* 39 (Dec., 1977), p. 449–461.

Hayes, J. R. *Cognitive psychology: thinking and creating.* Homewood, Illinois: Dorsey Press, 1978.

Hayes, J. R. and L. Flower. "Identifying the organization of writing processes." In *Cognitive Processes in Writing: An Interdisciplinary Approach.* Eds. Lee Gregg and Erwin Steinberg. Hillsdale, New Jersey: Lawrence Erlbaum, 1980.

Miller, G., E. Galanter, and K. Pribram. *Plans and the structure of behavior.* New York: Holt, Rinehart and Winston, 1960.

Newell, A. and H. Simon. *Human problem-solving.* Englewood Cliffs. Prentice Hall, 1972.

4 Problems and the Composing Process

Richard Young
Head, Department of English
Carnegie-Mellon University

Among the most significant of recent developments in rhetorical studies is a redefining of the composing process to include activities formerly considered to be, at most, ancillary to it. For at least three-quarters of a century composition has been concerned, on the whole, with problems of style and editing. In the last few years, however, interest has increased in those activities which precede the activity of writing, such as concept formation, invention (in the classical sense), and, perhaps most importantly, the discovery of judgments and generalizations which order and give meaning to experience. This interest has manifested itself in two ways: in research into the nature of these activities and, more often, in the creation of sets of operations (i.e., heuristic procedures) which enable one to carry out the activities more deliberately and efficiently. In short, a rhetoric of inquiry is emerging which complements the rhetoric of the finished word.

The development is encouraging since, historically, the importance of rhetoric in the academic curriculum has been closely related to its capacity for dealing with content and inquiry. But as significant as this work is, it doesn't go far enough. Traditional approaches have been criticized for arbitrarily segmenting what is a continuous process at a fairly late stage, usually at the rough draft, and for saying little or nothing about the activities which precede this stage. For example, Rohman and Wlecke argue that "traditional approaches to the writing process are ...inadequate if they fail to take account of the radically perspectival nature of writing. Typically such approaches stress only the virtues of hindsight—the 'rhetoric of the finished word'—without giving attention of the primary necessity of insight—the stage of discovery in shaping experience into perspective" (Rohman & Wlecke, 1964, p. 20). However, those working on concept formation and the discovery of ordering generalizations are open to a similar criticism (e.g. Rohman & Wlecke, 1964; Jennings, 1968; Larson, 1968; Stewart, 1972). They describe and illustrate procedures for controlling various cognitive acts but have little to say about *why* one performs these acts. They provide us with tools for doing something without explaining the motivation for doing it.[1]

Perhaps the reason is that in the classroom the teacher supplies the motivation when he gives the student an assignment. Unlike his classical counterpart, the modern rhetorician has tended to conceive of his art as a pedagogical rather than a psychological and social activity. And the peculiar needs of classroom instruction have tended to shape the art, resulting in distorted and incomplete notions about the composing process. In less artificial situations, when the writer is not responding to an assignment, what is it that sends him in quest of new concepts, judgments, and ordering generalizations?

These activities are, I believe, responses to cognitive needs. Inquiry begins with the need to readjust one's thinking to continually emerging problems. The heuristic procedures discussed with increasing frequency in our journals are attempts to specify acts we can engage in to make these adjustments (Young, 1976). And the finished work can be seen as a report on the adjustments we have made. To be sure, the work is also, simultaneously, an instrument for adjusting our relations with others, a response to a social problem. I would like, however, to limit the discussion to writing as a cognitive or expressive act rather than a social or affective act, and to consider its earliest moments. Such a bias leads us to ignore important features of the composing process while focusing on others, but it is justified if it yields useful insights and enables us to avoid being overwhelmed by complexity.

If a problem lurks somewhere behind every written work, then the nature of problems and procedures for dealing with them become relevant concerns for rhetoricians. What follows is an effort to explicate this stage of the composing process.

Problems do not exist independent of men. There are no problems floating around in the world out there waiting to be discovered; there are only problems for someone. For problems arise from inconsistencies among elements of the individual's cognitive system. We do not find problems, we create them. One's cognitive system, his Image of the world (Boulding, 1956), is composed of values, beliefs, opinions, organized and unorganized

---

[1]Lloyd Bitzer in his "Rhetoric Situation" (*Philosophy and Rhetoric,* Vol. 1, No. 1, January 1968) is a notable exception, as are Linda Flower and John Hayes in their work on problem-solving and the composing process.

information, all of which combine to form an exceedingly complex, more or less coherent system. A problem begins to take shape when one element of the Image is perceived to be inconsistent with another, as, for example, when I begin to see that two theories which I have accepted are incompatible, or when a sentence I have written violates my knowledge of English grammar, or when actions of our government violate values to which I am deeply committed.[2] A problem, then, is a special kind of psychological event.

It follows that because each of our cognitive systems is more or less unique, the problems which each of us has will also be more or less unique. For instance, a social system which is for the most part consistent with one person's image may be radically inconsistent with another's. Roy Wilkins, the former president of the NAACP, remarked once that white Americans cannot believe that the system which serves them so well is as cruel and ruthless and brutal as the Negroes in the ghettos know it. Someone who says he can't see what you're getting all worked up about is no doubt being quite honest. He really can't. The experience to which you respond with so much agitation simply does not clash with anything in his Image. The magnitude of the inconsistency may also differ, so that what is a great problem for one is inconsequential for another.

If, as some say, one's Image is his map of the world, it is a highly unusual map, for it is continuously in the process of readjusting itself. Conservative forces operate within the Image to maintain its consistency and stability; when one becomes aware of an inconsistency in his Image, pressures develop to eliminate it. Karl von Frish, whose simple and elegant experiments with bees are models of scientific research, describes the origin of a forty-year investigation this way:

> About 1910 a famous ophthalmologist, Professor C. von Hess, performed many experiments on fishes, insects, and other lower animals. He tested them while they were in a positively phototactic condition—that is, under circumstances where they moved into the brightest available light. He found that in a spectrum the animals always collected in the green and the yellow-green region, which is the brightest part of the spectrum for a colorblind human eye. Therefore, von Hess asserted, fishes and invertebrates, and in particular bees, are totally colorblind. If this is true, the colors of flowers would have no biological significance. But I could not believe it, and my skepticism was the first motive

---

[2]The summary of the origin and nature of problems presented here is based, in part, on Leon Festinger's *Theory of Cognitive Dissonance* (Stanford: Stanford Univ. Press, 1965). Festinger's theory seems particularly useful for our purposes, more so than comparable theories, because problems are seen as needs which lead to actions in the external world as well as in the mind, and because of the broad definition of dissonance. For a discussion of alternative theories, see Roger Brown's "Models of Attitude Change," in *New Directions in Psychology* (New York: Holt, Rinehart and Winston, 1962).

which led me to begin my studies of bees about forty years ago (von Frisch, 1960, p. 4).

His inquiry grew out of an awareness of the inconsistency between von Hess' assertation and his own belief that the colors of flowers were biologically significant. For him at least, the problem was sufficiently important to warrant years of work.

The awareness of inconsistencies in one's Image produces the wrinkled brow and uneasy feeling characteristic of the earliest stage of inquiry. If the inconsistency is sufficiently important, if we are sufficiently uncomfortable, we set about eliminating it. But how do we get enough control over this felt difficulty to begin systematic investigation? Usually we cannot press our inquiry to a satisfactory conclusion without first having a clear idea of the problem we are trying to solve. The more novel or complex the problem, the more essential it is that we understand it as clearly as possible. A false start at this stage of the inquiry affects all subsequent stages; for what begins poorly is likely to end the same way. "One may have the most rigorous of methods during the later stages of investigation," says F. S. C. Northrop,

> but if a false or superficial beginning has been made, rigor later on will never retrieve the situation. It is like a ship leaving port for a distant destination. A very slight erroneous deviation in taking one's bearings at the beginning may result in entirely missing one's mark at the end regardless of the sturdiness of one's craft or the excellence of one's subsequent seamanship (Northrop, 1965, p. 1).

Control over a felt difficulty begins with its analysis and articulation (which seem to be mutually dependent processes). And this leads those of us interested in the art of rhetoric to ask the following question: Can we develop a set of operations, a heuristic procedure, which can help us articulate problems?[3]

Two important components of any problem are already apparent, i.e., the clashing elements in the Image. It seems reasonable that these must be made explicit in an adequate statement of a problem. These in themselves, however, do not constitute a complete statement; together they constitute only a description of a *problematic situation.* A complete statement also includes a specification of the *unknown*—i.e., a statement of what it is that will enable us to eliminate, or at least mitigate, the inconsistency. Since this remains to be discovered, it is unusually stated as a question. A complete statement of a

---

[3]For a more complete answer than the one given here, see Chapter 5 of Richard Young, Alton Becker, and Kenneth Pike's *Rhetoric: Discovery and Change* (New York: Harcourt, Brace and World, 1970).

problem, then, has three basic components: the two clashing elements of the Image and the unknown.

A statement of the unknown is actually a partial description of the solution (Reitman, 1965, pp. 125–165). As such it serves two functions: (1) it serves as a guide for inquiry, for it specifies essential features of the solution; and (2) it enables us to know when we have found it, for the solution will match the description. Riddles, which are a special kind of unknown, illustrate clearly its descriptive character. "What goes on four feet, on two feet, and three, but the more feet it goes on the weaker it be?" But riddles are designed to puzzle whereas a well-stated unknown facilitates inquiry. As John Dewey points out,

> an unknown decides which specific suggestions are entertained and which are dismissed; what data are selected and which rejected; it is the criterion for relevancy and irrelevancy of hypotheses and conceptual structures (Dewey, 1938, p. 108).

This can be illustrated with a simple example. Everyone has had the experience of being unable to recall a name which he knows perfectly well; there is a peculiar gap in his consciousness where the name should be. Here is a problematic situation for which the missing name is a solution. Usually we can give a partial description of the name. We may know, for instance, that it begins with "B" and has more than one syllable. Our inquiry is guided at the outset by this description. We seek our solution not by searching through all the names that we know but through a sub-set having these two characteristics (Brown & McNeill, 1966, pp. 325–337). The unknown solution, then, is not totally unknown; it is partially known, and a well-stated question includes this partial knowledge.

Stating the two components of the problematic situation and then the unknown is a simple procedure for helping one move consciously and deliberately toward an adequate statement of the problem without waiting for unpredictable insights and without an excessive number of false starts. If it does not guarantee an adequately stated problem, it at least increases the chances of producing one. As far as I know, there are only two other procedures for stating problems in rhetoric. The first is the doctrine of *stasis* developed by Greek and Roman rhetoricians. It is a method for locating the issue to be argued in a court of law and as such has a limited applicability. Furthermore, it appears to be more concerned with questions to be argued than with problems to be solved. (See, for example, Quintilian, *Institutio oratoria* 3.6.80-104.) The second procedure requires the writer to *classify* and *state* problems as problems of fact, value, means, probability, and meaning (Graves and Oldsey, 1963). Although this can help to sharpen our thinking, it is not a very powerful procedure. What is really being classified is the unknown, and an unknown cannot be stated adequately without first understanding the problematic situation. For it is a careful study of the problematic situation which largely determines the features of the unknown. The classificational procedure fails to take account of the process I have been describing which begins with a feeling of psychological discomfort, moves through an analysis of its origins, and only then to a description of what will eliminate it. The inadequacy of the procedure illustrates the need for research on the psychological phenomena we seek to control and on the relative effectiveness of our heuristic procedures.

Extending our definition of the composing process to include the earliest stage of inquiry has several important implications for the teaching of writing. For one, it encourages the instructor to create a classroom situation which more nearly approximates actual writing situations. When a teacher assigns a topic to the entire class, he does create a problem for the student, but it is the wrong kind. The impulse to write seldom springs from the student's effort to develop and maintain an ordered and meaningful Image of the world, but rather from a desire to pass the course and avoid the various punishments which he knows await him if he fails. What student would ever write an essay comparing Ophelia and Desdemona or describing the furnishings of his room unless he were coerced into it by a teacher? He has better things to think about. As an alternative, the student can be helped to isolate and come to terms with his own problems, any problems, so long as they are *for him* genuine and interesting.

Not all inconsistencies which we find interesting, however, compel us toward solutions. Some may strike us as so curious or so charming that we settle our attention on them, and they become the subjects of discourse. Consider, for example, the "fabulous realities" Ken Macrorie urges his students to note and record; they are what I have called here *problematic situations*. Once attuned to them, we find them everywhere:

> I stood in the checkout lane behind a boy who looked about sixteen. He waited for the clerk to begin ringing up his package of Pall Malls, then reached out and added five packs of bubble gum (quoted in Macrorie, 1970, pp. 38–39).

The mind lingers with the inconsistency. Who the perceiver is determines whether the boy's unexpected behavior becomes an end in itself or the motive for further inquiry. But there is a larger generalization to be made here. Macrorie seems to me correct when he says that "the looking and discovery involved in producing fabulous realities is not a trick and not an exercise. It is the way good writers see" (Macrorie, 1970, p. 41).

It is, of course, possible, and at times desirable, for the teacher to present students with a problem rather than encourage them to find their own. But the problem should be presented in such a way that it becomes real and important to the students, so that they make it their own. We can develop various heuristic procedures for doing this. Abelard, for example, developed one which is well worth close study. Called *Sic et Non* (Yes and No), it juxtaposed contradictory statements by acknowledged authorities on an important issue, such as whether it is ever lawful to kill someone. If his students accepted the statements as authoritative (Abelard often quoted the Church Fathers and the Bible), they were faced with a problematic situation: the authorities know the truth, yet they contradict each other. Or as Abelard described the procedure, "when a number of quotations from [various] writings are introduced they spur the reader and allure him into seeking the truth in proportion as the authority of the writing itself is commended" (quoted in Norton, 1909, p. 19). The procedure, he continues, stimulates "tender readers to the utmost effort in seeking the truth" (Norton, 1909, p. 20).

The discovery of a significant problem and the discovery of a reasonable solution are or can be exciting and intrinsically rewarding activities, and they provide strong incentives for communication. Once students have been adequately instructed, they have little trouble with that traditional problem of composition courses—finding something to say. Adequate instruction includes not only instruction in the nature and articulation of problems but sharpening the student's awareness of his own cognitive life and encouraging him to believe that events in it are worthy and appropriate subjects for investigation. Students, and teachers, often regard problems as signs of personal incapacity—the good student is supposed to have answers, not problems. But problems are more profitably seen as opportunities to be seized. They mark the points at which the mind is ready to grow. Students also tend to see classroom problems as divorced from the "real" world and the genuine problems which it poses for them. It takes considerable effort and ingenuity by teachers to help students discover that a writing class provides an opportunity for confronting significant events in their psychological lives.

Although it is often easy to ignore the problems of others, we have difficulty ignoring problems that are, for us, real and important. Coming to terms with our problems is necessary for preserving our psychological stability and for adjusting ourselves to a changing, often enigmatic world. Thus, problems are important motivations to action; none of us needs to be prodded to solve a real problem any more than we need to be urged to eat when we are hungry. Much could be done to solve the teacher's perennial problem of student motivation if our methods were rooted in these facts of human behavior. A redefinition of the composing process to include this earliest stage of inquiry would result in a more adequate concept of rhetorical invention while encouraging the development of instructional procedures which reflect the profound interest we all have in our psychological lives and the great desire we have to create order and meaning there.

ACKNOWLEDGMENTS

Work on this paper was supported in part under Contract OEC-3-6-061784-0508, U. S. Office of Education. An earlier version was one of several papers submitted to the U. S. Office of Education as *Studies in Language and Language Behavior*, Progress Report VIII, February, 1969.

REFERENCES

Boulding, K. *The Image.* Ann Arbor: University of Michigan Press, 1956.

Brown, R., & McNeill. D. The "tip of the tongue" phenomenon. *Journal of Verbal Learning and Verbal Behavior*, 1966, *5*, 325–337.

Dewey, J. *Logic: The theory of inquiry.* New York: Henry Holt, 1938.

Graves, H. F. & Oldsey, B. S. *From fact to judgment.* New York: Macmillan, 1963.

Jennings, E. M. A paradigm for discovery. *College Composition and Communication*, 1968, *29*, 192–200.

Larson, R. Discovery through questioning: A plan for teaching rhetorical invention. *College English*, 1968, *30*, 126–134.

Macrorie, K. *Telling writing.* New York: Hayden, 1970.

Northrop, F. S. C. *The logic of sciences and the humanities.* Cleveland, Ohio: World, 1965.

Norton, A. O. *Readings in the history of education: Mediaeval universities.* Cambridge, Mass.: Harvard University Press, 1909.

Quintilian, *Institutio oratoria*, Trans. H.E. Butler. London: Heinemann, 1920.

Reitman, W. R. *Cognition and thought: An information processing approach.* New York: Wiley 1965.

Rohman, D. G. & Wlecke, A. O. *Pre-Writing: The construction and application of models of concept formation in writing.* Washington, D.C.: Cooperative Research Project No. 2174, Cooperative Research Program of the Office of Education, U. S. Department of Health, Education, and Welfare, 1964.

Stewart, D. C. *The authentic voice: A pre-writing approach to student writing.* Dubuque, Iowa: Wm C. Brown, 1972.

von Frisch, K. *Bees: Their vision, chemical senses, and language.* Ithaca, N.Y.: Cornell University Press, 1960.

Young, R. Invention: a topographical survey. In Gary Tate (Ed.), *Teaching composition: 10 bibliographic essays.* Fort Worth, Texas: Texas Christian University Press, 1976, pp. 1–43.

5 Revising

Ellen W. Nold
Stanford University

Recent research indicates that one of the major differences between skilled adult writers and unskilled adult writers is the way they revise. Sommers (1978) found that skilled adults first revised globally and then revised locally: they added and deleted large chunks of discourse first, and then considered their sentences and words. Unskilled writers, on the other hand, were stuck on words; they very seldom added or deleted paragraphs or changed the structure of sentences. They viewed revision as "finding the right word" and changing their prose to conform to the rules of written English as they understood them. Indeed, Beach (1976) suggested that adult sophistication of the revising strategies would be an excellent indicator of the developmental level of adult writers. In this chapter I explore a simple model of the writing process that illustrates the differences between skilled and unskilled adult writers. I caution against accepting notions like Beach's without proper control of other important variables, like subjective difficulty of task. Finally, I discuss the pedagogical implications of the model.

A SIMPLE MODEL OF THE WRITING PROCESS

Writing may usefully be viewed as a solution to a complex communication problem. Writers formulate discourse, often extended, for absent audiences to achieve their own and their readers' goals. Writers' communication problems are often ill-defined: there are many optimal solutions. Feedback from the audience is often delayed and difficult to assess.

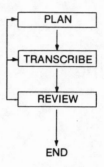

FIG. 1.   A model of the writing process.

When psychologists study the formulation of other solutions to complex problems, they typically identify three activities: *planning* the solution, *carrying out* the plan, and *reviewing* the results to judge if they meet the criteria for a good solution. For writing we can schematize the process as in Figure 1. The recursive arrows on the left of the diagram in Figure 1 remind us that planning, transcribing and reviewing are not one-time processes. As their texts grow and change, writers plan, transcribe and review in irregular patterns.

Revising is *not* a subprocess in the same way as planning, transcribing and reviewing are; rather, it is the *retranscribing* of text already produced. Writers retranscribe because they have decided, after reviewing text or their plans, that portions of the text are not what they had intended or not what their readers need. But in order to retranscribe, writers must be able to generate a more acceptable solution. If they cannot, they will not change their text. This analysis of revising shows that revising strategies cannot be inferred from the text alone: writers indeed may want to revise, but not be able to because they lack more promising solutions.

Let us circle back and flesh out this bare-bones scheme of the writing process, defining the psychological constraints on the process, the development of the subprocesses and the functions of each of the subprocesses. Each of the subprocesses of writing is assumed to involve focal attention and to be circumscribed by the well-known limits of short-term memory. Thus, all three subprocesses cannot operate simultaneously, even when a skilled writer completes an easy writing task. In fact, when most writers complete a task of moderate difficulty, even one subprocess probably overloads processing space. Thus, skilled adult writers must employ strategies to handle the overload on their attention; in fact, one of the differences in the processes of skilled writers may be the conscious application of these strategies in writing.

In addition, each of the subprocesses relies for its raw materials on knowledge, beliefs and other constructs in long-term memory (LTM). The raw materials may be generated just for the solution of the writing problem at hand, or they may be generated long before. The richness and accuracy of these materials in LTM affect both ease of writing and quality of the product. As a simple example, consider spelling. If writers do not have a rich and accurate store of remembered spellings, their writing can be slowed by overload on attention, and their texts may be judged illiterate.

There are two principal ways that individuals can increase the total workload handled by their limited attention: (1) by making various elements of the process routine, in order to decrease the processing *space* (attention) they require and (2) by applying a broad range of strategies over *time* to attend to all important elements of the process for a high-quality performance. Developmental psychologists often argue that processing *space* does not usually change over individuals' lifetimes: as they mature, their space is merely used *longer* (as attention-span increases) and *better* (as various tasks become routine and as they learn to apply load-reducing strategies).

Flavell (1977) speculated that both the planning and reviewing subprocesses are late-developing abilities:

One late-developing behavior is carefully shaping and tailoring a message under novel, unfamiliar conditions or constraints, as in some of those problem-solving type communications tasks of the earlier tradition. If you have to "solve" a "communication problem," rather than just say "what comes naturally" in a familiar communicative interchange, then you may have to consciously analyze, evaluate and edit candidate messages. Similarly, if your listener indicates that he did not understand your message, you may have to reanalyze and reevaluate it in order to construct a more adequate one (p. 178).

One reason that children may not feel the need to plan or review messages may be that they overestimate all their cognitive abilities, like their ability to memorize (Flavell, Friedrichs and Hoyt, 1970). Naive about how limited their attention is, children act as if it is equal to any task at any moment.

Recent experiments have shown that necessary activities for both planning and reviewing, such as examining the *message* for faults and taking the role of audience, are indeed late-developing. Markman (1977), for example, found that young children are unlikely to recognize the inadequacy of instructions given them. Her finding supports Robinson's (1976) deduction that young children are likely to blame the failure of instructions on the *listener* not the speaker. Cooper and Flavell (1972; reported in Glucksberg, Krauss and Higgins, 1975) deduced that by sixth grade, many children are aware of the need to take the role of audience, though they cannot effectively act upon or maintain that awareness. Cooper and Flavell tested five components of role-taking behavior with second and sixth graders:

existence, the awareness of...perspectives in general; *need,* knowing that analyzing perspectives is useful...; *prediction,* the ability to infer the task-relevant role attributes of...another; *maintenance,* the ability to maintain these inferences over time...; *application,* the ability to apply (that) awareness...to particular situations.

In response to two different tasks requiring talking about a new experience to an adult and to a child, the second-graders' performance was primarily accounted for by the first three components, while the sixth-graders' performance was accounted for primarily by the last two.

Moving to research more obviously directed at writing, we find that Crowhurst (1977) lends support to Cooper and Flavell's analysis by reporting that sixth-graders do not significantly vary the syntactic complexity of their writing when communciating to a best friend or to a teacher, but tenth-graders do. But even much older students—those in college, for example—have considerable difficulty responding to readers' needs. In exploring Flavell's (1968) theory that a speaker first encodes a message for himself and then revises it for an audience, Flower (1979) attempted to describe the structure and style of *writer-based prose* as opposed to *reader-based prose* written by college students. The differences are consistent, though Flower has not yet shown that they arise from different (or extended) generation strategies. Though promising, the concept of role-taking ability has not yet been operationally defined precisely enough to be a *predictor* of writing competence, though the work of Scardamalia, Bereiter and MacDonald (1977) is a step in this direction.

THE SIMPLE MODEL ELABORATED

If we elaborate our simple model, we can determine where the willingness to examine the *text* for faults and to take the role of the *audience* fit in to the writing process. We can also use this model to predict what might impel young writers to revise and what criteria might be considered by writers quite late in their development.

Planning

The planning subprocess of a skilled adult writer results in three products, stored in memory to be used in transcribing and reviewing. The planning subprocess uses as raw materials memories (knowledge, experiences and beliefs) stored in LTM before writers begin to write. Also stored are knowledge and experiences they consciously generate in order to solve the particular communication problem at hand. The three products of the planning subprocess are:

1. a representation of the writer's intended meaning;
2. a representation of the writer's intended audience—its knowledge, experiences and beliefs as well as its purpose(s) in reading;
3. a representation of the persona the writer wishes to project through his or her writing.

These products constrain each other and may force changes in each other as planning progresses. For example, a given meaning may not be able to be communicated to a given audience within given constraints of space. When writers notice such conflicts, they resolve them in planning.

Though none of these products of the planning subprocess are necessarily verbal, the planning subprocesses of skilled writers are often accompanied by note-taking, especially if the task is difficult. These notes can range from sketchy phrases to elaborate sentence outlines.

Transcribing

In the transcribing subprocess skilled adult writers are constrained by their global plans about meaning, audience, and persona. They draw from language knowledge (syntax, vocabulary, orthographics) to produce writing. During this local planning and execution at least seven other kinds of constraints may demand attention:

Semantic layout Writers feel constrained to represent faithfully the contours of their intended meaning—that is, to subordinate incidental information and to highlight crucial information. In addition, writers must manage given and new information to assure their readers' comprehension (Clark and Haviland, 1977). *Given* information may be:

1. explicitly specified previously in the same text,
2. reasonably inferred from information in previous text by the intended audience, or
3. reasonably assumed that the audience already knows.

Writer may need to keep a representation of their intended audience in mind as they form sentences and choose words.

Syntax Writers must form sentences to follow the grammar of their language and make them simple enough to understand, but not too simple. Syntax is itself constrained by choices about semantic layout and by the grapholect. To respond fully to these constraints, writers must bear in mind the abilities of their intended audience.

Grapholect   Hausen (1966) defined *grapholect* as a dialect of English used in formal written texts addressed to wide and/or educated audiences. Its requirements are stated in the many handbooks of usage published in America; among them are proper distinction between *between* and *among* and a prejudice for most strings of words punctuated as sentences to contain a subject and tensed verb. These constraints do not require the writer to envision the needs of any particular audience.

Word choice   The word choice of skilled adult writers is subject to at least four constraints:

1. how closely the word mirrors their intended meaning;
2. what the intended audience associates with the word;
3. how the word functions in the discourse (is it a key term?); and
4. how the word strikes the writer's aesthetic sense.

In addition, syntactical choices also constrain word choice. To respond fully to the constraints of word choice, then, the writer must consider the knowledge and experiences of his particular audience.

Physical layout   Constrained by the semantic layout and reflecting its grossest and finest contours, are headings, paragraphing, lists, graphics, spacing words, and handwriting.

Orthographics   Unconstrained by any considerations of audience and meaning, orthographics are the conventions of spelling and punctuating written English. In the case of unskilled writers bent on producing correct English, lack of orthographic knowledge sometimes determines word choice and syntactic structures.

Motor skills   Handwriting or typing may take up attention during the transcribing process though not in skilled adult writers, unless they use an unfamiliar machine. These can affect and constrain some aspects of the physical layout.

Figure 2 summarizes the constraints between different classes of possible attention-takers during the planning and transcribing subprocesses of a skilled adult writer. Note that the arrows flow from the products of the planning subprocesses to the transcribing subprocess: semantic layout (which further constrains) word choice, syntax and physical layout. Word choice and syntax are even further constrained by each other, by the grapholect and, for unskilled writers, by the orthographics of English. (That is, unskilled writers bent on correctness often do not use words they cannot spell or structures they cannot punctuate.) Note that no arrows flow to grapholect, orthographics

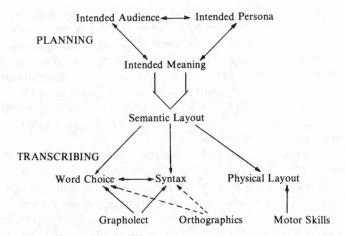

Arrows represent direction of constraint.
Broken arrows indicate constraints for unskilled writers but not usually for skilled writers.

FIG. 2. Constraints between the classes of possible attention-takers during the planning and transcribing subprocesses of a skilled adult writer.

and motor skills; these are not constrained by the particular communication task at hand. Thus, they can be (and usually are) taught and judged without reference to particular communication tasks. But that is a point to be explored further in the next section.

Reviewing

The raw materials of the reviewing subprocess are memories of the text: what it said, how it sounded, how it looked. Writers usually refresh their memories by rereading portions of the text: the last letter written, the last phrase, the last clause, the last paragraph(s). They may evaluate them, ie., match them against their intentions. The complexity of the review subprocess is bounded by the depth of the planning subprocess that has preceded it: writers cannot match the text against their intentions if they have not elaborated upon them. Similarly, if they have not conceived the audience or their own persona, they cannot evaluate their text against these. Texts written with minimal planning—say free writing exercises chronicling random thoughts—can be reviewed only against criteria that are constant across all communication tasks: adherence to the grapholect, to orthographic constraints, to standards of legibility. Young writers—who normally do not make elaborate plans about meaning, audience and persona—can be expected to review their texts only against the conventions of written English they hold in memory; older children or adult unskilled writers can be expected to review against *their* intended meaning first, unaffected by audience constraints either in reviewing or planning. Only when writers become quite skilled and sophisticated socially can they imagine and respond more than rudimentally to the varying needs of different audiences. We know that children vary their language when talking to younger children, and we know that the complex tasks inhibit children's ability to respond to the needs of younger ones (Shatz, 1978). We hypothesize, then, that even children can succeed at an easy writing task for an audience younger than they are.

Reviewing includes reading and evaluating. I have already discussed what can happen when writers judge that their texts can be improved. But evaluating also can lead to the decision that their text is even *better* than intended. To judge a text against intended meaning, however, requires that writers must conceive their *text's* meaning (for an audience) separately from their *intentions*. Correlated with role-taking ability, this ability to construct a separate text meaning is late-developing.

In determining if their texts have followed the conventions, older writers meet a similar problem: if they read their own texts for meaning, they are likely to miss many errors in conventions. A different style of reading is required of older writers, one that slows them down to look at the details. This style, well-mastered by proofreaders, must be consciously learned and applied by writers.

Revising revisited

In revising, writers add or delete elements of the text—letters, punctuation, words, phrases, clauses, sentences, paragraphs—because they have evaluated them as faulty *and* can think of a good way to change them. What is interesting about studying revision is (1) tracing the development of the subprocess of reviewing and (2) inferring the underlying representations (meaning, audience, writer) and knowledge (language, conventions) against which writers may be evaluating their texts.

But extreme care must be taken in studies that purport to help us understand the composing process—particularly review and revision—that these inferences are not based on false premises. Let me discuss a study on revision by the National Assessment of Educational Progress (1977) that makes four major errors. I cite this study so that other researchers will avoid them.

Incorrect assumption: Revision is a one-time process that occurs at the end of a writing session.

The NAEP gave nine-, thirteen- and seventeen-year-olds a writing assignment on which they wrote for fifteen minutes in pencil. They were given pens and thirteen additional minutes to revise their work. Forty per cent of the nine-year-olds, 22% of the thirteen-year-olds, and 32% of the seventeen-year-olds made no revisions in pen. No attempt was made to account for the *pencilled* revisions made on the *pencilled* draft.

Incorrect assumption: Difficulty of task makes no difference in the writers' discernible revising.

The NAEP gave nine- and thirteen-year-olds the same task: to make a report on the moon for their science class. The students were given six facts about the moon, but told that they could add others if they wished. The seventeen-year-olds were given a different, easier task: to write a complaint to a grocer who had given a younger family member bruised peaches. As Table 1 shows, thirteen-year-olds revised more than nine-year-olds in nearly every category, but seventeen-year-olds revised *less* than thirteen-year-olds in nearly every category. One cannot infer from the data that beyond thirteen, writers review less: the seventeen-year-olds probably revised less because the task was easy enough that they performed well on the first draft. They evaluated their first drafts and did not find them lacking.

What is interesting about the NAEP data is that the Moon Report task was probably easier for the thirteen-year-olds than the nine-year-olds, because the

TABLE 1
Kinds of Revisions Made by NAEP Students

		9-year-olds* Moon Report	13-year-olds Moon Report	17-year-olds† Letter
Cosmetic	% all	12.4	11.5	5.4
	% revisers	20.6	14.3	8.0
Mechanical	% all	27.6	48.9	26.5
	% revisers	46.0	62.8	39.0
Grammatical	% all	22.1	36.9	10.2
	% revisers	36.9	47.3	15.0
Continuational	% all	20.4	21.7	—
	% revisers	34.0	27.8	—
Informational	% all	25.2	47.6	39.4
	% revisers	42.3	61.0	58.0
Stylistic	% all	25.8	52.7	40.1
	% revisers	43.0	67.5	59.0
Transitional	% all	6.1	24.2	7.5
	% revisers	10.3	31.0	11.0
Organizational	% all	6.6	17.7	4.8
	% revisers	11.0	22.7	7.7
Holistic	% all	3.6	4.1	7.5
	% revisers	6.0	5.3	11.0

*Two figures are given (% all and % revisers) because a different percentage of students in each age group revised in pen: 60% of the 9-year-olds, 78% of the 13-year-olds and 68% of the 17-year olds.

†For 17-year-olds no raw data were released by the NAEP. Data for % revisers were derived from a bar graph. Data for % all were derived from % revisers. Accuracy of this data is assured to plus or minus three percentage points.

older students had in their long-term memories more facts about the moon, had written more school reports and had better control over the conventions of written English. But the older students made *more* revisions than the younger. These data suggest a complex developmental relationship between knowledge and the increasing use of strategies: because the thirteen-year-olds knew how to review and revise when asked to, they produced more revisions than the nine-year-olds *even though* the task was easier for them to begin with. In addition, the thirteen-year-olds evidenced the fastest growth over nine-year-olds in two categories: organizational and transitional. We can infer with some confidence that the thirteen-year-olds made far more changes in organization because their planning had matured enough to allow them to conceive of the discourse as a whole, with large chunks that could be rearranged to meet the audience's needs. A similar interpretation could be advanced for the addition of transitional devices: thirteen-year-olds were learning to mark the contours of their arguments so that their readers could not miss them. This increasing flexibility and concern for the reader is indeed the sign of predictable cognitive and social development.

Generally, researchers can expect that the more difficult the task, the more revising behavior they can expect from children above the age of thirteen. This hypothesis is reasonable because of the writer's limited processing space: when given a difficult task, the writer must attend to many aspects at once. Performance, even on well-learned conventions of writing (such as spelling or sentence structure), can be expected to deteriorate on the first draft. Maimon and Nodine's research (1978) clearly shows this phenomenon for college-age writers. But given enough time, writers who review will catch errors and infelicities they have made because the task has been difficult.

But this hypothesis must be modified because of individual differences in writing strategies: holding task difficulty constant, I hypothesize that for writers above thirteen, revision is inversely related to the amount and success of the preceding planning processes. Those writers who prefer first to write off the top of their heads should revise extensively more than others who plan extensively before beginning a draft. Before making inferences about the sophistication of a particular writer's review processes, the researcher must control for task difficulty, strategical style *and* the previously-mentioned ability to generate alternatives.

Incorrect assumption: Evidence from the text is the only data needed in analysing revising behaviors.

In order to analyze usefully the revising behaviors of writers, we need to infer with confidence the impetus for their revisions: in making a change, is the writer's primary consideration (1) following conventions of written English, as he or she understands them, (2) bringing the text's meaning closer to that intended, or (3) making the structure and meaning of the text more accessible to the reader (in other ways than the merely orthographic and grapholectic)? More simply, reviewing Figure 2, does the impetus for each revision come from the planning process *down* or from the conventions *up?* What mixture do we find?

Changes in the first three NAEP categories on Table 1—cosmetic, mechanical and grammatical—are impelled by the writer's understanding of conventions. But continuational and informational changes give more *information* to the text. They may be caused by the need to express new meanings generated by the writing process or the need to flesh out a preexisting plan for the audience's benefit. If continuational changes stem only from a growing number of things to say and informational changes stem only from additions for an audience's sake, then the pattern of the data suggest that between nine and thirteen, writers revise more to elaborate and clarify meanings for an audience and less to add new, unplanned meaning. This interpretation is consistent with the one we have already made about the changes in organizational and transitional categories between these same age groups. But unless we ask *writers* about the impetus for their revisions— particularly in hazy categories like *stylistic* or *holistic*—we cannot interpret our data with confidence.

Incorrect assumption: Reporting raw numbers of revisions is useful.

The NAEP study indicates the *amount* of revising that students did, but little about the final *success* of their efforts. One sub-study compares only the effects of organizational revisions made by nine-year-olds and thirteen-year-olds. Perl (1978) shows us that beginning adult writers make many revisions on their first drafts, but their efforts often result in worse drafts rather than better ones. We must study what the writer has left undone before inferring deficiencies in the writer's knowledge or strategies.

PEDAGOGICAL IMPLICATIONS

Though the simple model of the writing process presented in this chapter suggests clear *caveats* for researchers, its implications for teachers— particularly teachers of writers between six and twelve—are not so clear. One implication, however, is that even the conception of the writing process as *prewriting, writing and rewriting* oversimplifies. Planning occurs regularly in the middle of draft writing, not only before transcribing. Rewriting, which textbooks place at the end of first-draft writing, actually occurs throughout the writing of the draft. In fact, as Perl (1978) has shown for college-age unskilled writers, revising can interfere mightily with transcribing: her unskilled writers spent so much time worrying about the conventions that they sometimes had trouble producing grammatically acceptable sentences. Though we have no experimental evidence about how adult unskilled writers might profitably be instructed to change their writing processes, there is encouraging evidence from the classrooms of New York that changing unskilled adult writers' strategies can go a long way towards ameliorating the effects of their uncertain command of the conventions of written English. Consider these two texts from an adult writer, cited in Shaughnessy (1977):

> (1) Yesterday I saw something horrible. As I was walking down the street. I saw a man and his dog. Though this was a average man and his dog. This was a man beating his dog to death. Which made me sick. I scream for him to stop, though I didn't get any answer from the man....
>
> (2) ... The first assignment we had was a writing assignment. I made so many mistakes that it was truly ridiculous. The teacher returned my paper for me to correct it. The teacher helped me correct it and find the reasons why I made the mistakes.
>
> The second writing assignment we had was a little more difficult. I had my heart in this assignment not to make any mistakes, but I was wrong. I made fewer mistakes but they were there. This time I had to find them myself and understand why I made them. I found most of them but I really couldn't understand how I made such idiotic mistakes. This is where proof reading comes in. If I had proof read my papers there wouldn't have been that many mistakes....

It is hard to believe that the second sample was written only one month after the first. In that month, the writer could not have adequately learned the conventions required to produce such a perfect draft on the first try; rather, as her second paper explains, she has learned proofreading strategies. Given these powerful strategies and enough time, she can produce a conventionally acceptable draft. Her behavior is now closer to the skilled twelfth-grade writers that Stallard (1974) studied, whom he found spent significantly more time on a given writing task than a random group of twelfth graders (a mean of 40.6 minutes compared to 22.6 minutes). During this longer time, they wrote insignificantly more words (343 compared to 309) but made significantly more revisions (184 as compared to 64).

In addition, we do not know either how best to foster planning for meaning and planning for audiences or how best to aid review of those plans or the texts based on them. The work of cognitive and developmental psychologists suggests that it may be useless to teach planning (and review based on this planning) before a certain developmental stage. Though we may reasonably hypothesize with Flavell (1968) that planning for meaning might first occur and later be complicated by planning for audiences, we do not understand the subprocesses of writing enough to plan research-based curricula for the elementary and secondary schools. We need this understanding to assure that everyone can apply both knowledge and strategies to solve communication problems.

ACKNOWLEDGMENTS

The writing of this paper was supported by a grant from Exxon Educational Research and Development Fund.

REFERENCES

Beach, R. (1976) Self evaluation strategies of extensive revisers and nonrevisers. *College composition and communication,* 27: 160-164.

Clark, H. H. and Haviland, S. E. (1977) Comprehension and the given-new contract. *Discourse production and comprehension.* Norwood, N. J.: Ablex Publishing, 1-40.

Cooper, R. J. and Flavell, J. H. (1972) Cognitive correlates of children's role-taking behavior. Mimeographed copy: University of Minnesota.

Crowhurst, M. (1977) *Audience and mode of discourse effects on syntactic complexity at two grade levels.* Unpublished doctoral dissertation: University of Minnesota.

Flavell, J. H. (1977) *Cognitive development.* Englewood Cliffs, N. J.: Prentice-Hall.

Flavell, J. H., Friederichs, A. G. and Hoyt, J. D. (1970) Developmental changes in memorization processes. *Cognitive psychology,* 1: 324-340.

Flavell, J. H., Botkin, P. I., Fry, C. L., Jr., Wright, J. W. and Jarvis, P. E. (1968) *The development of role-taking and communication skills in children.* New York: Wiley; reprinted by Krieger, 1975.

Flower, L. (1979) Writer-based prose: A cognitive basis for problems in writing. *College English,* 41: 13-18.

Glucksberg, S., Krauss, R. and Higgins, E. T. (1975) The development of referential communication skills. *Review of child development research,* 4: 305-345.

Hausen, E. (1966) Linguistic and language planning. *Sociolinguistics,* ed., W. Bright, The Hague: Mouton.

Maimon, E. and Nodine, B. (1978) Measuring syntactic growth: errors and expectations in sentence-combining practice with college freshmen. *Research in the teaching of Engish,* 12: 233-244.

Markman, E. (1977) Realizing you don't understand: a preliminary investigation. *Child development,* 48: 986-992.

National Assessment of Educational Progress (1977) Write/rewrite: an assessment of writing skills. Denver, Colorado: U.S. Government Printing Office, Writing report #05-W-04.

Perl, S. (1978) *Five writers writing: case studies of the composing processes of unskilled college writers.* Unpublished doctoral dissertation: New York University.

Robinson, E. and Robinson, W. (1976) The young child's understanding of communication. *Developmental psychology,* 12: 328-333.

Scardamalia, M., Bereiter, C. and MacDonald, J. (1977) Role-taking in written communication investigated by manipulating anticipatory knowledge. Photocopy: York University.

Shatz, M. (1978) The relationship between cognitive processes and the development of communication skills. *Nebraska symposium on motivation,* ed., B. Keasey, University of Nebraska Press.

Shaughnessy, M. (1977) *Errors and expectations: a guide for the teacher of basic writing.* New York: Oxford University Press.

Sommers, N. (1978) Revision strategies of experienced writers and student writers. Unpublished speech, Meeting of the Modern Language Association, December 28, 1978.

Stallard, C. K. (1974) An analysis of the writing behavior of good student writers. *Research in the teaching of English,* 8: 206-218.

6

How Children Cope with the Cognitive Demands of Writing

Marlene Scardamalia
York University

> "I have all my thoughts in my
> mind but when I come to a
> word I can't spell it throws
> me off my writting."
> —Tenth-grade student

"The proposition that it is theoretically impossible to learn to write has the ring of truth," says Peter Elbow (1973, p. 135). Too many interdependent skills are involved, and all seem to be prerequisite to one another. To pay conscious attention to handwriting, spelling, punctuation, word choice, syntax, textual connections, purpose, organization, clarity, rhythm, euphony, and reader characteristics would seemingly overload the information processing capacity of the best intellects. For the skilled writer we may suppose that many aspects of writing are automated and that cognitive space-saving strategies make writing possible without inordinate demands on processing capacity. For the beginning writer, however, very little is automated and coping strategies are lacking. The beginning writer is in a predicament that amply justifies Elbow's statement about the theoretical impossibility of learning to write. Nevertheless, most children do write, and some even enjoy it. This paper examines children's writing in an attempt to analyze how children at different levels of writing development cope with cognitive demands of two different writing tasks. In both of these tasks the focus is on a single cognitive demand—the demand associated with coordinating content ideas. For mature writers this is probably the overriding challenge of expository writing, yet its development has received little attention in the research literature.

The ability to coordinate ideas has great developmental significance. The ability to coordinate one's own perspective with that of another marks, in Piagetian theory, the transcendence of childish egocentrism (Piaget, 1926); the ability to consider two criteria simultaneously opens the door to cross-classification (Inhelder & Piaget, 1969); and the ability to coordinate weight and distance underlies the logic of proportionality requisite for formal solutions to balance problems. This growing ability to coordinate concepts is illustrated by judgments in balance problems. The child's judgments are initially based on weight (or distance from the fulcrum) alone. Next, the child considers distance and weight factors simultaneously. If weight leads to the judgment that one side of the balance will go down while distance leads to the opposite conclusion, the child cannot resolve the dilemma. Finally, the child resolves such dilemmas by coordinating both weight and distance on both sides of the fulcrum (Siegler, 1976). Much of the story of cognitive development may be construed as taking progressively more variables into account during single acts of judgment (Bachelder & Denny, 1977a, b; Case, 1977; Pascual-Leone, 1969, 1970).

Thus it seems reasonable to expect children's developing expository abilities to show developmental patterns similarly based on increments in information coordinated simultaneously. The ability to coordinate ideas at increasingly complex levels may well underlie advances such as: (a) movement from loosely connected to tightly connected discourse (ability to coordinate increasing numbers of related ideas); (b) movement from unelaborated to elaborated discourse (ability to coordinate increasing numbers of successively reported ideas without straying from the intent of the communication); (c) movement from a single-argument thesis defense to defense that anticipates counter arguments (ability to coordinate an increasing number of reasons bearing on a position); (d) movement from single-episode narration following a chronological sequence to narration with several sub-plots (ability to coordinate increasing numbers of related events within a common thematic structure); and (e) movement from egocentric, non-communicative to decentered, audience-oriented prose (ability to coordinate different points of view).

The emphasis of this paper is on the cognitive demands associated with the coordination of increasing numbers of ideas in writing. The paper does not focus on the cognitive demands of syntax or vocabulary—the linguistic devices by which such coordinations are expressed. High level coordinations of ideas can be achieved through several simple sentences or through a single complex sentence. Likewise, complex thoughts can be conveyed with a relatively sophisticated or unsophisticated vocabulary. Examples of children's writing show that they often fail to coordinate ideas when it is safe to assume they have the linguistic competence to express the coordination, and they sometimes produce coordinations without using adult-like linguistic devices. Research in the development of writing abilities has typically focussed on children's acquisition of the linguistic devices for expressing ideas (Hunt, 1965; Loban, 1976; Mellon, 1969; O'Hare, 1973). While use of these devices is inevitably correlated with the final writing achievement (O'Hare, 1973), the use of various linguistic devices is never the end of writing development. This study is an attempt to get closer to the end of writing development—to the attainment of complex coordinations of ideas.

To determine children's level of ideational coordinations in writing, two tasks were presented singly to children at different ages. These tasks exemplify ways in which writing can require the coordination of ideas at increasing levels of complexity. The first task was a simple matrix task where children were instructed to convey in writing the information contained in the four cells of the matrix. Information in each cell could be conveyed without reference to information in any other cell, or it could be conveyed by interrelating the content of any one or all of the four cells. The second task was one in which children were asked to defend a thesis. Here children could discuss a single point of view or could incorporate opposing viewpoints at varying levels of complexity. The method adopted in this research involves characterizing children's performance as *level 1, level 2,* and so on, according to the number of content schemes they appeared to be able to coordinate in these writing tasks. A characterization of a child as level 1 does not mean that the child is judged incapable of attending to more than one content scheme at a time. The child may well have additional attentional capacity deployed elsewhere, on the mechanics of writing, for instance. What a level 1 classification means is that, however much attentional capacity the child might deploy altogether, his writing exhibits attention to only one idea at a time. Thus, we examine writing to determine how many idea units the child has explicitly related and, hence, coordinated.

Our classification system follows Pascual-Leone's lead in defining different levels of task difficulty according to the number of mental units coordinated simultaneously (Pascual-Leone, 1969, 1970). Like Pascual-Leone the number of figurative schemes (or units of task content) that subjects coordinate in a single mental operation is the basis for classification. However, unlike him, we have not attempted a step-by-step reconstruction of the child's thinking process. This would have required a much deeper understanding of the composing process than we presently have. Rather, we have chosen to analyze those expressed ideas that had to be taken into account simultaneously to produce the most complex idea coordination displayed in a child's writing. Different levels of idea-coordination are then analyzed to determine what these different levels might tell us about developing writing abilities.

Converting Matrices to Sentences

The first task was one in which the information to be communicated in writing was provided to children in the form of a matrix. An example is presented below.

	STATE	
	Michigan	California
Climate	cool	warm
Fruit Crop	apples	oranges

(Row group labelled "AT HARVEST")

The children were taught how to read matrices and then were instructed to write a paragraph or sentence containing all of the information in the matrix. The matrix was in front of the child throughout the writing task.

The matrix task was designed to fulfill two purposes: (a) to provide discrete units of task information that could be combined at any chosen level of complexity, and (b) to provide information in as language-free a manner as possible, thereby minimizing external influences on the child's attempted integrations. Differences in levels of complexity were determined by analyzing the relationships the child made among the independent cells.

In the description of matrix tasks, and of other tasks to follow, the terms *figurative scheme* and *unit of task information* are used interchangeably to denote chunked bits of information. In the matrix task information from a single cell (including row and column labels) constitutes a chunk (e.g., "In the state of Michigan the climate is cool").

At the lowest level of integration (level 1) the writing lacks integration. For example:

> In the state of Michigan the climate is cool. In the state of Michigan the fruit crop is apples. In the state of California the climate is warm. In the state of California the fruit crop is oranges.

This writing sample is considered to be a level 1 production because only a single unit of task information at a time is presented. There is no coordination of even highly related units of information.

At the next level (level 2) two units of task information are integrated. For example:

> In Michigan the climate is cool *and*
> the fruit crop is apples.
> In California the climate is warm *and*
> the fruit crop is oranges.

Consider the first sentence. In order to avoid the redundant use of the phrase *In Michigan,* it was necessary to consider the information from two cells simultaneously. Similarly, in the second sentence the same type of operation was performed in order to avoid the redundant use of the phrase *In California.*

At the next level (level 3), three units of task information are integrated. The products of the integration take at least two forms. First consider the following example:

> In Michigan the climate is cool *so* their
> fruit crop is apples.
> In California the climate is warm *so* their
> fruit crop is oranges.

The form of the first sentence suggests more than an appreciation of redundant information. It suggests an appreciation of the cause-effect relationship between climates and crops. This cause-effect relationship itself is assumed to be a scheme that is used in the integration process. By integrating the *cause-effect* scheme with the two schemes from the level 2 operation the child achieves this more advanced level 3 operation. It could be argued that this seemingly higher-order integration is more an indication of what the child knows about the relation between climate and crops than it is an indication of processing capacity. To be sure, the relevant information must be available in order for the child to integrate it, but that does not alter the fact that the successful use of such information depends on a level 3 integration. We find the same pattern on matrices from a variety of content areas, and we find children successful on level 2 integrations but not on level 3 integrations (e.g., they say "In Toronto in winter it is cold *but* they drink hot chocolate" rather than "*so* they drink hot chocolate"). Still, experimentation with artificial information allowing for the control of knowledge factors would obviously be an asset to research with matrix tasks.

	Michigan	Ontario
Climate	cool	cool
Fruit Crop	apples	apples

"In Michigan and Ontario the climate is cool and the fruit crop is apples." This sentence, although it combines all the information in four cells, can be produced by a series of two-scheme coordinations: (a) combine "In Michigan it is cool" with "In Michigan they grow apples" to obtain "In Michigan it is cool and they grow apples" (This is the same two-scheme coordination discussed above); (b) by a similar two-scheme coordination, obtain "In Ontario it is cool and they grow apples;" (c) combine the two (identical) main clauses into one clause; (d) combine the two prepositional phrases into one compound phrase; "In Michigan and Ontario."

What about the phrase, "In *both* Michigan and Ontario..."? It seems likely that this slight refinement involves a three-scheme integration.

Problems in Defending a Thesis

Above, I considered levels of achievement on a writing task with a controlled format and short responses, describing the tasks we are using and their interpretation. Below I attempt a comparable delineation of successive achievements within the less controlled format of children's essays. In this essay task children were asked to write for 15 minutes on the topic "Should students be able to choose what things they study in school?" In reviewing the protocols of these children it became obvious that staying on a topic was an achievement in itself. Accordingly, I have assumed that the topic is a figurative scheme that must be coordinated with others.

Level 1   The effort to isolate level 1 behavior began with an attempt to imagine the consequences for writing if one were unable to purposefully coordinate two units of task content. It seemed reasonable to assume that under such conditions a child would fail to elaborate on the topic, or would engage in disconnected discourse, or would engage in connected discourse (rather like story-telling) that strayed from the topic. While there may be other consequences, these were the ones initially considered. A great number of the above consequences appeared in the protocols. An example of disconnected discourse, or possibly a failure to elaborate, is the following (in this and all subsequent examples, children's spelling and punctuation were preserved):

> In School We Should Be Able To Do Any Kind Of We Want To Do We Are Free We Could Do Anything We Want God Us Free We Could Do Anything We Want To Do I'd Like Spelling And Math In School We Should Do It Any Time We Want.

The following two examples represent connected discourse that strays from the topic.

> Should Students Be Able Choose What Things They Study In School.
> Yes, I think we should. Because some subjects are hard like math. And because the teachers give us a page a day. I think the subjects that we should have is Reading. Because that is easyest one. I think we should't have math, science and social studies. Because in social studies and science we have to write up notes and do experments. I think *math* is the *worst* subject. And I *hate spelling* to. Because in spelling there are so many words to write and they are all *hard*. And they waste my time. I think school shouldn't be to 3:45. I think it should be to *2:00*. I think school is *too long*.

> Spelling
> Spelling is my subject because I like it because it is fun to do it, and right after one lesson I can go on to another lesson. Spelling sounds exciting, to me because I can get high marks, and when I have Spelling tests, I get high marks like: 25 out of 25, and 24 out of 25, and those look like good marks to me.

In writing the second protocol above it appears as if the child carried out a chain of operations, but that these operations did not require the simultaneous coordination of two schemes. The child begins with a figurative scheme representing his interpretation of the topic, generates a related idea, and writes it down. The first idea serves as inspiration for the second, but the two are not integrated; the first merely triggers the second. Since the child does not hold both the topic and subsequent idea in mind, the next thought likely will be inspired by whichever of these two schemes is more salient, although it is also possible that a salient but completely unrelated thought will enter.

In the first protocol above the child's thinking seems to be dominated by the idea *we should be free* (which presumably was inspired by the topic). He continually returns to this idea and in so doing fails to effect sequential coordination of ideas. The result is discourse that appears disconnected. It could also be argued that the child never returns to the topic because he never strays from it, in which case what he has written would better be classified as failure to elaborate (i.e., fixation on one idea). In either interpretation, it seems clear that the child is not coordinating information.

The two longer paragraphs above, provided as examples of connected discourse that strays from the topic, represent the most typical kinds of level 1 production. If the child does not apply the requisite integrative capacity, then it seems inevitable that his attempts at elaboration will result in his losing hold of the topic. I suspect that the child's productions at this level are controlled by some affective scheme. That is, the child hits on an emotionally charged content scheme that triggers a host of associated memories. Mennig-Peterson

& McCabe (Note 1) have shown that with 3- and 4-year-olds an affectively laden scheme such as a bee sting can produce detailed memories of past events that children elaborate rather coherently. Within Pascual-Leone's theory of Constructive Operators (1970), such results would be classified as A-boosted. That is, only one affective scheme, the one serving to cue relevant memories, is involved, and no attentional effort is required to keep it activated. Such a scheme would explain how young children can produce such elaborated constructions around some topics while not being able to do the same with others (i.e., with ones that fail to spark personal associations). In both examples above the child failed to hold onto the topic presented. But that topic seemingly has cued more relevant associations for each child, and these cued associations carry the child through to the end of the paragraph. In the first example there is some sense of topic maintenance, but only at the beginning. In the second example there is no sign of a return to the question that inspired the discourse. Bereiter (Note 2) has labelled this kind of production *associative writing.*

The above analysis implies that *narrative writing* about a single episode would fit into a level 1 category. In such writing the associative mechanism follows a time sequence: each event would trigger the next. On the other hand, *expository writing,* which requires organization of content beyond the associative, should not be possible at this level.

Level 2   Level 2 children, children who integrate two figurative schemes, have considerable advantage over level 1 children. Coordination of two figurative schemes implies that level 2 children can effect more than associative integrations of two consecutive ideas; they should be able to purposefully subordinate and coordinate ideas. For example, they are able to coordinate their most recent idea with the topic. However, a level 2 child should not be able to interrelate two consecutive ideas and simultaneously place them in proper relation to the topic. A number of protocols, one of which is presented below, seemed to fit this general description:

> Should children choose what they want to study on? Do you think children should choose what they want for social studies? I do. Because, would you like to study on something you don't like? Would you like to study on Brazil or Peru? Would you like to study on these countries?! Or other countries that are almost unknown to mankind? No. Not I. Who would suffer? We would if we had to study on countries like Brazil and Peru? No! We would only find half as much as is known to man! No! We shall not suffer on this case!! No we won't. Who, tell me who, would like to study on a country almost unknown to mankind?! Almost no one! Only a few! I wouldn't do it! Not at all! We won't suffer doing this. In fact we won't do it at all! Will we?! No! We won't do it!!
>
> Thank you

Notice the continual return to the topic (as somewhat redefined by this child) of freedom from the oppression of set curricula. It follows from the assumption that a child at this level cannot both interconnect consecutive sentences and simultaneously place them in proper relation to the topic; he must either develop his current idea *or* connect the current idea and the topic. The child in the present case seems to have alternated between these choices, first developing his Brazil-Peru idea to include the whole host of "countries totally unknown to mankind," then dropping that line of reasoning and returning to the theme of combating oppression. He runs through this two-unit cycle twice (Do you think children should choose....No. Not I. and Who would suffer....we won't do it!!) and then ends.

An interesting additional phenomenon is suggested in the above protocol. The child seems to display a sense of audience, in that he addresses the reader. Sense of audience minimally demands the coordination of two points of view, one's own and another's. Thus the appearance of such behavior is consistent with a level 2 analysis. Note, however, that it is the child's tone, not his content, that conveys a sense of audience. His content actually ignores the great mass of people who are enchanted by unknown places. It seems likely, therefore, that the child's audience-related stance is another affect-laden scheme—a sort of oratorical wrath—that sustains itself without attentional effort, lending a unified tone to the essay but contributing nothing to the coordination of ideas. Since all of a level 2 child's processing capacity is taken up coordinating pairs of ideas and staying on topic, we would not expect him to simultaneously adjust sentences to meet specific audience needs.

Since connected or consistent discourse itself implies awareness of another point of view (the point of view *not* to be presented) and since a sense of audience likewise implies awareness of another's perspective, it is reasonable that both behaviors should appear, in rudimentary form, at level 2. It may be the case, however, that extended *and* consistent elaboration actually demand the active rejection of ideas from the opposing perspective—in which case we would not expect extended elaboration to appear until level 3. Obviously, a good deal of research is needed to determine the relationship between processing demands and adjustments to other points of view.

The next protocol illustrates another level 2 performance with a different structure from that of the previous example:

> Should Students Be Able To Choose What Things They Study in School.
> Students are very sneaky and lazy. Most children would probably choose recess all the time but I still think that it is good.
> Only is it good though, if the subjects are limited to 4 or 6 things such as Reading, Math, Social Studies Science, art or French. The students though, would probably all ways pick art and not get work done....

Here the dominant idea seems to be that students are lazy and that given choice they would not act responsibly. Yet the author wishes to defend the idea that students should get to choose their school subjects. While the author appreciates that the two ideas he has presented are contradictory (a level 2 ability), he cannot resolve the conflict, so he is left with a pair-wise comparison of ideas that does not further his position. He seems to need some third scheme to break this set, or alternatively to give up one of the two ideas and concentrate on the other.

Informal work I carried out with a neighbor child suggests some features of level 2 behavior worth pursuing. The child and I took turns writing sentences on a topic he had chosen. Each time it was my turn to add a sentence to *our* paragraph I made a point of writing sentences that both followed his and related back to the topic, doing my thinking out loud in an attempt to model the process. But the child invariably generated his sentence from the one I had just written and ignored the topic sentence. His performance could thus be classified as level 1. Yet if left to his own devices, he could both stay on topic and produce connected discourse. The child was ten years old. The interruption of the two-person task seemingly caused regression to level 1 behavior, suggesting a rather tenuous grasp on the process of topic and theme integration. There did not appear to be a purposeful switching back and forth between the immediate thought and the larger context of the paragraph. This switching demands cognitive control over the process of writing, as well as the availability of sufficient processing capacity. The lack of a purposeful switching strategy may indicate that the *invention of such a scheme is more demanding than its execution.* Alternatively, this was likely the first instance in which the child met any demand for such a scheme, and we would not expect invention under such conditions. Whatever the case, the child's ability to work from both topic and theme when not interrupted suggests that it may be of use to bring such a process under conscious control.

By virtue of being able to coordinate three figurative schemes simultaneously, the level 3 child should be able to do more than integrate the topic with some immediate or salient thought. The child should now be able to do some pre-planning, by holding onto the topic while also holding two unwritten thoughts in mind. An example of a level 3 production indicating such qualities follows.

> I think you should not be able to choose your own things to study because of a lot of reasons. The first reason is that some kids might pick easy subjects to learn. Also because I wouldn't know what to learn about it, or write about. I think it alright for projects to do at home to pick a subject but not at school. If you they were to pick there own book for reading theyed propely pick the easiest one there. For math they would propely just do grade one and two work, and not learn any new things. School won't be like school if you picked your own subject.

The phrase, *because of a lot of reasons,* reflects a kind of thinking ahead that seems to require integration of at least three schemes—the topic and at least two supporting ideas. (Even the rhetorical use of the phrase *because of alot of reasons,* while perhaps not tied closely to the child's thinking, suggests pre-planning exemplary of level 3 productions). After the phrase *for alot of reasons* the writer proceeds to present two ideas in coordinate form: *The first reason...* and *Also....* Accomplishing this should also require integration of three schemes. To preserve the parallel structure signalled by the word *also* in the second supporting point, the writer would have to hold in mind the second point and the thesis, as well as the first point with which the second point must be placed in coordinate relation.

After the second supporting point the coordinate structure breaks down. The writer holds on to the topic and does not repeat herself, but she begins stating points that are subordinate to other points already made (such as *If they were to pick there own book...* which appears to elaborate upon the first point, *that some kids might pick easy subjects to learn*). The coordinate structure, however, probably could have been maintained if the writer had possessed an executive strategy for testing coordinate structure (Bereiter, personal communication). Then it would have been sufficient to hold in mind the topic and the new sentence under consideration, while comparing the new sentence with sentences already written. But lacking such a sophisticated bit of rhetorical knowledge, as we presume to have been the case, the writer could have maintained a coordinate structure only by simultaneously considering all the points previously made. Given a level 3 solution, we should expect this effort to break down just where it did.

The concluding sentence in this example shows another kind of integration not found in the productions of lower-level students. This summary sentence appears to show a three-scheme integration, uniting the conclusion with the thesis and also with what may be called the tenor of the intervening content.

Match and Mismatch between Task and Capacity

It was noted at the outset of this paper that the complexity of writing tasks is to a large extent determined by the writer. This was evident in the protocols examined in the preceding section, where expressing a position on an issue was implicitly defined by different children as anything from a free association task to one of considering alternative positions.

The possibility exists that a child may attempt to construct text at a level of complexity that is beyond his capacity, and consequently will produce an objectively unsatisfactory piece of writing. For instance, a child functioning at level 1, and thus capable, under the right conditions, of producing a reasonably comprehensible series of expressive statements, may set out to produce a thesis supported by a reason, fail to produce a reason that relates to the thesis, and thus produce an anomaly like, "Yes, Richard was cruel because they were all Danes" (quoted from Collis & Biggs, Note 2). At a higher level, a child may attempt to produce a thesis, a supporting fact, and a qualification to the supporting fact (calling for level 3 integrative abilities), but fail to see that the qualification undermines the thesis. Thus, again, the child produces an argument that seems inferior to what he would have produced if he had stuck to a lower level of task complexity—to giving only a thesis plus supporting facts, for instance. Note that these failures, if one is to call them that, are not linguistic failures. On the contrary, the child will often have used a mature syntactical form but filled it with unsuitable content.

If the limitation is primarily a cognitive one, it is reasonable to ask how children can set themselves cognitive tasks that are too complex for them. Isn't the setting of the task itself evidence of a higher level of processing? The answer to these questions probably depends on the conditions under which the child is writing. A likely possibility is that a child who sets himself a level 3 writing task and then deals with it by level 2 processing is usually a child who under more facilitative conditions could process information at level 3. For most children writing is not a situation that facilitates cognitive processing, and so we frequently find children tackling writing tasks that they are unable to handle.

In the following discussion protocols are characterized as, for instance, *level 2 task, level 1 performance.* The level of the task is defined by the level of processing that would be required to coordinate the ideas set forth or implied in the protocol. The level of performance is judged, as in the preceding section, by the complexity of the coordination actually achieved.

Level 1 Tasks   Since children at level 1 do not successfully coordinate figurative schemes, an obvious way in which they can avoid inconsistencies is by simply not elaborating on their statements. Thus a successful level 1 attempt would be one in which the subject simply presented a position with no support. The following example illustrates a level 1 task with level 1 performance:

"Yes I think we should be able to pick our own subjects." This was one child's complete composition, and its brevity no doubt reflects lack of motivation as much as rhetorical strategy. Be that as it may, it does show that by sticking to a level 1 task the child has successfully avoided inconsistencies. A level 1 inconsistency is impossible because an inconsistency minimally implies an attempt to integrate two units of content—a level 2 task.

Level 2 Tasks   In this example the child tries to provide support for his position, but the support statement is not successfully integrated with the position statement.

The following is a level 2 task: level 1 performance:

> No they shoud not be able choose what to study because sometime if there are
> subjects that are not very interesting and don't teach you a thing

Notice the attempt to use an *if-then* construction (*if there are subjects...*) in support of his position that students should not choose. Considering just the *if-then* construction (a two-unit coordination) it can be seen that the child failed to execute it successfully. Yet the simple deletion of the word *if* would yield the statement "sometime there are subjects that are not very interesting and don't teach you a thing," a perfectly reasonable support for the argument that students should be free to choose their own subjects. However, the child is trying to support the opposite position. So he has additionally failed in this two-unit position-support integration. Had the child simply stated his point of view with no attempt to elaborate it he would have been classified as successful at level 1.

A successful level 2 attempt to integrate position and support ideas is presented below as a level 2 task, level 2 performance:

> I don't think students should be able to choose their own subjects because then
> they would pick some dumb topics like *shoes.*

The supporting information presented after the word *because* is perfectly comprehensible and consistent with the argument.

Level 3 Tasks   Children at level 3 generally tried to integrate some qualification into their otherwise level 2 position-support structure. Below is a level 3 Task, level 2 performance in which the child succeeded with the position-support structure, but did not successfully integrate his qualification.

> Students should because some people are good in some subjects and others
> aren't. The others who aren't good might be good in different subjects, while still
> some are bad.

In her first sentence this child presents her position and a clearly relevant supporting statement—a level 2 performance. It is not clear what she was trying to do in her second sentence—perhaps explain the connection between her position and her supporting reason, perhaps elaborate on the reason, perhaps qualify it. In any event, the sentence is clearly not integrated with the preceding two ideas; it is merely juxtaposed. The result is a statement that is partly redundant, partly irrelevant, and that adds nothing to the argument. Compare this performance with that of a child who succeeds in integrating a qualification to his support statement in a level 3 task, level 3 performance:

> I think they should because it would be funner than dooing borring things. The students could probably get highter marks dooing something he wanted to than something borring but they could skipe an important lesson and go into life not knowing what it was. In a way it is good and in a way its bad. I think they should be able to choose some things, but there should be somethings they should study.

In this protocol we see a good example of thinking being carried out through writing, something that becomes possible to a limited extent with level 3 processing. The child has stated a position and a supporting reason, then seen a difficulty with the position and ended up by modifying his position. Notice that the child has provided two supporting ideas for his initial position in favor of free choice: it would be *funner* and students would get higher marks. His integration of these ideas into one supporting argument itself suggests a three-scheme integration--the two ideas and the thesis, combining to form the assertion that free choice would lead to higher marks because of students' studying things that interested them.

Then comes a thought opposed to the thesis: *students might miss learning important things.* It requires only a level 2 process to recognize the conflict between a thesis and an argument and thence, perhaps, to reverse one's thesis. But in the present case the child does not reverse his thesis; he modifies it to accommodate the opposing argument, and this kind of constructive thought, I hypothesize, minimally requires level 3 processing.

When a child can consider simultaneously his thesis, his support for it, and the opposing argument, he can appreciate the situation as a problem to be solved; whereas, if he can consider only two of the three schemes at a time, the best he can do is weigh the opposing arguments and come out for or against his thesis. What *appreciating the situation as a problem* means is that the output from evaluating thesis, support, and opposing argument simultaneously is a new scheme which constitutes a problem definition. The problem in this case seems to be: how to reconcile the thesis and the opposing argument. In applying a problem-solving strategy to this problem, at least three schemes must be handled simultaneously: the thesis, the opposing argument, and the tentative solution that is being tested for adequacy.

In this level 3 problem-solving process, the supporting argument is left out of consideration. The child, indeed, shows no evidence of recognizing that his modified thesis (allow free choice of some things, make others required) is at some variance with his original supporting argument, in that he would now have students required to study some boring things. To have searched for a new scheme that reconciled thesis, opposing argument, and supporting argument as well would, however, have required a level 4 process.

Level 4 Tasks In the orienting sentence of the following protocol we see what appears to be a solution to problems surrounding freedom to choose subjects, a solution generated after having considered conflicting ideas. Thus the child seems to have anticipated opposing positions to an argument, unlike the above child who recognized a difficulty with his position after he had presented it. Yet on closer analysis we see that while the child anticipated opposing positions, she did not deal with them.

Level 4 Task: Level 3 Performance:

> Should You Be Able To Choose What Things You Study in in School.
> This question really depends on the grade you are in (or you are talking.) If you are in elementary school, the subjects should not be *your* own choice, but (the teacher's and) the people who are working for the board of education. In this way, the subjects will give you an idea on, what you have to prepare, for your future and how well you are doing and also understanding them (the subjects). Junior High School's have the same idea as elementary schools, except for the more homework we receive and the work becomes much harder. The way the Junior High School's are organized is fine, in my opinion. We have a few subjects to choose from and that will be enough for us; (to choose from) since our option subjects are just for our entertainment and extra knowledge. I am very pleased with my educational subjects and I think we should leave our schooling programs the way it is.

The child's first sentence implies that she is going to coordinate two *if-then* clauses: *If you are in a lower grade then...* and *If you are in a higher grade then...* This coordination of two positions that in themselves imply two-unit coordinations would demand the simultaneous coordination of four units of task content. The demand is somewhat comparable to that for the highest level of achievement on the Michigan-California matrix problem discussed earlier in which the child has to work out a proportionality problem (i.e., a is to b as c is to d). But consider what the child does instead of working at this level. She takes one side of the question, the side dealing with children in lower grades. She claims, to paraphrase her, that if you are in elementary school then the board should have control. Having presented this two-unit *if-then* position, she integrates a third elaboration scheme (that this course of action will provide good training for the future). Now we expect her to follow through with the alternate *if-then* construction, implied in the introductory sentence, about conditions in higher grades that make the situation there different. But the child never deals with such ideas. She simply discusses how junior high school is rather like elementary school and that she likes it that way. Here we have an instance in which the language used leads to expectations of higher levels of integration than are actually employed.

Out of the eighty grade-eight protocols (the highest grade tested to date) there was one example of a child successful at coordinating conjectures from both sides of an argument. Here is a level 4 task, level 4 performance:

Should You Be Able To Choose Your Subjects

Chose is an important thing but a very tricky thing to fool with. I feel that chose of school subjects should be something that is done carefully. A young child given a chose would pick the easy subjects with no foresight into his future. But choose in his later years could be very important. To develop his leadership qualities. To follow and develop his interests and charictor to his fullest. So with these facts I come to the conclution that chose of subjects should not be given until about the age of fifteen. You can not condem or praise what you know little about. Until the age of choise a full and general cericulum should be given. It is not up to the school board to decide your life and until you are old enough to decide it is not your dission ether.

Seemingly, this child is able to take a single factor, *choice,* and work out complex relationships surrounding it. He, like other children, considered the fact that when you are young, you may not make very wise choices. But his method of coping with this factor is quite different from theirs. Other children figure out a way to eliminate factors problematic to their point of view. For example, one girl decides that parents should come into the picture in cases with young children, that parents of *those students* should talk it over with their child. She has simultaneously considered her thesis, an objection to it, and a solution to the objection (a three-unit integration). She therefore seems to feel justified in dismissing the age factor, and proceeds to deal with an unrelated problem. Other children simultaneously consider their thesis, an objection to it, and support for the objection. They thus lose hold of their original support of their position and switch to the other side of the argument. Whatever their course of action, the common feature of these three-unit integrations is that factors are considered one-by-one and a relevant scheme is dismissed rather than integrated.

In the above protocol we see the synthesis of opposing arguments. What clearly distinguishes this child from others is that he appreciates a dilemma surrounding the question of choosing subjects, an operation which demands a four-scheme integration. His introductory statement provides warning that there is no simple solution to the dilemma he sees: choosing is good (position) because choosing is educational (support); but choosing is bad (position) because young children cannot evaluate future consequences of choices (support). By coordinating these schemes simultaneously the child can re-group the four units and recognize that the position *chosing is good* is contradicted by the fact that young children cannot appreciate future consequences; alternatively, the position *choosing is bad* is contradicted by the fact that choosing is educational. The child therefore recognizes that neither position is acceptable and that a different position must be found. If the child has an alternative solution available in his repertoire (perhaps some stock solution such as *let's compromise* or *different people need different things*) this may be triggered by the child's appreciation of the dilemma. Otherwise the child will have to apply a problem-solving strategy.

Let us stop and consider how the present situation differs from that found in the level 3 protocol where the child came to grips with a problem. In that case the child gave attention to one thesis (that students should choose what they study), support for it, and an argument against it (that students might miss something important). He did not give attention to the contrary thesis that students should not choose their own subjects. Thus the problem he faced was that of reconciling his chosen thesis with the argument against it. In the present case the child gives attention to both theses and to the objections to each. Thus his problem is a more complex one. He does not have a chosen position but rather sees the question of curricular decision-making as an open one. He must, therefore, hold three things in mind while searching for a solution: the issue of curricular decision-making, the idea that young children are incompetent to choose, and the idea that choosing is itself an important educational activity. Holding these three ideas in mind while testing possible solutions against them constitutes a level 4 task. From the protocol, it is impossible to tell whether the solution arrived at by the child (no choice up to age 15, free choice thereafter) came from such a level 4 problem-solving process or whether it merely reflects a ready-made compromise or *split the difference* strategy that is elicited whenever a dilemma is perceived. In any event, the perception of the dilemma itself entails a level 4 coordination of schemes.

This protocol is unique in another way. It does not stop with the proposing of a solution. The writer then goes on to consider the difficulty of who should decide what young children should study. He does not get very far with this problem (very likely because of time limitations). What he does do, however, is enough to illustrate the ability that is inherent in level 4 performance to generate a coherent *line of thought.* If the preceding analysis is correct, it is only when one can consider four ideas simultaneously that one is in a position to sustain the dialectical process of thesis, antithesis, synthesis, new antithesis, and so on. It takes simultaneous attention to thesis, antithesis, and the supporting case for each to perceive the need for a synthesis, and it also takes a level 4 process at the least to generate a novel synthesis.

Educational Implications   The writing of the children with whom I have worked reflects great difficulty in putting thoughts together in writing. It may surprise some readers to learn that these children range in age from ten to fourteen years and that most of them were from academically high achieving classes. It seems ironic that writing, considered by some the crucible of literate thought (Goody & Watt, 1963; Havelock, 1973; Olson, 1977), actually presents obstacles to complex idea coordination.

There is a paradox underlying children's difficulties with idea integration in writing. Young children who are particularly constrained by limited resources do less planning, less note taking, less revising and less reading than adults. Even at the high school level research conducted by Stollard (1974) shows that only 40% of a randomly selected group of students ever stopped and looked back to see what they were writing. Thus the very activities adults use to break up this complex activity into manageable subroutines are what children fail to take advantage of. Not only do adults plan ahead, stop to reread, to revise and to organize their thoughts as they develop them sequentially, they frequently do this through a series of drafts. In this sense writing is the opposite of reading. In reading the beginner often does in pieces what the skilled person does as a single complex act. In writing the beginner tries to do as a single complex act what the skilled person does in pieces.

Students do not generally get the kind of feedback needed to help them restructure writing into a more efficient series of acts. Consequently, the dilemma they face is a serious one. First we give them tasks requiring more resources than they currently demonstrate—a situation where effective problem solving has been shown to be delayed, if not halted (Scardamalia, 1977). Then we expect them to invent sophisticated strategies while working on the very kinds of tasks on which they demonstrated inefficient strategies in the first place.

One proposed solution to the dilemma posed by the demandingness of writing has been to remove concerns for correctness. There are several problems with this solution, the most important of which is that it is not clear such an approach addresses the problem. First, telling children they need not be concerned with correctness does not insure that they won't be. The highly advantaged children who supplied the protocols for this study were for the most part brought up on this supposedly benign kind of treatment. After eight years their writing is still cramped and distorted by the difficulties of handling mechanics. Lack of instructional emphasis on correctness has not freed these children from concern; it has simply meant that they have not mastered the mechanics of writing and so are doomed to go on worrying about them.

Furthermore, recent evidence indicates that concerns with mechanics are not the major impediment to presentations of coherent ideas in discourse. By grade 6, children who are producing written text—and thus dealing with difficulties due to mechanics—produce text more coherent than that produced when they were dictating essays (a condition in which interference due to the mechanical demands of writing is eliminated) (Scardamalia, Bereiter, Goelman, in press.)

Removing concerns for correctness does not appear to be an effective means for lowering demands of idea coordination in writing; nor does practice alone. West (1967) reports that studies on teaching methods consistently show that *practice alone* is not very effective. Careful reading of essays combined with analytic discussions of ideas, presentation of functional writing assignments, and intensive evaluation were effective strategies when combined with practice; but practice alone was never found to be the most effective teaching strategy. I believe such findings point to a serious fallacy in the whole conventional approach to writing—the belief that when students engage in complex writing tasks they are actually engaged in all the complex problems of writing. Stollard's research suggests that this is not true, as does much of our recent research on the thinking that children bring to their writing. Papers presented at the 1980 AERA meetings ("Knowledge Children Have but Don't Use in Their Writing") address this topic directly.

We seem to have been brought full circle to the "ring of truth" in Elbow's proposition that "it is theoretically impossible to learn to write." But it is important to keep in mind that current research does not support this proposition. It makes clear there are no simple solutions; but it also suggests reasons to be encouraged. An important reason is the eagerness with which children seize on more adult-like composing strategies, executive procedures that permit them to sustain a more complex composing process. There are many ways around problems children face (Bereiter & Scardamalia, 1981; Scardamalia, Bereiter and Fillion, 1981; Scardamalia & Bereiter, in press). The challenge to researchers and educators is to understand the various cognitive processes that accompany writing, their demand characteristics, and how the multiple processes involved in writing get coordinated. Then, rather than our willy-nilly ignoring, subtracting from, changing, or adding to the demands we place on children, we will be in position to help them coordinate all the demands, while living within the constraints of their processing capacities.

ACKNOWLEDGMENTS

The research that this paper is based on has been supported by the Social Sciences and Humanities Research Council of Canada. I wish to express my indebtedness to Carl Bereiter whose insightful criticisms and constructive comments have been invaluable. In particular I would like to thank him for assistance in reviewing, step-by-step, the task analyses reported. My thanks also go to members of our research team, Valerie Anderson, Bob Bracewell, and Brooks Masterton, for providing the data needed for these analyses.

REFERENCE NOTES

1. Mennig-Peterson, C., & McCabe, A. *Structure of children's narratives.* Paper presented at the biennial meeting of the Society for Research in Child Development, New Orleans, March 1977.
2. Collis, K. F., & Biggs, J. B. *Classroom examples of cognitive development phenomena.* ERDC Funded Project 7/41, University of Newcastle, undated.

REFERENCES

Bachelder, B. L., & Denny, M. R. A theory of intelligence: I. Span and the complexity of stimulus control. *Intelligence*, 1977, *1*, 127–150. (a)

Bachelder, B. L., & Denny, M. R. A theory of intelligence; II. The role of span in a variety of intellectual tasks. *Intelligence*, 1977, *1*, 237–256. (b)

Bereiter, C. Development in writing. In L. W. Gregg & E. R. Steinberg (Eds.), *Cognitive processes in writing*. Hillsdale, N.J.: Lawrence Erlbaum Associates, 1980.

Bereiter, C., & Scardamalia, M. From conversation to composition: The role of instruction in a developmental process. In R. Glaser (Ed.), *Advances in Instructional Psychology*, Vol. 2. Hillsdale, N.J., Lawrence Erlbaum Assoc., 1982.

Case, R. Intellectual development from birth to adulthood: A neo-Piagetian interpretation. In R. Siegler (Ed.), *Children's thinking: What develops?* Hillsdale, N. J.: Lawrence Erlbaum, 1978.

Elbow, P. *Writing without teachers*. London: Oxford University Press, 1973.

Goody, J., & Watt, J. The consequences of literacy. *Comparative Studies in Society and History*, 1963, *5*, 304–345.

Harrel, L. E. A comparison of the development of oral and written language in school-age children. *Monographs of the Society for Research in Child Development*, 1957, *22* (3).

Havelock, E. A. Prologue to Greek literacy. In C. Boulter (Ed.), Lectures in memory of Louise Taft Semple, second series. Cincinnati: University of Oklahoma Press for the University of Cincinnati, 1973.

Hunt, K. *Grammatical structures written at three grade levels*. Champaign, Ill.: National Council of Teachers of English, 1965 (Research Report No. 3).

Inhelder, B., & Piaget, J. *The growth of logical thinking from childhood to adolescence*. New York: Basic Books, 1958.

Inhelder, B., & Piaget, J. *The early growth of logic in the child*. New York: Norton & Company, Inc., 1969.

Loban, W. *Language development: Kindergarten through Grade Twelve*. Research Report No. 18. Urbana Ill.: National Council of Teachers of English, 1976.

Mellon, J. C. *Transformational sentence-combining: A method for enhancing the development of syntactic fluency in English composition*. Research Report No. 10. Urbana, Ill.: National Council of Teachers of English, 1969.

O'Hare, F. *Sentence Combining: Improving student writing without formal grammar instruction*. Research Report no. 15. Urbana Ill.: National Council of Teachers of English, 1973.

Olson, D. R. From utterance to text: The bias of language in speech and writing. *Harvard Educational Review*, 1977, *47*(3), 257–281.

Pascual-Leone, J. *Cognitive development and cognitive style: A general psychological integration*. Unpublished doctoral dissertation, University of Geneva, 1969.

Pascual-Leone, J. A mathematical model for the transition rule in Piaget's developmental stages. *Acta Psychologica*, 1970, *63*, 301–345.

Piaget, J. *The language and thought of the child*. London: Kegan Paul, Trench, Trubner & Co. Ltd., 1926.

Savin, H. B. & Perchnock, E. Grammatical structure and the immediate recall of English sentences. *Journal of Verbal Learning and Verbal Behavior*, 1965, *4*(5), 348–353.

Scardamalia, M. Two formal operational tasks: A quantitative neo-Piagetian and task analysis model for investigating sources of task difficulty. In G. I. Lubin, J. F. Magary, & M. K. Poulsen (Eds.), *Piagetian theory and the helping professions*. Los Angeles: University of Southern California Publications Dept., 1975.

Scardamalia, M. Information processing capac demonstration using combinatorial reasoni

Scardamalia, M., Bereiter, C., & Fillion, B. *Wr composing activities*. Toronto: OISE Pres Publishing Co., 1981.

Scardamalia, M., & Bereiter, C. The develo capabilities in children's composing. In N *Language: A Developmental Approach*. Lc

Scardamalia, M., Bereiter, C., & Goelman, H. In M. Nystrand (Ed.), What writers know: discourse. New York: Academic Press, in

Siegler, R. S. Three aspects of cognitive develc

Stallard, C. K. An analysis of the writing behav *of English*, 1974, *8*, 206–218.

Vinh Bang Evolution de l'écriture de l'enfant à Niestlé, 1959.

West, W. W. Written composition. *Review o*

7 Writing is not the Inverse of Reading For Young Children

Charles Read
University of Wisconsin, Madison

We have all heard writing and reading described as *encoding* and *decoding,* respectively. This metaphor suggests that writing begins with ideas stored in some representation and consists in substituting some other representation, according to an algorithm or code. Reading, then, consists of the inverse procedure by someone who is in possession of the same code. This paper questions this assumption and presents evidence from children's writing which suggests that writing and reading are not inverses for children in the early grades. One implication is that children's writing ought to be studied on its own terms, and not merely as an outgrowth of reading. Another implication is that the type of representation which is optimal for beginning reading need not be optimal for beginning writing.

Having introduced the encode-decode metaphor, I should explain that my purpose is not merely to complain about a figure of speech. No doubt we all recognize that this commonplace metaphor is simplistic and perhaps misleading in various ways: the creation of an idea in writing is very different from the apprehension of one in reading. The two processes differ in the high-level integrative skills that they require, as well as in their motivation and context. In schooling, too, writing and reading are seldom parallel; first-graders get much more practice (and greater facility) in reading than in writing, typically. My concern, though, is with an assumption which is very widely held and of which the encode-decode metaphor is merely one frequent expression, namely, that reading and writing are mirror-images at their cores.

It would seem that writing and reading, to be effective, must be inverses. Mathematically, two functions are inverses if the second function, applied to the output of the first, leads back to the starting point. Square and square root are inverses in this sense: the square root of x^2 is always x. Similarly, as you read my writing, you should re-construct essentially the message that I am trying to convey. If not, then one or both of us is failing to read or write properly. In the special case of the same person doing both jobs, I should be able to write a message at time one and re-construct that message at time two. This is the essence of the encode-decode metaphor, and it seems a modest enough requirement. For reading and writing to accomplish their purposes, it would seem that they must be inverses in this limited sense. Yet I believe that young children do not begin with this assumption and that although they can read and write, their reading and writing are not inverses.

A stronger notion of *inverse* would require not only that the two processes have opposite effects overall, but that they proceed through the same steps in opposite directions, i.e., that every step of one process must be the inverse of a corresponding step of the other. In arithmetic, this would require that if we compute squares by multiplying, we must compute square roots by dividing, for instance. Since I deny that young children's writing and reading are inverses in the weaker sense, I must also deny that they are inverses in this stronger sense. Admittedly, any attempt to compare reading with writing is considerably handicapped by the fact that there is no generally-accepted analysis of either task, especially no analysis which seriously claims to be formal and complete. I will simply point up certain aspects of the two tasks which are not parallel.

This paper has two more general aims, as well. It suggests that we need to define more precisely *where children are* as they embark on reading and writing, that is, what expectations and assumptions they hold, what levels of representation they find natural, and how these starting points may differ from their ultimate destinations. It points out that some assumptions we have taken for granted about the processes of reading and writing, types of representation, and levels of difficulty, are in fact empirical assumptions that may be wrong. Finally, this paper argues that writing is not necessarily more difficult than reading. Young children often take an approach to writing that avoids much of the complexity.

My contention that reading and writing are not inverses is based on samples of writing of children at ages 4, 5, and 6 which I have collected in studying young children's spelling. Consider the following example:[1]

Example One
WONS A LITOL GROL WOS WOKIG IN HR GORDIN INTIL SE GOT
KOT BIY A ROBR AND TIN SE SKREMD AND TIN HR MOM AND
DAD KAM OUT AND HLPT HR OWT OV THE ROBRS HANDS AND

---

[1]These are not based on the child's pronunciation, which is standard Upper Midwestern American. Nor was the spelling GAOL based on any antique British influence.

TIN TAY KOLD THE POLES AND TIN THE POLES TOK KAR OV THE ROBR AND POT HIM IN THE GAOL.

(age 6, 3 approx.)

In the examples cited in this paper, I have inserted spaces between words, corrected backwards letters and other faulty printing, and have occasionally made a judgment involving an unclear letter. I have not otherwise altered the spelling. Appendix A presents interlinear translations, in case they are needed.

The most significant fact about Example One (and the others to be cited) is that when she wrote it, the author could already read frequent words and high-redundancy texts in standard orthography. The girl who wrote Example One could at the same time read words such as "once, little, girl, was, her, she, by, then, and came," in standard spelling with ease. In other words, there can be a stage at which children have two distinct systems, one for reading standard spelling and another for writing in their own invented orthography. Both systems can be effective, and the nonstandard spelling system does not necessarily affect the reading system adversely. I will return to this issue later.

Invented spellings have several characteristics which I have explored in other publications (Read, 1975, Ch. 2; 1980). Some of the more interesting ones, such as the spelling of phonetically similar vowel sounds with the same letter and the omission of pre-consonantal nasals, do not appear in this (relatively late) example. We can see the common device of using a letter to represent its own name, as in *HLPT* and *SKREMD*. There is also the spelling of /š/ with *S* and / ǯ / with T, as in SE (she), TIN (then), and TAY (they). The main characteristic of these spellings which distinguishes them from standard orthography is that they are derived segment-by-segment, with the names of the letters in mind, along with the letters' common sound values. Clearly, the process which this girl used to spell was basically distinct from the process she used to read. At this stage, she created, rather than retrieved, the spellings of familiar words. This separation has been characteristic of at least two dozen children whose beginning spelling I have studied.

Others have observed the same kinds of invented spelling. Beers (1974) and Gentry (1977), for example, studied spelling patterns in first grade over the course of a year. They see these invented spellings as one part of an orderly stage-like development. Moreover, Beers and Gentry made their observations in Virginia, a different dialect region from either Boston or Wisconsin, where I have collected evidence.

It is clear that the children who create these spellings do not share our assumption that spelling must be standardized. In Example One, having written OUT in line three the author is not deterred from writing OWT just four words later. When one considers that English (not to mention its ancestors) was written for about one thousand years without standardized spelling, one realizes that there is nothing odd in this. Young children have no reason to share the cocnern for widespead literacy, printers' convenience, and language *correctness* which led historically to the adoption of standardized spelling.

More surprisingly, these children also do not assume that we must have a unique spelling for each sound, as many reformers recommend. In Example One GOT, KOT, WOS, and POT all have the same vowel spelling and the same general structure, even though all of them have different vowels ($/a/$ $/ɔ/$, $/ʌ/$, and $/ʊ/$, respectively) in this girl's speech. This willingness to generalize spellings, or to categorize sounds, is also characteristic of the children I have studied.

One final observation, although it is not shown in Example One, is that children at this age frequently write with little concern for an audience. They write notes to themselves which they cannot read later, and they write invitations to playmates who they know cannot read. Our son, age six, writes signs, mostly of the KEEP OUT variety, addressed to his sister, age four, who cannot read a word of it. In fact, many of the salient properties of beginning spelling reflect writing that is not really intended to be read: the invented spellings of even familiar words; the absence of standardization; and the use of a single spelling for a wide range of (phonetically similar) sounds, an even wider range than in standard spelling, in some instances. Quite often, even the author cannot read this spelling; I have asked children to read me stories that they themselves wrote only a day or two before, and if they have forgotten what they wrote, they usually cannot reconstruct it from their own spelling.

We have plenty of examples of adult writing that reveals an aloof disregard for the audience, of course. One variety oozes from centers of learning and other large bureaucracies. By comparison, children's lack of concern for audience, even when the audience is themselves, seems both more innocent and more profound. The writer of gobbledygook is careless only at the sentence level and above; his spelling and punctuation are likely to be nearly flawless. As Richard Lanham (1974) has pointed out, pretentious prose serves a higher cause than clarity: it conveys the writer's office, social role, and claim to expertise. I contend that children, on the other hand, are not necessarily trying to convey anything. They are far less interested in the *product* than we are, and more involved in the *process* of writing something down. A child will labor for hours to write down a story, and when it is finished, he or she may show it to you. Then, however, his interest in it is ended; it is rare that he will make any effort to keep it and even rarer that he will read it. Teachers have long made similar observations about children's art.

At any rate, whatever a child's purposes—and they are undoubtedly multiple—the writing of young children who can read seems to show that for them, the two processes are fundamentally different. We tend to think of a reader/writer as having acquired a set of literacy skills, which relate print to sounds or to messages. We are tempted to suppose that the reader/writer simply accesses this collection of skills, starting at one end or the other, depending on which task is being carried out. Schematically, our conception looks like this:

read

PRINT⇐ = = = = = = = ⇒ SKILLS ⇐ = = = = = ⇒ MESSAGE

write

FIG. 1

Such a schema *may* be correct for the skillful adult; but it is not appropriate for the young child. A child may have had considerable experience in reading the word *was,* for example, but that experience has no necessary impact on his writing.

For additional evidence of this point, consider Examples Two through Five below. These are a report of a trip to the dentist, a set of recipes, a story modeled on the Oz stories, and a school composition after a visit to a computing center, respectively. Our son created them at ages roughly equally spaced between 4, 9 and 6, 1. These illustrate again the initial independence of reading and spelling. At the time that our son wrote the Woozy story, for example, he had had considerable experience in reading, including some of the Oz stories. He was well-acquainted with words such as *some, city, follow, yellow, brick, road, want, with,* and *started;* and yet he created his own spellings for all of these and more. For the absence of standardization, compare CINPYEUTER with CINPYOUTER in Example Five, for instance.

Example Two
THAY BROT MY TETH AND THEY POT A FILEN IN THEY
HAD A SPETHOL DRIL IT IS FOR TACIN OUT CABDES

(age 4, 9)

Example Three
BLUE BERE PIE

FRST A PAWD OF BLUEBERES. THAN AD SOM GIGRBRED THAN
BAC IT FOR 10 SEKIS.

CAK

FRST 4 CUPS OF SHGR. TEN AD 2 CUPS OF BUTTR THAN AD SOM
FRASTNG.

KUKES

FRST AD GIGR BED. THAN PUT IN 5 CUPS OF CHAKLIT CHIP
(age 5, 4 approx.)

Example Four
THE WOOZE OF OZ

ONE DAY THER LIVED A WOOZE, IN A SMALLL HOUSE. ONE
DAY SOME TRAVRS CAME. AND ASKED HOW TO GO TO
THE EMRLD CITE. FOWL THE YELLO BRIK RODE WAS THE
REPLIY. DO YOU WONT TO GO WITHE US? O.K. SO THEY
SITRTED THER GRNE. AFTER THEY HAD WAKEED 4 MILS
THEY FOWD A SNASWANAPZANA. IT LOOKED LIKE AN
OTAPUS BUT IT HAD 100 LEGS. THE STRAIGRS SED HELO
AND THE SNASWANAPZANA SED HELO. I CAN SHOOT
WATER BLITS SIAD THE SNASWANAPZANA. THE WOOSE
SIAD WELL I CAN SHOOT FIRE. LES FRGT UBOUT ALL THAT
SIAD THE SNASWANAPZANA WARE ARE YOU GOING? HO
TO THE EMLD CITE I CAN GET YOU TO THE EMRLD CITE IN
A SEKINT SIAD THE SNASWANAPZANA (Picture of smiling
snaswanapzana.) O.K.! SIAD THE TRAVLS AFTER THE RIDE
THEY WENT TO OSMA AND OZME SIAD THAT THE WOOZE
WOOD ROOL ALL OZ.   (age 5, 8)
THE END

Example Five
THE CINPYEUTER

THE CINPYEUTER IS BIG. IT CAN STOR OBAT 5,000 WORS AT
ONE'S. THER ERE TAPES THAT STOR WORDS. THER ERE
TOW WASE OF TAKEING TO A CINPYOUTER, ONE IS BY A
TRMINL THE OTHER IS BY A CADE.   (age 6, 1)

Comparing Example Two with Example Five, one cannot miss the
development that has taken place; note the standardization of -*ing* endings,
for instance. This development was gradual, however; over a span of a year
and a half, invented spellings of familiar words by no means disappeared.
From a few observations, it seems that even children older than six or seven
will continue to create their own spellings, if their home and school remains
tolerant. On the other hand, children who have suddenly faced new criteria, as

in moving to a new school, have been able to change the basis of their spelling quickly, presumably because they already knew the standard spellings from their reading experience.

Children also adopt the comparatively abstract characteristics of standard spelling only gradually. Note the two instances of SED, followed by six instances of SIAD, in Example Four. The standard spelling, being neither regular nor phonemic, is subject to confusion at first. An even more striking case is the apostrophe in ONE'S (Example Five). Here a morphological marker of standard spelling is applied on a more nearly phonetic basis, without regard for meaning. Having introduced examples from our own son, I should re-emphasize, perhaps, that I have seen the asymmetry between reading and writing in many children. I use these writings from our child only because it has been convenient to collect a series of dated examples under known circumstances.

Writing, as young children approach it, remains close to the surface of language; they devise ways of representing individual sound-segments and syllables. Frequently, they resolve the problem of what to say and how to say it by letting their writing resemble their speech, as in the following first-grade composition:

Example Six
TODAY IS FALL NO TOMAERO IS FALL
YES TODAY IS FALL WEL JAST FRGT IT
THE LEEVS AER FALLING
THE LEEVS AER FALLING
AND TAY TRNE DIFRINT COLRS

I am not suggesting that writing is thus made easy—indeed both reading and writing are difficult for some children—but I contend that these tasks are quite different in level of abstractness. Some children invent rather concrete representations, namely spellings based on letter-names and phonetic similarities. Using these concrete spellings, some start writing before they learn to read (Chomsky, 1975a).

The reading process admits no such surface-level strategy. A reader cannot simply ignore the writer's choices and preferences, as young writers often ignore the needs of their readers. The reader is inevitably in the position of trying to re-construct another person's ideas, a problem that doesn't arise in writing as young children approach it. Consequently, as a reader, one usually makes use of the context, including what one knows about the author and the book, what one has read previously, the illustrations, and so on. This context is quite variable in its usefulness; in many books for young children, the entire message can be derived from the illustrations alone, while in other cases, context tells the reader very little.

The reader must also identify segment-, syllable-, and word-length units written in standard orthography, which is highly abstract. The reader cannot choose what level of abstractness he finds reasonable, as children do in writing. Admittedly, we do not yet know precisely what units are employed in the processes of reading, but it is surely safe to say that these units are less directly related to speech sounds and phonetic relationships than in young children's spelling.

Finally, the reader must momentarily store units which have been identified and later integrate them into a meaningful message. This process, too, is complex at several levels, from *blending* segments into syllables, to extracting meaning from sentences in which intonation is not indicated, to relating sentences to each other in discourses which may be, for instance, ironic or humorous. In short, the key difference between reading and writing is that in reading, someone else has chosen both the message and the level of representation, while in writing as young children do it, no one else is necessarily involved. The result is that the two processes need not have any components which are truly inverses.

Other investigators have noticed the discrepancy between reading and spelling at the early stages. Bryant and Bradley (1979) suggest, on the basis of experiments, that children with a reading age of about 7½ years tend to spell on the basis of sound/spelling correspondences, but read by recognizing longer units. The subjects in most of the experiments actually represented two groups: normal readers with a mean chronological age of 6 years, 10 months, and backward readers with a mean chronological age of 10 years, 4 months, the two groups having the same mean IQ and average reading performance. Both groups exhibited the lack of parallelism between reading and spelling. Bryant and Bradley's most striking evidence for the use of different strategies in the two tasks is that there were words which some children spelled correctly but could not read, as well as the reverse.

In her fascinating study of the development of her son's literacy, Glenda Bissex (1980) observed a similar discrepancy. She notes that her son used varied strategies at an earlier age in reading than in spelling. In particular, he relied heavily on context in reading at a time when he was still spelling in a strictly segment-by-segment fashion. As Bissex points out, the use of varied strategies is important to self-correction, but this capacity develops later in spelling than in reading.

Uta Frith (1978) has observed a contrast between reading and spelling in some twelve-year-olds, comparing the reading performance of good and poor spellers, both groups being of normal intelligence. Frith remarks:

> The paradox that deserves some explanation is how input processes (reading) and output processes (writing) can be divorced to such an extent that one

functions well, the other poorly. The written word is both stimulus and product. How is it then that some people can read but cannot write?

She goes on to show, through a series of experiments, that her poor spellers were indeed good readers in ordinary circumstances but that their difficulty could be brought out in tasks which required converting print to sound. The impairment that Frith observed may be quite different, in both mechanism and social significance, from the contrast between spelling and reading in young children, but it supports the potential separation of the two processes.

What, then, are the prospects for further research? What issues are reopened or cast in a new light if one accepts that early writing and reading are not parallel? The partial independence of these skills surely suggests a renewed importance for research on the development of writing considered as a distinct skill rather than as an extension of reading. It suggests, moreover, the importance of research on the early stages of writing development, in which we can see the origins of at least the surface skills more distinctly. Clearly a major focus also ought to be on the period in which reading and writing come together, in that the sound/spelling systems merge. Does this reflect a linguistic development, a growing ability to internalize a highly abstract spelling system? Does it reflect cognitive maturation, an ability to treat two activities as reciprocal? Certainly children's early writing exhibits the egocentricism that has often been associated with children's spoken language (Piaget, 1926; Vygotsky, 1962), that is, language that is not addressed to anyone and is not meant to evoke a response from any listener. Can we trace cognitive development in writing, as Piaget traces it in speech?

To what extent do the two systems, reading and writing, finally merge, and what is the influence of reading experience on this merger? In adults, reading and writing are surely inverses in the weak sense: when we read our own writing, we recreate the idea that was written down, at least roughly. In simple cases, and in some difficult ones, this holds true even when the writer and the reader are different people, much to the benefit of all of us. But are these processes inverse in the stronger sense, being mirror-images step-by-step? Or are they more like the finding of squares and square roots: squaring typically proceeds by multiplying, but square root-finding is not efficiently carried out by dividing alone. What differences are there among individuals, in the extent to which the two processes are parallel in detail? For example, for some people, nearly any word which is familiar in reading is available in spelling, while for others this is far from true. Frith (1978) showed not only that her poor spellers read differently than her good spellers, but also that the poor spellers were good readers, in ordinary tasks. Thus, their ability to read and write standard spelling differed—quite substantially, it seems.

Finally, what are the effects of early experience in writing? Why do some children approach writing like drawing, while others do not approach it voluntarily at all? Having seen the enthusiasm with which some children take it up, I can only speculate that one reason that other children write only under duress is that they have learned from parents, siblings, or teachers that it is a difficult task, mine-strewn with the danger of being wrong. What difference does it make in the long run if children are allowed to use superficial spellings for a few years at first? What difference does it make if children gain pleasure in writing at an early age? These questions remain regrettably vague and undeniably difficult to investigate, but nonetheless central.

Instructional Implications.   Meanwhile, what about present educational policy and practice: what suggestions does this point of view about early-stage writing carry for the teacher? Even without knowing the answers to the questions posed above, I am persuaded that voluntary writing in the primary grades is valuable. Teachers in grades K-2, at least, should encourage children to write, free from concern about standard spelling, or, at first, the demands of a reader. Rather, teachers and parents can look upon early writing in roughly the same way that they regard children's art, as an expression which is created with pleasure and which is not expected to be adult-like.

Carol Chomsky (1975a,b) has taken the lead in recommending this policy to teachers and parents generally. Both she and I are aware, however, of the constraints within which teachers and schools operate. Some parents are not happy to see their children bringing home nonstandard spelling with the teacher's approval. They see these spellings as the beginning of bad habits which may be difficult to correct. Nor would they be reassured to learn that some researchers consider such spellings a natural and interesting aspect of development. Teachers can only do what they think is possible in their community.

Teachers can begin by reassuring themselves and parents. It seems clear that nonstandard spelling does not imply difficulty in reading; for a child to write GROL does not endanger her reading of *girl* at all. Teachers and parents should be aware that some children begin to write before they begin to read, and that this order is understandable when one compares the two tasks from a child's point of view. Second, teachers can encourage children's growing awareness of their readers, as reflected not only in increasingly standard spelling, but also in more explicit transitions and statements of background information.

Even when teachers and parents do not impose adult expectations in these matters, children gradually become aware of the existence of an audience and of that audience's needs. Meanwhile, the audience gradually becomes more distant from the child, expanding beyond teachers, parents, and siblings.

Children who have extensive opportunities for writing in the primary grades may gain significant educational advantages. The process focuses their attention on writing in relation to speech, it promotes an awareness of themselves and their subject, and it provides an avenue for creativity which has no precise counterpart. A child who writes stories for pleasure and writes instructions to gain increased control over his siblings and peers is less likely to grow up feeling that writing is a fearsome and odious task to be engaged in only when it is socially required, as in thank-you notes. These benefits of early writing experience are admittedly difficult to quantify, but I think they are real. Once beginning writing and reading are seen as distinct, more freedom in writing opens up for both teachers and children. We can allow children to develop their facility and their awareness gradually, as we recognize that they begin with assumptions very different from those of a literate adult.

REFERENCES

Beers, J. First- and second-grade children's developing orthographic concepts of tense and lax vowels. University of Virginia, 1974. University Microfilms, 1975. No. 75-4694.

Bissex, G. L. *Gyns at Wrk*. Cambridge Mass.: Harvard University Press, 1980.

Bryant, P. E. & Bradley, L. Why children sometimes write words which they do not read. In U. Frith (Ed.), *Cognitive processes in spelling*. London: Academic Press, 1979.

Chomsky, C. Invented spelling in the open classroom. *Word, 27* (special issue: *Child Language Today*), 1975a, pp. 499-518.

Chomsky, C. How sister got into the grog. *Early Years,* November 1975b pp. 36-39, 78-79.

Frith, U. From print to meaning and from print to sound, or how to read without knowing how to spell. *Visible Language, 12,* 1978, *43-54*.

Gentry, J. R. A study of the orthographic strategies of beginning readers. University of Virginia, 1977. University Microfilms, 1979. No. 7901152.

Lanham, R. *Style: an anti-textbook*. New Haven: Yale University Press, 1974.

Piaget, J. [*The language and thought of the child*] (M. Gabian, trans.). Cleveland: Meridian Books, 1955. (Originally published, 1926.)

Read, C. *Children's categorization of speech sounds in English*. Urbana, Ill.: National Council of Teachers of English, 1975.

Read, C. Creative spelling by young children. In T. Shopen & J. M. Williams (Eds.), *Standards and dialects in English*. Cambridge, Mass.: Winthrop Publ., 1980.

APPENDIX A

Example One

WONS A LITOL GROL WOS WOKIG IN HR GORDIN
Once a little girl was walking in her garden
INTIL SE GOT KOT BIY A ROBR AND TIN
until she got caught by a robber and then
SE SKREMD AND TIN HR MOM AND DAD KAM OUT AND
she screamed and then her Mom and Dad came out and
HLPT HR OWT OV THE ROBRS HANDS AND TIN
helped her out of the robber's hands and then
TAY KOLD THE POLES AND TIN THE POLES TOK
they called the police and then the police took
KAR OV THE ROBR AND POT HIM IN THE GAOL.
care of the robber and put him in the jail.

(ages 6, 3 approx.)

Example Two

THAY BROT MY TETH AND THAY POT A FILEN IN
They brushed my teeth and they put a filling in.
THEY HAD A SPETHOL DRIL IT IS FOR TACIN OUT CABDES
They had a special drill. It is for taking out cavities.   (age 4, 9)

Example Three
BLUE BERE PIE

Blueberry Pie
FIRST A PAWD OF BLUEBERES. THAN AD SOME GIGRBRED
First a pound of blueberries. Then add some gingerbread
THAN BAC IT FOR 10 SEKIS.
Then bake it for 10 seconds.

CAK

Cake
FRST 4 CUPS OF SHGR. TEN AD 2 CUPS OF BUTTR
First 4 cups of sugar. Then add 2 cups of butter
THAN AD SOM FRASTING.
Then add some frosting.

KUKES

Cookies
FRST AD GIGR BED. THAN PUT IN 5 CUPS OF
First add gingerbread. Then put in 5 cups of

CHAKLIT CHIP
chocolate chips.   (age 5, 4 approx.)

Example Three

Example Four
THE WOOZE OF OZ

ONE DAY THER LIVED A WOOZE, IN A SMALL HOUSE. ONE DAY
One day there lived a Woozy, in a small house. One day
SOME TRAVRS CAME. AND ASKED HOW TO GO TO THE EMRLD
CITE.
some travelers came. and asked how to go to the emerald city.
FOWL THE YELLO BRIK RODE WAS THE REPLIY. DO YOU WONT
TO
Follow the yellow brick road was the reply. Do you want to
GO WITHE US? O.K. SO THEY SITRTED THER GRNE. AFTER
go with us? O.K. So they started their journey. After
THEY HAD WAKEED 4 MILS THEY FOWD A SNASWANAPZANA.
IT
they had walked 4 miles they found a snaswanapzana. It
LOOKED LIKE AN OTAPUS BUT IT HAD 100 LEGS. THE STRAIGRS
looked like an octapus but it had 100 legs. The strangers
SED HELO AND THE SNASWANAPZANA SED HELO. I CAN
SHOOT
said Hello and the snaswanapzana said Hello. I can shoot
WATER BLITS SIAD THE SNASWANAPZANA. THE WOOSE SIAD
water bullets said the snaswanapzana. The woozy said
WELL I CAN SHOOT FIRE. LES FRGT UBOUT ALL THAT SIAD THE
well I can shoot fire. Let's forget about all that said the
SNASWANAPZANA WARE ARE YOU GOING? HO TO THE EMLD
CITE
snaswanapzana. Where are you going? Oh to the emerald city.
I CAN GET YOU TO THE EMRLD CITE IN A SEKINT SIAD THE
I can get you to the emerald city in a second said the
SNASWANAPZANA (Picture of smiling snaswanapzana.)
snaswanapzana.
O.K.! SIAD THE TRAVLS AFTER THE RIDE THEY WENT TO OZMA
O.K. said the travelers. After the ride they went to Ozma
AND OZME SIAD THAT THE WOOZE WOOD ROOL ALL OZ.
and Ozma said that the Woozy would rule all Oz.   (age 5, 8)
THE END

Example Four

Example Five
THE CINPYEUTER

The Computer

THE CINPYEUTER IS BIG. IT CAN STOR OBAT 5,000
The computer is big. It can store about 5,000
WORS AT ONE'S. THER ERE TAPES THAT STOR WORDS.
words at once. There are tapes that store words.
THER ERE TOW WASE OF TAKEING TO A CINPYOUTER,
There are two ways of talking to a computer;
ONE IS BY A TRMINL THE OTHER IS BY A CADE.
one is by a terminal, the other is by a card.   (age 6, 1)

8 Toward a Developmental Theory of Writing

Roger W. Shuy
Georgetown University

Any discussion of the need for a developmental theory of composition must begin with an analysis of what is known about the acquisition of composition skills. Despite the broad-based and intensive attempts made to measure the level of writing ability in this country, these measurements, including the available standardized tests relating to composition, fail in the most important ingredient of all—knowledge of what to measure. In the national assessment of writing, (NAEP, 1972) for example, five age groups from primary through adult were assigned the task of writing a composition based on a stimulus picture of a forest fire. Several good things could be said about such a procedure. Unlike many composition assessments, this one actually was based on writing. Having accumulated these thousands of written compositions, however, the assessment staff had to determine criteria for scoring them. It was decided that a minimal cut-off point would be established and that the criteria for minimal cut-off would be mechanics. Thus, writing was defined, for the first time in this study, as spelling, punctuation, usage and capitalization. Since the mandate for measurement did not specify features of writing such as discourse cohesion, creativity, logic, tone or well-turned phrasing, no argument could be made against such a decision. Contextual concerns were also minimal in the national assessment, since the writers were never told who the audience for their composition might be. Nor were they given a chance to proofread their efforts.

Another more short-term comparative study of written compositions of 9, 13 and 17 year olds was carried out in 1970 and again in 1974, each time on national samples of 1500 students (NAEP, 1975). The report, issued by the National Assessment of Educational Progress, concluded that the writing of the 1974 17-year olds is less coherent, more simplistic and awkward than their 1970 counterparts while the same writing quality of the nine-year olds had slightly improved. Professional English teachers who served as test analysts were generally skeptical of the significance of the exam. Richard Lloyd Jones observed that the test "... is a very gross, not a very sensitive instrument, but happens to be the best we have right now." (*Washington Star,* November 19, 1975, p. A1). It seems to me that our ability as teachers to help learners understand specific problems, limitations, and strategies in writing is hampered by our lack of knowledge about how writing skills develop.

The rest of this paper, therefore, will address two basic issues: why we have had such a difficult time constructing a developmental theory of writing and what needs to be done to construct one.

PROBLEMS IN CONSTRUCTING
A DEVELOPMENTAL
THEORY OF WRITING

Invisibility of the Topic

One reason for our inability to understand writing in terms of development is the invisibility of the topic. Most people are aware that there is a relationship between language and writing, but they are in no way conscious of what this might mean. For years linguists have had to live with the idea that their field of study is not only undervalued by the general public but also that is is not even seen by them. Those who do perceive the relationship seldom see it in its fullest potential. That is, they may generalize about the desirability of people writing as they speak, but they do not identify the component parts of this phenomenon or their developmental characteristics. It has been clear to many researchers, for example, that children acquire their native language in orderly, developmental, sequential stages. It has been only recently, however, that this development has been identified in terms of its phonological and grammatical components (Dale, 1972). It is one thing to say that a child's language is underdeveloped or immature. It is something quite different to say exactly what is underdeveloped or immature about it.

Certain parallels are clearly evident among fields related to composition. In the field of second language learning, for example, it is likely that the five major component parts of language learning (phonology, lexicon, morphology, sentences and utterances) are all available to learners at all stages of development; but it is also likely that these vary tremendously in terms of their rate of development at different periods in their language development. Figure 1 depicts how this might work.

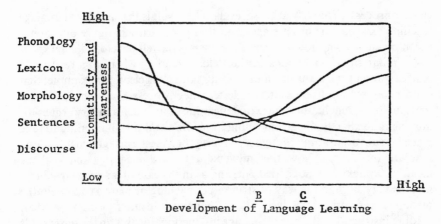

FIG. 1.   Schematic Representation of Rates of Development for Different Language Systems

At any given stage in the acquisition of the target language (onset, A, B, C, well developed), all systems are developing but at different rates and are in a sense, in different degrees of cruciality to the user and in different relationships to each other. Thus, in his communication, a learner at the onset of language learning will be developing greater awareness of phonology and lexicon, but the rate of development of these language systems will be lower as they become more fully developed. High rates of development at the sentence and utterance (discourse) level will occur later. Furthermore, it has been suggested that as a language system develops, it becomes automatized and consequently requires less conscious attention from language users. Thus, the curves in the figure can be viewed as depicting the extent to which the language user has to be consciously aware of processing the level of a given language system.

However much the experts might argue about the exact rates of development of language systems and levels of automaticity in Figure 1, there is general agreement that something like such a relationship actually exists, and this is the major point to be made from the illustration.

In reference to this figure, we might examine current materials related to second language teaching for what relationship exists between theory and teaching. The answer is, very little. In the field of English as a second language, for example, there is a primary focus on the component parts of phonology, lexicon and grammar, but even in these matters it is not at all clear how the decision gets made to focus or sequence one form with regard to another. Although context is provided in the form of sentences or utterances, little if anything is done to structure the teaching or materials to help the learner process effectively at these levels. The result is that much of language teaching exists at the onset stages and that good learners figure out, pretty much on their own, how to process at the more well developed stages.

A similar situation obtains in the field of reading where Figure 1 could easily represent the acquisition of reading skills. It is clear, for example, that good readers do not read letter by letter; they process by larger and larger units, up to and including contextual meaning units. Such a theory argues for moving immediately toward meaning in reading and for all learning to take place in realistic meaning contexts. There has been some disagreement among scholars on exactly how this movement toward meaning and realistic meaning context is to be carried out, and as in the case of language teaching, there is very little in the way of structured teaching or materials to help the reader process print effectively at the sentence and utterance levels. Most reading instruction, like most language instruction, focuses on the onset skills and leaves the more cognitive development to the learner's own discretion.

The invisibility of a more holistic theory of the science of composition, then, is quite predictable from what we see of the sister fields of second language teaching and reading. For one thing, the science of composition is invisible to those who view it only as a craft. Moreover, the cognitive aspects of composition are invisible to those who view it only as a set of skills. Finally, the utterance processing of composition is invisible to those who see it primarily at lower or smaller levels.

One of the most critical school subjects in terms of individualization is that of writing. One learns writing oneself, not as a group. It can be learned *in* groups, but the learning is individualized or it is not learning. Relatively little is known about individualization or learning styles in the development of language or writing, despite the rather large amount of attention given to individualization by educators. Figure 1 outlines the development of language systems essential to writing, but suggests a rather gross guess as to the developmental stages through which children pass in learning to write. At any given stage, the interrelationship of these language systems to one another will be in a somewhat different arrangement.

For a more finely grained analysis, for each of these five language systems in writing, similar developmental schemata could be created. Thus, for lexicon, we should be able, with research, to determine what the expected developmental stages and rates might be. For discourse, we could plot at what age anaphora or foregrounding, for example, begins to develop in children's writing. Once the component categories are determined and the developmental patterns are established, we might then have a basis for assessing the rates of development of different language systems in writing for individual children. It is possible, for example, that the developmental lines illustrated as a gross generalization in Figure 1 are different for different children. The gradual rise in the development of discourse competence in writing ability may be much more sharply developed in certain children, throwing off the ecology of the overall developmental scheme. The point here, however, is that no solid work on individualization of the language-related aspects of composition will be possible until we have a framework, based on research.

Surface Analysis

A second reason why it is so difficult to construct a developmental framework theory for composition stems from the fact that writing, like most school subjects, suffers from *surface analysis,* that is, writing is taught or assessed primarily in relation to its surface as opposed to its deeper semantic and syntactic features. As the National Assessment studies clearly indicate, it is only the surface level aspects of composition that are measured. That which is not measured is too difficult to see, too difficult to explain, too difficult to assess or all of the above. Recent litigation and legislation regarding bilingual education has brought this problem to courtroom prominence. Cities throughout the country are being called upon to measure the English language ability of the foreign born to determine whether or not they should be placed in bilingual education programs. New York City developed its own test measuring English ability in matters relating to phonology and morphology. Chicago and other cities followed suit. The state of Iowa was seriously contemplating the use of a test which asked a series of questions only about the child's parents' language, birthplace and length of residency in the United States. Most of these questions can be considered discrete-point measurements. Discrete-point tests are the usual first impressions which people have of language tests. The widely used Test of English as a Foreign Language (TOEFL) is a clear example. Such tests usually have multiple choice items, each item probing the knowledge of a particular fact about language. These tests can measure some of the language skills which a child has but only if we are willing to assume that the skill of language can be isolated and shrunk into a small component for measurement purposes. The problem with such tests is in how to select representative items.

In any language test, a severe problem arises when language is measured outside of its naturally occurring context. Language is always used in a specific situation, at a specific time with different participants for different purposes. Contextual factors heavily influence both language form and usage; language ability is, however, almost always assessed out of context, yielding, at best, an approximate indication of such ability. Probably the major reason why such tests remain popular is that they are reliable, easy to administer and score, and permit cross comparison of test results. One of the major problems with such tests is that they do not grow out of clear and adequate decisions about what matters most, e.g., content validity. Lack of content validity can come about as a result of lack of research on the topic, from an inability to express what the valid content is, from an inadequate theory or validity or from a kind of hopeless laziness which leads us to measure that which is easy to measure, whether it is valid or not.

I have introduced this discussion of language assessment to indicate that an adequate developmental framework for writing should be able to distinguish what is important to measure from what is not. Such information is not yet clearly available.

The Past Overpromise of Linguistics

A third reason why it is difficult to create a developmental theory of writing is that school people have become wary of the langauge aspects of composition. In the past, linguists have frequently tried to relate what they know about linguistics to the teaching of composition. These efforts have not been recognized as successes for several reasons. One problem is that composition required the analysis of cohesive discourse while linguists had been studying units much smaller and much less relevant to composition. In the forties and fifties, the focus of linguists was on phonology and morphology. In the sixties, the focus was on sentence syntax. Not until the seventies has the field of linguistics seriously turned its attention to areas of language which have promise for aiding the study of written composition.

Earlier studies of phonology held out high promise to composition teachers who were told that if they taught their students intonation, they could punctuate more effectively. Almost forgotten now are the books which taught that double cross juncture was something like a period and that plus juncture was like a comma. These notions were difficult to teach and frequently destroyed by counter-examples. The linguistic period of syntax focus offered, and provided, even less to the composition teacher. Several publishers converted to transformational grammar but were met with very little success. The teachers saw little evidence that their students could learn to write better by knowing transformational grammar and, of course, they were right. There is little reason to believe that knowledge of *any* grammar, traditional, structural, transformational or any other kind, will help children write better. Why should being able to talk about what they are doing help children do it any better? Is it important to have a metalanguage in order to talk? Of course not. Many teachers saw the failure of transformationally based pedagogy as a weakness in the theory. This criticism was doubly unfortunate since the available published materials trailed far behind developments in transformational grammar and were, at best, very poor representations of the theory.

By the seventies, therefore, composition teachers had grown wary of the influence of linguists in their business. They could do as well, if not better, with their own approaches. Whatever the science of writing had to offer, it was not being done well enough to be of any use.

One can hardly blame teachers for their lack of enthusiasm about the contribution of linguistics to their field, but some nagging, unanswered questions remain. If we are interested in determining how to express the assessment of writing ability, how to diagnose meaningfully and how to prescribe knowingly, we need a template which will provide a guide for such assessment, diagnosis and prescription. Such a template sounds quite a bit like a developmental theory of writing. Oral language specialists have already been successful with this phase of their research. In the field of reading, it is now clearly recognized that a developmental theory is critical to that field. To get such a theory, one must do some rather scientific things. The craft of writing can and does exist very well without the science. It uses the science without really being taught it. One learns from reading, from examples, from being edited, from listening and a host of other resources.

On the other hand, to determine how this development takes place, whether taught or not, we need some tools which have content validity (they efficiently measure what they claim to measure) and reliability (they are fair and can be replicated). The past contributions of linguistics to writing were only small pieces of such validity and were never shown to be reliable. Linguistics in the seventies can be characterized by an increased awareness and analysis of context and variability (sociolinguistics), by a deep concern with meaning (semantics, pragmatics) and by a focus on units larger than a sentence (discourse analysis). These three characteristics aid research in writing more than anything contemplated in linguistics before.

ISSUES FOR A DEVELOPMENTAL THEORY
OF WRITING

It would be nice if we could point to developmental research in written composition and build a theory on what is already kown. Short of this, we must construct a theory which contains as complete an array of accurate components as we can determine, placed into some sort of holistic configuration with a base line of time. In short, what seems to be needed is a kind of written composition counterpart to Figure 1. It is not at all clear what the components are in such a theory. Perhaps some of the same ones used in language learning or reading would obtain (e.g., lexicon, morphology, sentences and utterances) but probably not in the same ways, since writing is developed after language is rather thoroughly learned. It would appear, in fact, that the major components in such a theory would be discourse or utterance components—those aspects of writing which foreground,

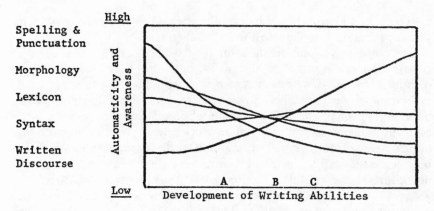

FIG. 2. Representation of Development of Writing Abilities

subordinate, equalize, relate, connect, alternate, open, close, continue, etc. If so, a schematic representation of the writing process may look something like Figure 2.

Representation of Development of Writing Abilities. Figure 2 displays the interrelationships of early skills such as spelling, punctuation and grammatical accuracy along with lexicon and syntax as rather high awareness and automatic phenomena. Errors in writing which relate to such language systems are often not a result of the students' lack of knowledge of their own language. Rather they result from an incomplete or inaccurate learning of the written representation of known oral language. With syntax, problems in writing are of two major types: those which represent spoken norms accuately but which are not acceptable in writing, and those which result from the process of writing itself. In the latter case, the slowness of putting thought to paper can, of itself, get in the way of accuracy. Discourse level ability starts rather low in automaticity and awareness in writing, but it is not at point zero. Even children beginning to write have language repertoires, sequential moves and rituals in their spoken language.

If we superimpose Figure 2 on to a similar scheme which illustrates actual teaching practice, we see that in the case of the field of second language learning, the early onset skills are taught much longer and much more slowly than Figure 1 would suggest. The same is true in the field of reading, where letter-sound correspondences are often taught for several grades, even to those who have mastered them, long after these skills should have retreated from pedagogical visibility into invisible automaticity. The result in both second language learning and reading is potentially disastrous. Boredom is enemy number one. Dislike of language or reading follows suit. Even more peculiar is the effort by measurement people to isolate these component parts in assessments of the gestalts of language learning and reading. There is no reason to believe that as these language (systems) become automatic they will be retained in memory in any way which is indicative of progress. One might as easily hypothesize that a system (access) which is crucial at onset stages but which is learned to the extent that it is automatic and, therefore, less aware to the learner, would show *decreasing* scores on a test which tries to measure it.

A generalization which can be made for the subjects of writing, reading and second language learning, then, is that early developmental skills, however important they may be as onset skills, simply cannot substitute for later, more cognitive strategies. Aligned with this generalization is the fact that at onset, developmental skills are generally taught far longer than they should be in all three subjects, and, that when these subjects are measured, wide confusion exists regarding what they mean. Figure 3 depicts this situation.

This figure reveals two problems which characterize the teaching of writing, speaking and reading: early skills are taught far longer than they should be and later strategies are seldom taught at all. The first is far easier to deal with than the second. If early onset skills are overtaught, it is a simple matter to reduce the time spent teaching them. But what can we do about helping writers learn to produce syntax and utterances more effectively? As usual, education is best at negative characteristics and less good at positive, building strategies.

If a developmental theory of writing is to create utterance-building strategies, it will be necessary for us to determine what these discourse units are and how they are acquired. It will come as no surprise to learn that the science is not there yet. We know about cohesion, about anaphoric devices, about foregrounding, sequencing, opening, continuing, closing, etc. from

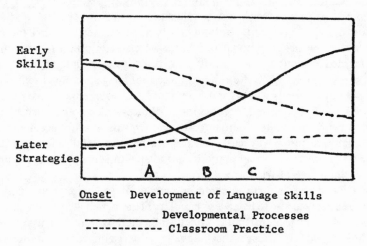

FIG. 3.   Comparison of Teaching and Assessment Practices with Children's Growth in Language Abilities (Reading & Writing)

studies of conversational analysis and discourse. There is no reason to believe that cohesive written prose will act much differently.

The purpose of this paper, then, is not to catalogue every instance of utterance building devices in writing. It is possible, however, to catalogue some misconceptions about discourse values and to suggest a strategy for building discourse competence. The remainder of this paper will deal with some of the traditional discourse efforts in writing showing, in each case, how the effort itself can go against what may be considered the natural discourse of written language.

The Effort to be Simple

In the current concern with unclear writing it is sometimes assumed that writers could write clearly and simply if only they wanted to. In general, however, this assumption is unwarranted. On the contrary, it appears that much of the obtuse, confusing prose which they write is the direct result of misguided attempts to be precise, clear, and straightforward.

The concept of language simplicity is, in itself, quite complex. Some astonishing and unfounded assumptions are frequently made about how people write clearly. Adults trying to talk to babies or small children often feel that they are using simple, even child-like language in their efforts to communicate. Linguists who have studied such efforts have found that the baby-talk of adults is not all simple, (Ferguson, 1966) and that often it is not even very similar to the way children speak. For children writing has proven to be more difficult than anyone would have guessed, and even many middle-level teaching materials suffer from an inability to distinguish between an adult concept of simplicity and a child's concept of clarity.

Most of the misconceptions about clarity in writing result from a failure to understand the organizational principles which determine the structure of well-formed sentences and well-formed discourses. A language is highly structured at all levels. But on the surface, a language presents itself to us as sentences made up of words (and, secondarily, of some small-scale syntactic units like infinitives and prepositional phrases). As noted earlier, most people, when they think of language, think of words. It is not accidental that vocabulary is a commonly used indicator of what is generally considered to be intelligence. After all, vocabulary drills and spelling occupy a major portion of early language instruction.

As a result of this focus, a common perception in language instruction is that the easiest feature to teach is vocabulary. That which is easiest to measure is vocabulary. The unfortunate conclusion, therefore, is that if you teach vocabulary, you will teach the language. This is, of course, dangerously wrong, for words and their arrangements are only surface manifestations of a larger linguistic system. *There are deeper principles* which serve to relate surface forms to meanings, and which link sentences together into a coherent whole.

The Effort to be Clear

Efforts to improve language ability are concentrated more at the word, phrase or sentence level than at the discourse level. The writing found in insurance policies is a case in point (Shuy & Larkin, 1978). Reading such prose leads one to the conclusion that there has often been a strong effort to limit the number of words used to refer to a given concept. The reader becomes convinced that the writer feels that if he were to use two or more terms for the same concept, a greater possibility of misunderstanding would ensue. This results in paragraphs like the following:

> Written notice and proof of claim must be *furnished* to the Home Office while the Insured is living and remains totally disabled. In event of default in payment of premiums, such notice and proof of claim must also be *furnished* within 12 months from the due date of the premium in default. Failure to *furnish* notice and proof as required above shall not of itself invalidate or diminish any claim hereunder if it is shown not to have been reasonably possible to have *furnished* such notice and proof and that such notice and proof were *furnished* as soon as was reasonably possible (Shuy & Larkin, 1978, page 308).

It appears, for example, that the authors of life insurance policies assume that substituting another term for a preferred term, *furnish,* like *supply, submit, provide, give* or some other term, would result in potential misreading of the intended concept. While they are lexically clear, however, the policy writers violate discourse rules which militate against repeated use of the same term. Clarity at the utterance level is sacrificed for clarity at the word level.

A conscious effort to be clear, then, can lead to unclarity of discourse on many occasions. Insurance policies fall into this trap and, in so doing, reduce the natural redundancy which language affords. Much of communication is based on a kind of conceptual triangulation. We write or speak an idea one way, then restate it another way in order to provide two views of the topic to our listener or reader. This redundancy is conventional in formal writing (the introduction tells the reader what you are going to say; the body tells it; the conclusion tells what you have just said). This is common in most exposition (the point is articulated and then illustrated -- a kind of realistic retelling). When writers use the same words or phrases over and over, they reduce the natural redundancy expected in communication. Thus, by limiting the numer of words used to refer to a concept, one reduces the communicative redundancy which the use of different words for that concept can provide.

The Effort to be Explicit

Another faulty approach to conscious improvement in composition is the assumption that in order to be clear, ones writing must be totally explicit. This notion grows out of a learning theory which supposes that people learn mostly what they are taught. In contrast, it appears that much language learning is self-generated rather than explicitly taught. Thus a new word in a familiar syntactic context will suggest all sorts of possibilities for clarity. For example, from the sentence, *I would like to purchase a dozen oranges and a pound of yellow gloppers.* the reader/listener knows a great deal about *gloppers* without ever hearing a definition. In that they can be purchased by the pound, we know that they are something like groceries. Since they are yellow, they are probably vegetables or a fruit of some kind. The point here is that the inferencing which goes on in either reading or listening adds redundancy of the sort which narrows down the possible meaning of even nonsense words such as *gloppers.*

In the case of much writing, a problem seems to arise not only from the effort to be asbolutely and totally explicit, but also from the desire to be totally and absolutely explicit in each sentence. For perfectly understandable reasons, writing frequently must be as accurate and explicit as possible. This leads the writer to think of all the real and potential conditions which might apply to any given statement. Linguistically, the result of such explicitness is a piling up of short phrases in sentences such as the following found in an insurance policy:

> The cash value of the Policy at any time while the Policy is in force on a premium-paying basis equals its cash value at the end of the period for which premiums are due and paid.
>
> Unless otherwise elected in writing, if any premium remains unpaid at the end of its grace period, a premium will be paid automatically by the Company to the next quarterly premium date (a) using any available dividend accumulations and (b) advancing any available loan value of the Policy as an automatic policy loan as of the date of the unpaid premium. The effort to be totally explicit in each sentence (an effort that also may help explain the constant repetition of the same words over and over) clearly interferes with the readability of these passages.

Sometimes this need to add explicit qualifications causes authors to pile on useless phrases, as in

> ...the Company will waive each premium falling due after the commencement and during the continuance of the total and Permanent Disability of the Insured.

It would be enough to say *during the total and permanent disability of the insured,* since any time that fell during that period would also have to be after its commencement and during its continuance.

The effort to be explicit, then, can actually lead to rather unreadable prose unless the writing is viewed in the total language system, at the lexical, syntactic and discourse levels. To achieve greater clarity in written prose will require that we make prose more consonant with the characteristics of the linguistic system. Efforts to be simple, clear and explicit can all interfere with the writer's ability to use the complete linguistic system when he writes. Since some attempts to make prose clear, precise and explicit superimpose considerations that contradict natural linguistic principles, writers must learn to write prose that incorporates the different levels of linguistic systems, i.e., spelling, punctuation, morphology, syntax, discourse in an interaction that communicates effectively.

Analyses of written language also run the risk of leading to neat little formulae for producing acceptable prose. Such a danger occurred recently in the previously mentioned effort to analyze insurance policy texts. Natural observation showed me that such policies contain an unusually large number of prepositions. The social scientist in me led me to do a simple preposition count which confirmed my hunch. The policy I examined contained one preposition for every 5.76 words whereas the prose of *Washington Post* columnist James Kilpatrick contained only one preposition for every eleven words. Closer examination showed that insurance policy prose has a strong preference for nominal over verbal forms. Policies tend to use phrases like *the death of the Insured* rather than *when the Insured dies; make an election of* rather than, simply, *elect* or *choose; before the commencement of the period of disability of the Insured rather* than *before the Insured becomes disabled,* etc.

To see some of the effects of this preference, let us consider the following sentence, dealing with a change of beneficiary in a life insurance policy: *The change will be effective as of the date of signing by the Owner, whether or not the Owner or Insured is living at the time of receipt at the Home Office.*

This is not a very difficult sentence to understand. By examining it closely, however, we can discover some of the problems that crop up in more complicated passages.

This sentence does not include any surface forms associated with the nominals signing and receipt which indicate what is to be received or signed. When these nominals are changed to their verbal forms (in the passive), an overt subject is needed. We decided to rewrite the passage to see if we could improve it. The result was as follows: *The change will take effect when the Owner signs it, whether or not the Owner or Insured is living at the time the Home Office receives it.*

In this rewritten version, regular discourse rules provide the referent of *it.* The surface structure here gives the reader a more explicit indication of what he needs to understand. Nominal forms like *signing* name an event or act, but hide many of the particulars of that act from view. On the other hand, full clauses, with their verbal forms, specify more completely the specific details of an event or act. Nominal forms with their prepositional phrase adjuncts are shorter, more compact, than clauses. On the other hand, they also require more "figuring out". While they simplify the surface form of a sentence, they put more strain on that part of linguistic system that lies beneath the water. It should also be noted that the rewritten versions contain fewer prepositional phrases than the original. The switch from nominal *signing* to verbal *sign* has, for example, permitted the use of an explicit surbordinating construction using when, rather than a prepositional construction like *on the date of*. Thus, analysis of different linguistic systems and their interaction in writing prose should be studied in relation to communicative effects on reader to understand principles of written communication, rather than applied in mechanical fashion.

A second recommendation is more lofty and ambitious. It is to suggest that future research in writing be devoted to ways of verifying or correcting the skeleton of a developmental theory of writing outlined here. Just what are the strategies employed by writers as they improve cohesion and skill? How are they acquired? At what age? Through what sub-steps or stages? No useful effort at assessing writing ability can get very far measuring entry-level skills at middle or advanced stages. What is needed is a better knowledge of where to tap. Then the tapping will be easy.

REFERENCES

Dale, Phillip. *Language development: structure and function.* Hinsdale, IL: The Dryden Press, 1972.

Ferguson, Charles A. Baby talk in six languages. *American Anthropologist,* 66:6.2. 103–14 (1964).

NAEP (National Assessment of Educational Progress). Report 10, Selected Essays and Letters. U.S. Government Printing Office. 1972.

NAEP (National Assessment of Education Progress). "Writing mechanics 1969–1974: A capsule description of writing mechanics," Report #05-W-01, Denver, Colorado: National Assessment of Educational Progress, 1975.

Shuy, Roger W. and Donald Larkin. Linguistic considerations in the simplification/classification of insurance policy language." *Discourse Processes* Vol 1, No. 3 July-Sept., 1978, pp 305–321.

It is interesting indeed to speculate about the semantics of this message, or about Tim's sense of his audience. But for the moment let us turn, instead, to the spelling. A couple of points are worth noting here. First, this small incident suggests why in studying children's spelling in the writing samples we are collecting we have decided to concentrate on the misspellings in children's compositions. While we have asked the teachers to indicate the kinds of asssistance given in the writing of each piece in our sample, we cannot be certain how a child came up with a conventional spelling. We can be more certain, however, that the misspellings are the child's own creations. There is, moreover, strong precedent in child language research for studying children's language *errors* (from the point of view of adult grammar) for what can be inferred from them about the linguistic strategies a child may have used in producing them (see, for example, Cazden, 1972).

Also noteworthy, of course, is Tim's rendering of *are* with the letter r. (His teacher had him read the note aloud, and confimed that he intended *you are,* not the contraction.) Tim's misspelling is all the more interesting for his evident confidence in it. He felt uncertain about the spelling of *world* and sought the help he knew was available; he apparently felt no such uncertainty about *are.*

Tim's strategy of relying on the sounds of a letter-name to represent the sounds in a word he writes is typical of many young children. Sometimes children use all of the sounds in the name of a letter, while other times they seem to make systematic uses of parts of letter-names. Carol Chomsky (1972a) describes one preschool boy's pleasure in discovering a spelling for the word *Kate* when he combined the two plastic letters K and T. Charles Read (1975a, b) found that for some preschool children, learning the names of the letters in the alphabet provides them the makings of a system for producing *invented spellings.*

Misspellings in the writing of first and second grade children in our sample show many of the characteristics Read and Chomsky found in the invented spellings of preschool children. We have found that such spellings as BOT for *boat,* LADE *for lady,* and DREST for *dressed* are not uncommon in the compositions of young children. Sometimes we can see evidence of a child sifting through the possibilities. One first grade girl's composition, for example, shows that she tried WIY, then Y, before finally settling on WY to represent *why.* Cazden (1975) suggests that Spanish-speaking bi-lingual children sometimes invent spellings which incorporate their Spanish accents, and she cites one child's DRRAGN for *dragon* as an example.

Other misspellings appear in the writing of the children in our sample which seem to result from strategies employing some knowledge of orthographic principles of spelling. Examples of this sort are BOTE for *boat,* DREEM for *dream,* and OF CORSE for *of course.* Sometimes a child's overgeneralized knowledge of the orthographic representation of grammatical morphemes seems to have been applied, as in the spelling of TOLLED for *told*. Still other misspellings suggest that the child has built a multi-syllabic word with what he knows about words of one syllable, as seems the case in a third grader's spelling of REEDICKYOULIS for *ridiculous*.

Certainly not all misspellings result from the child's use of purely linguistic strategies. We could search for a linguistic explanation for a first grade girl's spelling of ENTOURRASSTING for *interesting,* and no doubt we could find one. But my hunch is that, in the first place, the child simply recalled that *interesting* is a *long* word—based on having said and heard it, if not on having seen it. So deciding to use as many letters as she could, she then found a method (doubling consonants—what I heard one teacher call *The Mississippi Principle*) for accomplishing her goal. In many instances, it is difficult to unambiguously identify a child's strategy since more than one strategy can account for the child's misspelling.

Of the preschool children he studied, Charles Read noted that "In general, the children invented their own spellings by relating the sounds as they heard them to the letter names that they knew." Further on he adds that "the spellings appeared one to three years before the child entered school and continued in use until they were gradually replaced by standard spellings, usually as the child received formal instruction in reading and writing" (Read, 1975b, p. 332).

It is quite possible that children pass through distinguishable phases of development in the period between the production of spellings derived from letter-names and the consistent production of conventional spellings. As Read and others have noted, not all children begin spelling before they come under the influence of instruction. And, of course, not all children arrive at the ability to produce standard spellings consistently. Furthermore, there are many possible influences on a particular child's spelling performance. These include the characteristics of his spoken language, his reading experience, the instruction he has received, the attitudes and requirements of his teachers and perhaps of his parents, and his own conceptions of, and attitudes toward, spelling and writing. But despite all of these complicating influences it appears likely that for young elementary school children, learning to spell is essentially a developmental process much like those that contribute to a child's acquisition of spoken language. Viewed as a developmental process, spelling involves a gradual shift from invented spellings to producing conventional spellings. The problem is to understand better the orthographic rules children acquire as they shift from the idiosyncratic rules of their invented spellings to rules of conventional English orthography.

In practical terms, a fuller understanding of how children mature as spellers may suggest a reversal of the kind of policy illustrated by the teacher who told her students not to write *enormous* until they could spell it correctly—use *big* in the meantime, she said. Better descriptions of how children develop spelling skill may even provide supporting evidence for those teachers whose intuition and experience tell them that children just beginning to write should be encouraged to experiment freely with the new medium. And certainly, more information on spelling development in children who do eventually produce consistently standard spelling will be useful to us in helping children for whom producing conventional spellings is a struggle.

Syntax

Sentence structure has probably received the largest share of attention from researchers studying children's written language development. In an article in the *Journal of Child Language,* Richardson, Calnan, Essen and Lambert (1975) plot the results of a number of studies (Hunt, 1965; O'Donnell, Griffen, and Norris, 1967; Potter, 1969; Rosen, 1969; and their own) to show that older children tend to write longer and more complex sentences (t-units, actually) than do young children (Richardson, et al., 1975, p. 104). Also, O'Hare (1973), Mellon (1969) and others have reported studies suggesting that through instruction and practice in sentence-combining, children can be trained to write more complex sentences than they wrote before such training. So, while there is discussion among researchers and teachers about children's *syntactic maturity,* if syntactic maturity is associated with writing more complex sentences, then it is evidently a process that can be hastened by training (see O'Donnell, 1976).

It seems likely, too, that the complexity of a child's written syntax has something to do with how he reads, how much, and what—as well as how much and what he hears read to him. While there is a lack of research to support this conjecture, Carol Chomsky (1972b) has discussed the possible influence of reading experience, both visual and aural, on syntax in the school-age child's spoken language.

A child's speech patterns may also influence the syntactic patterns he writes. This is our impression as we begin to analyze the writing of the children in our sample, although we also notice a good many constructions that seem *writerly* and not like those common in the conversation of children. In this connection, it is interesting to note Jenefer Giannasi's (1976) report in her recent bibliographic essay on "Dialects and Composition," that research findings are divided on the issue of whether speakers of nonstandard dialects exprience special dialectal interference when they try to write what has come to be known as *Standard Edited American English.* One interpretation of these mixed findings is that the language considered *standard* in writing is a dialect unto itself, and that speakers of any dialect of American English experience some measure of dialect interference when they write.

As I have noted elsewhere (Gundlach and Moses, 1976), our plans to study several years' writing of a number of children have led us to two developmental questions concerning children's written syntax. The first is suggested by an observation made by Janet Emig (1971) in her study of the composing processes of high school seniors. Noting that literary style is partly a function of an author's preference for certain kinds of sentence structure, Emig observed that students, too, demonstrate in their writing individual preferences for certain syntactic constructions. Following this idea, the question we would like to pursue in studying the writing of elementary school children is this: If children demonstrate individual preferences in the syntactic structures they write, how dominant are these structures, and how long do they persist?

Richardson and colleagues suggest another aspect of written syntax worth exploring in longitudinal studies. Citing the results of studies by Rosen (1969, 1973), they assert that "a writer's sentence structure is affected by the kind of task set and the mode of discourse used" (Richardson, et al., 1975, p. 101). Here we have posed the following question for ourselves: Is a child's written syntax, within a *stage* of *syntactic maturity,* influenced by the dynamics of the writing task he is given and his response to it? While we cannot report any developmental evidence yet on this point, for what it is worth, college writing teachers regularly puzzle over the fact that their students writer fuller and more pleasing sentences in autobiographical sketches than in literary analyses.

The observation I have heard elementary school teachers frequently make about children's written syntax is that when a child first begins to write, his written sentences seem much less complex, more *primitive* than the sentences he speaks. What research there is appears to confirm this impression. Vygotsky (1962) found that in the language of Russian school children, spoken syntax was more mature than written, and O'Donnell, Griffin, and Norris (1967) noted a similar imbalance in the speech and writing of American third grade children. However, in the same study, O'Donnell and his colleagues found that in the language of *fifth* and *seventh* grade students, the reverse was true—written syntax tended to be more complex than spoken. The initial imbalance and the apparent *crossover* later on imply a shifting relationship between speaking and writing as children develop writing ability. This point and others I have raised in this brief discussion suggest that while the study of adult grammars may not be especially profitable for the writing student, the study of the grammar of children's writing may prove very useful to the teacher or researcher interested in children's writing development.

Discourse

Writing is a process of making, and what the writer makes is not a word or a sentence but a text, or a whole discourse. Children, if given the chance, compose whole discourses from the beginning of their development as writers. And as one observes the growth of a child's writing abilities, one would expect to see increasing length and complexity in the whole discourses the child writes.

One approach to the question of writing development at the discourse level has been simply to record the amount of writing children of different ages produce when given a specified writing task. For example, Myklebust found that when he administered his Picture Story Language Test to groups of children seven through seventeen years old, "there were consistent increments in story length for both sexes up through thirteen years of age" (Myklebust, 1973, p. 17).

There is also evidence, however, which suggests that simple length of written response to a given assignment varies greatly within a group of children the same age, and that length of text is not necessarily an index of other measures of written language development. Anyone who has taught writing has seen evidence of this sort, and the point is made rather dramatically in the results of a study reported by Richardson, et al. (1975). In this study 521 eleven year old children were asked to perform the following task:

Imagine that you are now 25 years old. Write about the life you are leading, your interests, your home life, and your work at the age of 25. (You have thirty minutes to do this.) (Richardson, et al., 1975, p. 102) Perhaps not surprisingly, the eleven year olds wrote compositions in response to this assignment ranging in length from fewer than fifty to more than six hundred words. And while length of the piece produced correlated with the child's score on a general ability test, length of composition did not predict length or complexity of sentences. That is, composition length did not correlate with *syntactic maturity*.

My impression as we gather our sample of children's writing is that elementary school children do indeed tend to write longer and more complex compositions as they get older and gain more writing experience. But it is also true that the length and complexity of any particular composition are related not only to the age and skill of the child who wrote it, but also to the writer's aims, his sense of what is required of him, and his personal reactions to the material at hand. Perhaps this is simply another way of saying that the characteristics of a written text are influenced in significant ways by the context in which it is written.

From a developmental point of view, an interesting question is whether the relationship between text and context changes as the child matures and develops as a writer. In this regard, James Moffett (1968) and James Britton and his colleagues at the University of London (Britton, 1970; Britton, et al., 1975), using different systems for classifying kinds of texts, both advance the general hypothesis that in developing as a writer, the child becomes able to write for increasingly remote audiences, about increasingly abstract subjects, and for an increasingly elaborate and differentiated set of purposes. While these points have been argued by Moffett (1968) and Britton (1970), it remains to obtain developmental data that empirically confirm them. Britton and his colleagues have investigated the validity of their system in describing the writing development of adolescents, with inconclusive but interesting results (Britton, et al., 1975). For a more extensive discussion of Britton's system of analysis in light of preliminary findings in our study, the reader may want to refer to our paper, "The Ontogenesis of the Writer's Sense of Audience" (Gundlach, Litowitz and Moses, 1979).

Early in their development as writers, children demonstrate a recognition that a written composition should have a coherent structure, as well as a *beginning-middle-end arrangement.* Often the first sign of this recognition are the storybook beginning—*Once upon a time*—and the concluding notation, *The End.* Even in the very short compositions of first grade children just beginning to write, this sense of the requirements of written discourse is sometimes clearly in evidence. Among the first compositions written by one six year old is this report from home: "Once upon a time my baby sister flushed a rag down the toilet."

As children are able to write longer compositions they tend to include more kinds of information in their writing and to arrange the information into more complex structures. In our research project, we have begun to look closely at the structure of children's written texts, concentrating first on narratives .We suspect that inquiry at that level of discourse will turn up both interesting common lines of development and important information about differences among individual children and their growth as writers. Little study has been made of the stories children write, but recent research into a number of related topics provides a stock of useful methods of analysis that may be adapted to the study of children's written narratives. In particular, researchers may want to examine theoretical studies of discourse (e.g., Applebee, 1978; Grimes, 1975; Halliday and Hasan, 1976), studies of spoken narrative (e.g., Labov, 1972; Botvin and Sutton-Smith, 1977; and Kernan, 1977), and studies of children's comprehension of stories (e.g., Frederiksen, 1977; and Stein, 1978).

While developmental theories may be derived from studies in which the variables in writing tasks are highly controlled, researchers ultimately will have to account for the structure of the compositions that children write under the less controlled conditions of normal school experience—and it is just this sort of *data* that teachers must interpret from day to day in their work. In examining the compositions children write in the course of school activities, we find that there is often a great range of structural complexity among the compositions produced by the children the same age, and sometimes considerable variation in the structure of compositions produced

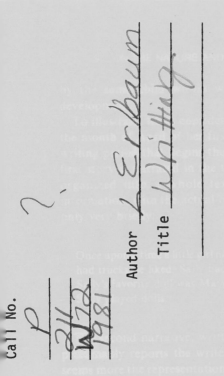

at would seem to be a single *moment* of

wo narratives written by a six year old girl in
grade year. Both were written during a free
morning routine of this particular class. The
ird person and seems obviously shaped and
. The text is dominated by background
rration of events coming at the end, and then

ned Sally had a brother named Sammy. Sammy
dolls she liked. Sam's favorite car was Toyota.
They had dinner then Sam played trucks and

n a week later, is cast in the first person and
s actual experience. Indeed the composition
f a fragment of experience than a consciously
shaped whole text; yet it does have a marked beginning and it ends with the same conclusive kind of sentence that marks the ending of the first narrative.

> One day I sad to my mother Mom. What dear she said. I want to go out. Then go out she said. And I played with my friends.

Complicating the question of how to determine this particular young writer's narrative *competence* is a third story, also composed in April of her first grade year. In this case the author, accepting an opportunity regularly offered to the members of her class, dictated her story to her teacher rather than writing it herself. Here is the text that the teacher recorded:

> Anna was a little girl. She was littler than her dog. She was littler than her sister. She thought she was littler than her goldfish, but it really wasn't true. She had a baby brother and she hadn't seen him yet and she thought he would be bigger than she.
>
> One day Anna went out, feeling small. Her friend came to play. They played dolls. Anna had a doll that was up to her hip. Her friend had one who was up to her knee. It was a very small doll.
>
> After they had a tea party, her friend went home. Anna went home and had dinner and got into bed with her doll and said her prayers. And in her prayers she wished to be bigger.
>
> "I think my wish will never come true," said Anna to her doll.

The writer is a lonely figure cut off from the stimulus and corrective of listeners. He must be a predictor of reactions and act on his predictions. He writes with one hand tied behind his back being robbed of gesture. He is robbed too of his tone of voice and the aid of the clues the environment provides. He is condemned to monologue; there is no one to help out, to fill the silences, put words in his mouth or make encouraging noises (H. Rosen, 1971, p. 142).

Phillip Lopate, a poet who teaches writing to children as a member of the Teachers and Writers Collaborative in New York, speaks of the solitude and concentration required of the writer. In an article on helping elementary school children make the transition from speaking to writing, Lopate notes that "writing is secreted from a more underground, ambitious part of the will than that nervous urge that generates speech" (Lopate, 1977a, p. 24). Of his own writing processes, Lopate says,

When I write seriously I need to go off by myself. For me, writing is a solitary and private act.... the only really useful advice I could give to someone who wants to be a writer is— *learn to be alone* (Lopate, 1977b, p. 74).

I have noted earlier Vygotsky's impression that the written language of young school children is considerably less complex than the language of their speech. Vygotsky explains the differences in 'product'—language forms in writing and in speech—in terms of the different cognitive demands of the two processes: "The discrepancy is caused by the child's proficiency in spontaneous, unconscious activity and his lack of skill in abstract, deliberate activity" (Vygotsky, 1962, p. 100).

Reading the writing of young school children one does sometimes get the sense of the young writer struggling to advance a message while trying to bring the technical problems of writing under control. And indeed the result is often writing with short, direct sentences, sometimes built from the syntactic elements of the writing assignment (when one has been made). Frequently, the content of such writing seems compressed and, sometimes, elliptical.

To illustrate, let us consider examples from two sets of compositions written by children in a first grade class. In the first case, the children had been making clay animals, and talking about the making and the animals themselves. Picking up a suggestion from one of the students, the teacher asked the children to try writing responses to this question: "What if your clay animal came alive?" (As usual, spelling help was available).

One girl wrote: *"What if my clay animal came alive it would be fun."*
Another girl wrote: *"I like my clay animal because it is fun to play with."*

These two responses do not take the matter very far, nor do they exhibit children fully engaged with meeting the assignment. More in the spirit of responding to the question is this next response, also written by a girl: *"if my clay animal came to lif he would crawl around."*

Here the writer describes what the animal might do if indeed it were alive. (Note the girl's conversion of *came alive* from the assignment to *came to lif* in her sentence.) Two more responses from this set show the first grade children recording their feelings about the prospect of having their play animals come alive. One girl wrote: *"I wish my clay cat was alive;"* while another girl wrote: *"When my clay animal came to alive he would change I wouldn't like it."*

One wonders of course about the constraints imposed on the children's sentences by the questions they were trying to answer. It is interesting, therefore, to consider the writing produced by other children in the same first grade class on the same day. These children chose, as an alternative to the clay animal assignment, to respond to a question referring to a recent power failure in the area: "What happened when the lights went out?" In the context of this writing assignment, which asked the children to compose from the material of remembered experience rather than from purely invented material, some children produced sentences which were very complex indeed. For example, one girl wrote: *"When the lights went off my mom was smart because she put two candles on the table."* Perhaps the amount of material these children had available to draw on and the amount of information they consequently had to convey led them to compose pieces that seem compressed. One boy wrote: *"one weeknight the lights went out and we had candles and we sleep in are Mom room and my Mom has wax."*

When a child is working with a still-developing mastery of punctuation, and, for whatever reasons, produces elliptical narrative sequences, the result can sometimes be strikingly ambiguous. This first grader, a girl, wrote: *"we were doing Fair shares and the lights went off and I was glad Mom was feeding the baby."* One possible reading of this piece might run along the following lines: the young writer was doing her domestic chores (*"Fair shares"*) when the lights went out, and she was delighted at the sudden event—work would have to cease. And, incidentally, her mother happened to be feeding the baby at the moment when the power failed.

Both Vygotsky, observing the writing of Russian children, and Connie and Harold Rosen, much more recently studying the writing of British children, add to their analyses of the difficulties children encounter in the writing process the notion that children have little use for writing. Vygotsky noted that when a child is pressed into the activity of writing during early writing instruction, "he has no need for it and has only a vague idea of its usefulness" (Vygotsky, 1962, p. 99). Connie and Harold Rosen wrote, "It is very easy to think of many reasons why a young child should not want to write, and very difficult to think of reasons why he should" (Rosen and Rosen, 1973, p. 85).

Our impression, from observing children writing and from reading what they produce, is rather different. In the school we have studied most extensively, children appear to have several important uses for writing. It also appears that when children are encouraged to explore freely the possibilities of writing they do not experience the writing process as merely a difficult and often frustrating process of preparing a message for the reader. Rather, they find value for themselves in the writing process (see Douglas, 1975), and make the activity of writing serve a variety of purposes. For example, sometimes children use the process of writing to fantasize. Consider the following story, written by a second grade boy at Halloween time. Note the shift from third person pronouns to first person as the action becomes intense—linguistic evidence of the young writer's engagement in the fantasy. Note, too, the curious resolution at the end of the narrative.

> Once upon a time there was a boy he saw a old house and he went in it. it was scary then he saw a ghost and ran away fast. The next day he went back and then he wan he got back he went upstairs Then he ran into a room The he hrd foot seps and hid undr a bed Then the thing came in it had big fangs the boy ran. it was after me and the door was locked and I was afraid wan I got home I said I got to write abot this mom.
>   The end

Children also seem to use writing to recall and savor personal experiences. For example, one first grade boy wrote: *"I play with my dad. I play darts with him."* In another piece of writing by the same first grader, we get the sense of a child summoning to mind (and paper) a favorite object in his life: *"I got a new bike. It is good. And fast. My bike is blue. I ride my bike for a long time."* Writing also seems to offer children an occasion for organizing the events of their daily lives (Britton, 1970), and for exploring cause and effect, and other relationships (see Bruner, 1975; Gundlach, 1977).

At other times the activity of writing seems to be for children a more purely aesthetic process, a process in which they make images and create moods. Here, for example, is a piece written by a fourth grade girl:

> In the morning the sun is firey red, surrounded by colors like pink, orange, blue, and red. Hours go by. The sun us soon over head. Then once in a while you see

an eclipse. You dare not look because you know it will blind you. Now it is over.
The sun slips by with another rainbow. The world is dark and everyone sleeps.

In these speculations about the uses to which a child may put the activity of
writing, we have been making inferences from children's compositions about
the nature of their writing processes. In general, these inferences suggest that
in the experience of children, the writing process may be related in function, at
least, to other activities in which children use representational symbols, such
as drawing, sculpting, drama, and other forms of symbolic play. This
hypothesis also seems consistent with our observations of children as they
write. In the primary grades, writing is very often undertaken in conjunction
with drawing (Graves, 1975; Gundlach and Moses, 1976). Indeed, Graves
suggests that for some of the seven-year-olds in his study, drawing was a
necessary prelude to writing (Graves, 1975, p. 236). We have observed
children occasionally producing a *sound track* as they compose—as in the
case of the second grade boy who made the sounds of a revving engine and
squealing tires as he drew a picture of a racing car, then wrote about the new
toy racing car he had recently acquired (Gundlach and Moses, 1976).

We also see indications of the relatedness of writing, drawing, and certain
kinds of play in children's comments about their own writing practices.
Seeking to learn about the implicit conceptions or "theories" of writing that
children hold, we have asked a number of children why they write, what they
like writing about, what working conditions they prefer when they are
writing, and, following Graves (1973), their notions about what "good"
writers know and do. One nine-year-old, asked what he enjoys writing about
and why, answered: *"Sea animals and people swimming. And I like writing
about them because it makes me think I'm sailing."* Responding to the same
question, a nine-year-old girl wrote: *"I like to write about horses because I
know a lot about them and I'm good at drawing them."* Bits of evidence such
as these persuade us that Vygotsky has pointed both researchers and teachers
in the right direction in suggesting that "make-believe play, drawing, and
writing can be viewed as different moments in an essentially unified process of
development of written language" (Vygotsky, 1978, p. 116).

What can be said, then, about the nature of the writing process as children
experience it? As we try to understand the earliest writing of children, we need
to view children's experience of the writing process from two complementary
points of view. First, we need to examine the ways in which the writing
process can be said to be *discontinuous* with other symbolizing processes in
children's lives—most notably the social process of speaking. Then we need to
explore the ways in which children's experience of writing activity may
be *continuous* with, in the sense that it extends the functions of, such non-
writing activities as drawing, sculpting, story-telling, and various kinds of
play.

To understand how the writing process fits into particular children's experiences, we need to take into account several factors that contextualize early writing development. For example, children's individual styles of symbol use (see Gardner, Wolf, and Smith, 1975) and characteristic play activities are likely to figure prominently as they begin to write. Also likely to be important in their early writing development are children's reading experiences and reading instruction, especially as these influence the children's conceptions of what writing is like and what its uses are. And, of course, children's early experience of the writing process, and the kinds of compositions they produce as a result, are no doubt significantly influenced by the sense they make of the writing instruction and advice they receive from teachers and parents.

As children mature, their experience of the writing process may be transformed several times through their school years. Some transformations may result from the children's advances in cognitive development—increasing intellectual endurance and dexterity will allow them to engage in more sustained writing activity and to become increasingly able to shift attention among the concerns of purpose, subject, audience, text strategy and linguistic convention. Older children's increasing ability to use language in ways not tied to immediate contexts (see Bloom, 1975) may lead them to use writing for more varied purposes, and eventually to develop adult-like specialized uses for it (see Olson, 1977). School experience and instruction may have similarly enabling effects, leading children, as they develop, both to a keener sense of how to affect their readers and to a fuller sense of writing as an extension of themselves and their ideas (Litowitz, 1977). It should be noted, however, that schooling can also have an intimidating and finally limiting effect on students' experience of the writing process, as Emig's (1971) study of the composing processes of twelfth graders makes clear.

If we are to understand the features we observe in children's written language, we shall have to investigate what children are doing when they write. We need to ask this question in three ways: What are children at a given point in development *able* to do as writers? What do they *choose* to do, given free rein? And what do they accomplish, given the various sorts of constraints to be found in a range of writing circumstances? Inquiry of this kind will need to explore writing on at least two levels. First, we need to learn more about how the cognitive processes of young writers result in the linguistic forms that appear in their compositions, from spellings and syntactic structures to elaborate plots or arguments. Second, as we pursue this research using the methods of inquiry and analysis of cognitive psychology and psycho-linguistics, we must also keep in view, and learn more about, how a child's written compositions are influenced by his own *theory of writing*—his notions of what it means to write and of what writers are supposed to do, and, no small matter, the child's evolving sense of himself as a writer.

It would be appropriate , were there space, to take up the question of how teachers figure into children's written language development and to discuss the cultural and social settings in which children learn to write and in which children and teachers interact. But these are themselves large subjects, and must be set aside for another time. Let us conclude, then, with passages from two recent books which have much to tell us about children and their writing, although neither addresses the subject directly. Mina Shaughnessy has written in her valuable guide for the teacher of writing, *Errors and Expectations:* "For the Basic Writing student, . . . academic writing is a trap, not a way of saying something to someone." For these students, she goes on:

> . . . writing is but a line that moves haltingly across the page, exposing as it goes all that the writer doesn't know, then passing into the hands of a stranger who reads it with a lawyer's eyes, searching for flaws (Shaughnessy, 1977, p. 7).

Shaughnessy's book offers much useful advice for those of us who would help older students find connections between the written langauge they are asked to produce and ideas they have to present. But how is it that these connections are lost somewhere along the way in schooling? This, too, is a question about the nature and development of children's writing. This paper has been concerned principally with children who can and do write. But what about those who cannot or will not? Or those who experience the writing process in the terms described by Shaughnessy? A starting point for tackling these questions can be found in the following remark about learning to read, made by Bruno Bettelheim in his book, *The Uses of Enchantment:*

> The acquisition of skills, including the ability to read, becomes devalued when what one has learned to read adds nothing of importance to one's life (Bettelheim, 1976, p. 4).

This is equally true of learning to write, it seems to me, and I suggest that we begin here in trying to understand why some children develop as writers and why so many do not.

ACKNOWLEDGMENTS

I want to acknowledge the invaluable assistance of Rae Moses and Bonnie Litowitz in the collection of data for this project.

REFERENCES

Applebee, A. N. (1978) *The Child's Concepts of Story.* Chicago: University of Chicago Press.
Bettelheim, B. (1976) *The Uses of Enchantment: The Meaning and Importance of Fairy Tales.* New York: Alfred A. Knopf.

Bloom, L. (1975) "Language Development," in F. D. Horowitz (ed.), *Review of Child Development Research*, Vol. 4. Chicago: University of Chicago Press.

Botvin, G. J. and Sutton-Smith, B. (1977) "The Development of Structural Complexity in Children's Fantasy Narratives," *Developmental Psychology*, Vol. 13, No. 4, pp. 377–389.

Britton, J. (1970) *Language and Learning*. London: Penguin Books.

Britton, J.; Burgess, T.; Martin, N.; McLeod, A.; and Rosen, H. (1975) *The Development of Writing Abilities (11-18)*. London: Macmillon Education.

Bruner, J. (1975) "Language as an Instrument of Thought," in A. Davies (ed.), *Problems of Language and Learning*. London: Heinemann.

Cazden, C. (1975) "Classroom Teaching Relived," *Harvard Graduate School of Education Association Bulletin*, Vol. 19, No. 3, pp. 12–13.

Cazden, C. (1972) *Child Language and Education*. New York: Holt, Rinehart and Winston.

Chomsky, C. (1972a) "Write Now, Read Later," in C. Cazden (ed.), *Language in Early Childhood Education*. Washington, D.C.: National Association for the Education of Young Children.

Chomsky, C. (1972b) "Stages in Language Development and Reading Exposure," *Harvard Educational Review*, 42, pp. 1–33.

de Ajuriaguerra, J. and Auzias, M. (1975) "Preconditions for the Development of Writing in the Child," in E. Lenneberg and E. Lenneberg (eds.), *Foundations of Language Development: A Multidisciplinary Approach*, Vol. 2. New York: Academic Press.

Douglas, W. W. (1975) "On Value in Children's Writing," in R. Larson (ed.), *Children and Writing in the Elementary School: Theories and Techniques*. New York: Oxford University Press.

Emig, J. (1975) "Hand, Eye, Brain: Some 'Basics' in the Writing Process." In Cooper and ODell, *Research on Composing: Points of Departure, 1978*. Urbana. NCTE.

Emig, J. (1971) *The Composing Process of Twelfth Graders*. Urbana: National Council of Teachers of English.

Frederiksen, C. H. (1977) "Structure and Process in Discourse Production and Comprehension," in M. A. Just and P. A. Carpenter (eds.), *Cognitive Processes in Comprehension*. Hillsdale, N.J.: Lawrence Erlbaum Associates.

Gardner, H.; Wolf, D.; and Smith, A. (1975) "Artistic Symbols in Early Childhood," in *New York University Quarterly*, Vol. 6, pp. 13–21.

Giannasi, J. (1976) "Dialects and Composition," in G. Tate (ed.), *Teaching Composition: 10 Bibliographic Essays*. Fort Worth: Texas Christian University Press.

Graves, D. (1975) "An Examination of the Writing Processes of Seven Year Old Children," *Research in the Teaching of English*, Vol. 9, No. 3, pp. 227–241.

Graves, D. (1973) "Children's Writing: Research Directions and Hypotheses Based Upon an Examination of the Writing Processes of Seven Year Old Children," unpublished doctoral dissertation, State University of New York at Buffalo.

Grimes, J. E. (1975) *The Thread of Discourse*. The Hague: Mouton.

Gundlach, R. Children as Writers: The beginnings of learning to write. In M. Nystrand, *What Writers Know: The Language, Process, and Structure of Written Discourse*. New York: Academic Press. (in Press)

Gundlach, R. (1978) "Tawking of Water: The Writing Process as Children Experience It." Paper presented at the Annual Meeting of the National Council of Teachers of English, Kansas City, Missouri, November, 1978.

Gundlach, R. (1977) "When Children Write: Notes for Parents and Teachers on Children's Written Language Development." Mimeographed paper distributed to parents of children in the Winnetka public schools, Winnetka, Illinois.

Gundlach, R.; Litowitz, B.; and Moses, R. (1979) "The Ontogenesis of the Writer's Sense of Audience: Rhetorical Theory and Children's Written Discourse." In Brown and Steinmann (Eds.). *Rhetoric 78: Proceedings of Theory of Rhetoric* an Inter-disciplinary Conference. Minneapolis: University of Minnesota.

Gundlach, R; Litowitz, B.; and Moses, R. (1977) "Text and Context in Children's Written Discourse." Paper presented at the Second Annual Boston University Conference on Child Language, October, 1977.

Gundlach, R. and Moses, R. (1976) "Developmental Issues in the Study of Children's Written Language." Paper presented at the First Annual Boston University Conference on Language Development, Boston, Massachusetts, October, 1976.

Halliday, M. and Hasan, R. (1976) *Cohesion in English.* London: Longman.

Hunt, K. W. (1965) *Grammatical Structures Written at Three Grade Levels.* Urbana: National Council of Teachers of English.

Kernan, K. T. (197)) "Semantic and Expressive Elaboration in Children's Narratives," in Ervin-Tripp, S. and Mitchell-Kernan, C. (eds.), *Child Discourse.* New York: Academic Press.

Labov, W. (1972) *Language in the Inner City: Studies in Black Vernacular English.* Philadelphia: University of Pennsylvania Press.

Litowitz, B. (1977) "Writing, Written Language, and Learning Disabilities." Paper presented at the Annual Meeting of the American Speech and Hearing Association, Chicago, Illinois, November, 1977.

Lopate, P. (1977a) "The Transition from Speech to Writing," in B. Zavatsky and R. Padgett (eds.), *The Whole World Catalogue 2.* New York: McGraw Hill Paperbacks.

Lopate, P. (1977b) "The Moment to Write," in B. Zavatsky and R. Padgett (eds.), *The Whole World Catalogue 2.* New York: McGraw Hill Paperbacks.

Mellon, J. (1969) *Transformational Sentence-Combining.* Urbana: National Council of Teachers of English.

Moffett, J. (1968) *Teaching the Universe of Discourse.* Boston: Houghton, Mifflin.

Myklebust, H. (1973) *Development and Disorders of Written Language,* Vol. 2. New York: Grune and Stratton.

O'Donnell, R. C. (1976) "A Critique of Some Indices of Syntactic Maturity," *Research in the Teaching of English,* Vol. 10, No. 1, pp. 31–38.

O'Donnell, R. C.; Griffin, W. J.; and Norris, R. C. (1967) *The Syntax of Kindergarten and Elementary School Children:* A Transformational Analysis. Urbana: National Council of Teachers of English.

O'Hare, F. (1973) *Sentence-Combining: Improving Student Writing Without Formal Grammar Instruction.* Urbana: National Council of Teachers of English.

Olson, D. R. (1977) "From Utterance to Text: The Bias of Language in Speech and Writing," *Harvard Educational Review,* 47, pp. 257–281.

Potter, R. R. (1967) "Sentence Structure and Phrase Quality: An Exploratory Study," *Research in the Teaching of English,* 1, pp. 17–28.

Read, C. (1975a) *Children's Categorization of Speech Sounds in English.* Urbana: National Council of Teachers of English.

Read, C. (1975b) "Lessons to be Learned from the Preschool Orthographer," in Lenneberg and Lenneberg (eds), *Foundations of Langauge Development: A Multidisciplinary Approach.* New York: Academic Press.

Richardson, K.; Calnan, M.; Essen, J.; and Lambert, M. (1975) "The Linguistic Maturity of 11-year-olds: Some Analysis of the Written Compositions of Children in the National Child Development Study," *Journal of Child Language,* Vol. 3, No. 1, pp. 99–116.

Rosen, C. and Rosen, H. (1973) *The Language of Primary School Children.* London: Penguin Education.

Rosen, H. (1973) "Written Language and the Sense of Audience," *Educational Research,* 15, pp. 177–87.

Rosen, H. (1971) "Towards a Language Policy Across the Curriculum," in D. Barnes, J. Britton and H. Rosen, *Language, Learner and the School,* revised edition. London: Penguin.

Rosen, H. (1969) "An Investigation of Differentiated Writing Assignments on the Performance in English Composition of a Selected Group of 15–16 Year Old Pupils." Ph.D. Thesis, University of London.

Rummelhart, D. (1975) "Notes on a Schema for Stories," In D. G. Bobrow and A. Collins (eds.), *Representation and Understanding: Studies in Cognitive Science.* New York: Academic Press.

Shaughnessy, M. (1977) *Errors and Expectations: A Guide for the Teacher of Basic Writing.* New York: Oxford University Press.

Stein, N. L. (1978) "How Children Understand Stories: A Developmental Analysis." Technical Report No. 69, Center for the Study of Reading, University of Illinois at Urbana-Champaign.

Vygotsky, L. S. (1978) *Mind in Society: The Development of Higher Psychological Processes,* ed. by M. Cole, V. John-Steiner, S. Scribner, and E. Souberman. Cambridge, Massachusetts: Harvard University Press,

Vygotsky, L. S. (1962) *Thought and Language,* ed. and translated by E. Hanfmann and G. Vakar. Cambridge: MIT Press.

Weigl, E. (1975) "On Written Language: Its Acquisition and Its Alexic-Agraphic Disturbances," in E. Lenneberg and E. Lenneberg (eds.), *Foundations of Language Development: A Multidisciplinary Approach.* New York: Academic Press.

10 Text and Content: An Investigation of Referential Organization in Children's Written Narratives

Elsa Jaffe Bartlett
Sylvia Scribner
The Rockefeller University

One of the principal obstacles to the development of more effective writing instruction is ambiguity about the processes which enter into the construction of a coherent written text. While cognitive and linguistic theory is often used to explain lapses in coherence in the written discourse of children, few analytic methods are available for objective and precise assessments of the cognitive and linguistic component processes involved in coherent text production.

The research described in this chapter is concerned with one aspect of coherence, namely, skill in referential organization. By referential organization, we mean the construction of expressions in written texts which guide the reader in relating new information to old. In any extended discourse, a listener or reader must keep track of incoming information and construct an organized representation of the objects, characters, events and opinions described. How do skills in constructing and communicating an organized representation develop in children? And what linguistic and cognitive difficulties do they encounter? If it is true that the construction of coherent discourse depends in crucial ways on the construction of appropriate referring expressions, then it is clear that a better understanding of the development of referring skills will contribute to efforts to improve children's writing.

Those concerned with the assessment of children's writing have taken note of the importance of referential organization. Holistic measures of writing skill often require that evaluators attend to this dimension in one way or another (Educational Testing Service, 1976). However, no analytic schemes have yet been developed that enable one to identify and assess linguistic and

153

than single noun phrases. When Warden (1976) asked children to construct more extended spoken discourse, he found evidence for a fairly protracted period of development. Warden's subjects ranged in age from three to nine years. While even the youngest children used the definite article to construct anaphoric phrases, only nine year olds followed the adult pattern of using the indefinite article in their construction of introductory phrases. Investigations of the development of pronominalization indicate a similar pattern: deictic meanings seem to be acquired early (de Villiers, and de Villiers, 1974), but full mastery of the co-referential functions of pro-forms may not be achieved until the junior high school years. (See, for example, Chomsky, 1969, and studies cited in Palermo and Molfese, 1972). Indeed, Loban (1976) reports a marked *increase* in the referential ambiguity of pronouns in children's spoken discourse beginning at about seventh grade and persisting at least through the ninth, reversing the typical developmental trend. Since Loban's data are longitudinal, this result cannot be attributed to sampling differences and is thus all the more impressive.

This work indicates that acquisition of referring expressions can hardly be an all-or-none phenomenon, since children are able to use these linguistic forms with at least some of their meanings in some communication situations and linguistic contexts at a relatively early age. What the research suggests is that some contexts may tax the linguistic (and perhaps cognitive) resources of the child more than others. This may be due in part to an interaction of a context with the resources available in the language for accomplishing reference in that context, in part, to an interaction of a context with the child's knowledge of these resources and, in part, to an interaction of a context with the child's strategies for constructing certain kinds of referring expressions appropriate in that context. Thus we will want to pay particular attention in our analyses to the contexts in which referencing errors occur, since it may be only by taking context into account that we can begin to understand the nature of children's difficulties.

THE STUDY AND ITS STORY SAMPLE

Stories analyzed in this study were collected during the 1975–1976 school year and were elicited as part of an evaluation of a creative writing program developed by the Teachers and Writers Collaborative. (A description of the research appears in Teachers and Writers, 1976.) The stories were elicited by a research assistant in New York City elementary, public school classrooms, with assurances to the children that they would not be graded and that their stories would not be shared with anyone else. To elicit the narratives, the assistant wrote the following story topic on the board:

A man leaves his house. His body is found the next morning.

In her instructions, she stressed that the sentences she had written on the board were not necessarily the opening sentences of a story but "An idea or a spring-board... write a story using this idea. Think about what might have happened..."

From these written narrative texts, a sample was selected representing the work of 52 children in two public schools at the following grade levels:

Grade level	Number of texts
third	7
fourth	11
fifth	23
sixth	11

Each child contributed one text to the sample. All children were reading at or above grade level.

Analytic Scheme

The scheme we applied in the analysis of these stories provides information about the referential status, linguistic form and referential location of noun phrases. It is similar to a scheme developed by Rochester and Martin (1977) to analyze referring expressions in the spoken discourse of adults, but differs in that it provides more complete information about the wording adopted by writers in various contexts.

Referential Status. Noun phrases were divided into two categories: *introductory* phrases which instruct the reader to enter a new element into the evolving representation of the text, and *phoric* phrases which instruct the reader to find a referent elsewhere, either in the text or (rarely) in the communication situation itself. Appendix A at the end of this chapter lists the categories that were employed to clarify the referential status of noun phrases.

Linguistic form. Noun phrases were also categorized in terms of their form. Introductory phrases occur in such forms as the following:

1) Once a *man* left his house. (indefinite & noun)
2) *Jim* ran down the street. (proper name)
3) A woman once lost *her purse*. (passive & noun)

Phoric noun phrases are typically constructed as pro-forms or as definite noun phrases that include an article or a demonstrative:

4) John bought a new car but *he's* having trouble with *it*. (pronouns)
5) John bought a new car but *that car* causes a lot of trouble. (demonstrative & noun)
6) John bought a new car but *the car* is a real lemon. (definite & noun)

Definite noun phrases can be further characterized in terms of their wording: in some cases, the introductory noun is repeated; sometimes an elided version is constructed and sometimes a new noun is used:

7) John has a son. *The son* is five.
8) John has two cars. *The two* are lemons.
9) John has a son. *The boy* is five.

Location of referents. Referents of phoric noun phrases are usually located in the preceding text or in the communication situation:

10) John was unhapppy. *He* left home.
11) Now put down *this paper*.

In some cases, the location of a referent will require an inference:

12) John found a flashlight. *The batteries* were dead.

These have a complicated relation to other elements in the text: on the one hand, the definite article tells the reader to search elsewhere in the text for the appropriate referent, but if the reader does so, she will find that batteries have not been explicitly introduced. A close semantic associate (flashight) has, however, and it is presumed that the notion of batteries is implied by the word flashlight. Technically, then, *the batteries* could be counted as an introductory noun phrase but given its close relation to a flashlight, the phrase could also be phoric, albeit one which requires an inference for its interpretation. We have arbitrarily adopted the former designation (introductory-inferential) (Appendix A).

Characterizing Children's Referring Expressions

As we might expect, sixth graders produced substantially longer stories than other children in the sample. There was an increment at each grade level, with third graders producing an average of 103.4 words and sixth graders, 227.6. For this reason, data will be reported in terms of proportions rather than absolute numbers.

In all, the children produced a total of 1660 referring expressions, of which only 68 (4%) were judged by coders to be ambiguous or misleading. Despite

TABLE 1
Percentage of Introductory and Phoric Referring expressions and their text location at each grade level.

| Grade Level | Introductory | | | | | Phoric | | | |
| | Total | Begin. | Text Location | | Total | Begin. | Text Location | |
			Middle	End			Middle	End
Third	41	37	30	33	59	23	39	38
Fourth	40	39	29	32	60	31	35	34
Fifth	43	38	33	29	57	30	33	37
Sixth	37	42	26	32	63	31	34	35

the generally successful quality of their referencing, it should be noted that two-thirds of the children produced at least one ambiguous expression. The proportion of introductory and phoric phrases at each grade level is presented in Table 1. It is about the same across the four grades, indicating that children seem to provide about the same ratio of old to new information in their texts despite the differences in story length.

Table 1 also shows the distribution of introductory and phoric phrases across a text. To obtain these percentages, we divided each text into thirds and tallied the proportion of introductory and of phoric phrases across the three segments of each text. We might have expected to find a preponderance of introductory phrases at the beginning of these narratives, but the distribution appears to be remarkably even across the segments at all grade levels. This suggests that in developing their narratives, children continued to add new information at a reasonably uniform rate.

We were curious to know whether these children would rely on a particular linguistic device in constructing referring expressions. For example, would they rely on pro-forms in constructing their phoric phrases and indefinite articles in their introductory ones? As we can see from Table 2, about one-fourth of their introductory expressions were constructed with indefinite

TABLE 2
Percentage of Introductory Expressions Having These Linguistic Forms

| Grade Level | Linguistic Form | | | |
	Indefinite Article	Proper Name	Definite Article + Inference	Other
third	21	10	23	46
fourth	22	8	16	54
fifth	28	8	14	50
sixth	18	14	12	56

TABLE 3
Percentage of Phoric Expressions Having These Linguistic
Forms

| | Linguistic Form | | |
Grade Level	Pro-Form	Lexical Repetition	New Wording
third	73	21	6
fourth	62	29	9
fifth	64	29	7
sixth	83	12	5

articles and another 10% consisted of proper names. Comparable data on adult discourse are not available, although Warden's (1976) data suggest that adults might use a much higher proportion of indefinite articles.

It has sometimes been suggested that children produce a large proportion of introductory expressions that require an inference for their interpretation, but as we can see from Table 2, the proportion of these in this sample is fairly low. The closest we can come to comparable adult data are reported in Rochester and Martin's (1977) study of spoken discourse. In this study, normal adults participated in an interview and in addition, were asked to describe a set of cartoons and retell a story. Analysis of their referring expressions shows that between 7% and 11% required an inference, a figure somewhat lower than that obtained for our subjects but not substantially so.

Table 3 indicates that children's preferred strategy in the construction of phoric phrases was to use a pro-form. The rest of the time, they tended to rely on a repetition of the introductory expression (e.g., John bought a car. The car was a lemon.). Only occasionally did they construct new wording. (John has a son. The boy is five.)

To summarize, then, the overwhelming proportion of referring expressions produced by our children was unambiguous. New and old information seemed to be evenly divided across the beginning, middle and end segments of a given text. The children had no clear preference for a particular linguistic device in the construction of their introductory expressions, but in the majority of instances they seemed to rely on pro-forms in the construction of their phoric expressions. In a sense, we can view this characterization of children's successful referring expressions as a context against which to view their unsuccessful attempts and it is to these that we now turn.

Characterizing Children's Errors and Ambiguities

Ambiguous or uninterpretable referring expressions were produced by 35 (67%) of our writers. The proportion of subjects producing errors was roughly the same at the third (57%), fourth (64%), and fifth (65%) grades, but rose to 82% in our sixth grade sample. Given the small size of this group, the increase may reflect nothing more than sampling error, but it is possible that it indicates a real increase in ambiguity, perhaps similar to that observed by Loban (1976) in his older subjects. The overwhelming majority of referring expressions produced by these 35 writers was readily interpretable, an observation which suggests that their difficulties do not reflect a complete ignorance of the way in which referencing is accomplished. However, the quality of their referencing seemed to vary substantially within a given text.

For example, in the following sample, the writer has produced interpretable discourse up to *the man,* at which point, the referencing becomes quite misleading: our first expectation is that *the man* refers to the dead man, and it is only after we read the rest of the sentence and called on our pragmatic knowledge of what it is that dead men can and cannot do that we realize these words refer to the husband and not the friend.

> There was a man and every night he would go to a bar and get drunk. His wife didn't like this at all. One day she could not stand it any more. She thought he should be taught a lesson so she took the man who her husband always went out with and killed him. She put him in the bath room and the next morning *the man* got up to wash his face. He saw the dead man dead. . . .

Such variability within a single text was common in our sample and led us to suspect that children's difficulties may depend to a large extent on the context in which the referencing must be accomplished. When we examined actual instances of ambiguous or misleading references, we found that in 54 (79%) of the cases, the ambiguity occurred within a single type of context, one in which the writer attempted to make anaphoric reference to one of two same-sex, same-age characters who were interacting in the narrative. Children's usual linguistic devices (pro-forms and common noun phrases, such as *the man* or *the boy*) will fail to make differentiations in such contexts, and so it is not surprising to find that this is where most ambiguities occur.

What is less clear is the nature of the difficulty. Are children unaware of the special requirements of this sort of referential context? Or do they make some faulty but at least partially appropriate attempt to accommodate their referencing to these contexts? To address this question, we compared the referring expressions produced by children in these more complex contexts with those produced in contexts where characters of different sex and age interacted. In all, a total of 166 different story characters appeared in our corpus: 94 in the more complex and 72 in the simpler contexts. When we examine the referring expressions produced in the two types of context, one interesting difference emerges: the *variety* of referring devices increases in the more complex contexts. Thus, while children are likely to use one or at most

TABLE 4
The relation of context to the number of different referring
expressions used to designate each story character

Linguistic Context	Number of story characters	Number of different referring expressions used to designate each character			
		one	two	three	four
Complex contexts (another character has same sex, same age)	94	24	40	29	1
Simple contexts (no other character has same sex, or same age)	72	41	25	2	4

two different types of devices in referring to an individual character in a simple context (e.g., a pro-form and a general noun phrase: There was *a man* and *he* went out), in a complex context children are more likely to use two or three different ones (e.g.,: There was *a man* named *Jim* and *he* went out). (See Table 4: X^2 = 30.85; d.f. = 3, $p < .01$.) Clearly, then, in complex contexts children adopt referencing which, in its variety, provides them with greater flexibility and the potential for making fine distinctions. This suggests that our children may indeed have been aware of the difficulties inherent in these contexts and may have attempted to adjust their referencing accordingly.

That most of their errors occurred in these contexts, suggests that their adjustments were not always successful. But it is unclear whether these failures are due to an inability to choose appropriate devices or to some more transient or momentary difficulty. To consider this question, we can examine the kinds of devices used by writers in the complex contexts, in order to determine whether these could, in principle at least, make the required differentiation between the two same-age, same-sex characters. Four kinds of devices exist: two that make the required distinction (naming a character and using a distinguishing categorical label, such as *a robber, a friend*) and two which do not (using a non-distinguishing label such as *a man* or *a person* and using a pro-form). In our sample, there were 47 pairs of interacting same age, same sex characters. To address the question, we tallied the devices used by each writer to refer to each of the two characters when the pair *first* interacted in the text.

In 40 instances (85% of the cases), children selected devices which could, in principle, make the required distinctions. For example, in 13 cases (28%) the writer differentiated between the characters by using the non-distinguishing term (*a man*) for one and a distinguishing categorical label for the other.

(Typically, it was the assailant who was categorized and the labels included such terms as *thief, robber, kidnapper, cannibal.*) In another 11 instances (23%), the writer named each character. Other combinations included the use of a name together with a distinguishing term (5 instances) or a non-distinguishing term (5 instances); the use of two distinguishing categorical terms (3 instances) or a distinguishing term and a pro-form (3 instances). Thus, the majority of writers knew how to select devices which made the requisite distinctions. That 36 of the 54 ambiguities observed in complex contexts occurred after children had already accomplished at least one unambiguous reference to one of the characters (in a context in which both were interacting) suggests that for some children ambiguities may arise from temporary lapses rather than any lack of basic knowledge.

In the case of 7 of the 47 pairs of interacting same-age, same-sex characters, however, writers failed to use devices which differentiated between the two characters. It is possible that these children failed to realize the implications of such a context for referencing, but it is also possible that the difficulties arise less from any basic lack of awareness than from an inability to choose appropriate devices. When we examine the actual texts, we find some slight evidence that children who initially produced inadequate constructions, changed their strategy as they went along, an observation which suggests that the difficulties resulted more from faulty selection than from a failure to appreciate the ambiguities inherent in their first wordings. For example, in the following text the writer first labels each character with the words *a man.* Then she goes on to provide more definite descriptions, based on the content of the story:

> A man left his house at night. He was walking in an alley and while he was walking he said to himself, "somebody or something is following me." So he started running and tripped on a piece of metal and a man shot him. *The man that got shot* had a gang of men and he wouldn't pay them for the work they did so *the man behind him* was in the gang and shot him.

In the following instance, although the writer provides himself with an adequate distinguishing label at the beginning of the story (the name *Harry*), he fails to use it at first and instead relies on the nondistinguishing term *the man* and the pronoun *he* to identify both characters, with predictably confusing results:

> One day a man named Harry left his house. He was going to the movies. A man was standing outside of *his* front door. *He* didn't know it. *He* walked out side the door. *The man* took him buy the mouth Harry bit him the man pushed him on the ground Harry fell on his face....(Italics, ours)

> Referencing in the preceding texts is clearly awkward at times, particularly when the writers attempt to provide additional differentiating information through the use of definite descriptions (e.g., the man that got shot). But such

awkwardness need not necessarily mean that these writers are unable to accomplish referencing at all. Indeed, one might speculate that these writers are in some sense aware of the deficiencies in their referencing and are struggling to find a set of linguistic devices which will in fact accomplish what they intend. We might also expect that such children would benefit from instruction designed to develop a greater range of referencing devices for use in complex contexts of the sort encountered here.

Consistency in Children's Texts

It is sometimes suggested that children will have difficulty keeping in mind the evolving structure of their texts during the process of composition, presumably because of the demands which the task of writing makes on the child's cognitive processes. In an attempt to consider this hypothesis, we examined the spatial and temporal consistency of our texts to see if any contradictory statements occurred. For example: Did characters or objects seem to be in two places at once? Did characters or objects change in number or in other essential characteristics? Were the temporal sequences contradictory?

On the whole, we found that writers did construct a consistent spatial and temporal organization for their texts. Although children sometimes had difficulty accomplishing certain kinds of referencing, it was almost always possible to arrive at some consistent, non-contradictory interpretation of the text. To be sure, there were childish misconceptions, particularly about the motives and social structure of the adult world. But there were very few instances in which the writer actually failed to construct a consistent set of events.

In this particular corpus, we have only been able to find four possible examples of inconsistent text. In text one, sequences 1 and 2 can be interpreted as stating that the character opened the door twice.

Text One:[1] There was once a girl who lived in an apartment building and she was living very happily. Then a man knocked on the door and said let me in I'm your brother but she didn't have a brother but *she let him in anyway*$_1$ but got a gun *and opened the door*$_2$ and as soon as he came in she shot him....

In text two, sequences 1 and 2 may indicate that Harry left his house twice.

Text Two: One day *a man named Harry left his house*$_1$ he was going to the movies. A man was standing outside of his front door. He didn't know it. *He walked out side the door*$_2$....

---

[1]In this and the following texts, the children's spellings and punctuations have been retained. (Italics ours)

In text three, sequence 3 suggests that the man had gone indoors although sequences 1 and 2 place him outside in the park and there has been no indication in the text that he has changed location.

> *Text Three:* Me and my friends were playing *in the park.*₁ We was running *in the park.*₂ And we saw this man drinking whisky. He started running after me and my friends and then he fell *on the floor*₃ flat faced. Then the cops came.

Finally, in text four the defining characteristics of the object in sequences 1 and 2 are inconsistent: in sequence 1, there are two knives and in sequence 2 (which appears to have the same referent) there is only one.

> *Text Four:* A man... was walking out of his apartment... When he put the key in the door two black men jumped out at him. They both had pocket knifes one stuck it in his throat and they heared a nois they got scared and dropped *the knifes*₁... the police didn't find know clues but some figer prints on *the knife.*₂

With these four possible exceptions, then, we have found that the story events constructed by children in our sample are temporally and spatially consistent. Since the texts in our sample were produced by eight to eleven years olds who already had several years of instruction in writing, it is possible that younger children will have greater difficulty constructing consistent story events. It may also be true, however, that younger children will show their inexperience not so much by a lack of consistency as by the production of simpler (but nonetheless wholly consistent) texts.

SUMMARY AND CONCLUSIONS

Our analyses of referential organization have led us to the following tentative conclusions. Despite the fact that most of the referring expressions in the children's texts were successful, more than two-thirds of the children produced at least one ambiguous construction. The majority of these occurred in what we have termed complex contexts. Comparison of the referring expressions produced in simple and complex contexts showed that children adopted a more varied set of linguistic devices in the more complex contexts, a finding which suggests that they were sensitive to differences in the referential requirements of the two contexts. Furthermore, a look at the devices themselves suggests that most were, in principle at least, adequate for signaling the required distinctions and that most ambiguities occurred *after* successful referencing had already been accomplished at least once in the same context. This pattern of results suggests that for these children difficulties arose not so much from any lack of basic awareness of the referential requirements inherent in these contexts or from any basic inability to choose appropriate linguistic devices, but rather from more momentary and transient performance factors specific to the context in which referencing occurs. The specific nature of the cognitive and linguistic processes operating in complex contexts remains to be understood.

These findings also have implications for future research on the writing of upper elementary school children. What they suggest is that the difficulties these children experience in using referring experiences are likely to depend in important ways on context. It appears reasonable to expect that context will also be important in other aspects of children's writing. Analyses of children's writing must, therefore, incorporate some characterization of the relation between the particular aspect of language under study and the contexts in which it occurs. This chapter has demonstrated how an analytic scheme can be developed and used to assess referring expressions in children's writing in a way that is sensitive to contextual factors. A similar research strategy should prove fruitful in investigating other aspects of children's writing.

ACKNOWLEDGMENTS

This research and preparation of this paper were supported by Grant No. 765–0410 from The Ford Foundation to Teachers and Writers Collaborative. Data were collected as part of an earlier study supported by the National Institute of Education (Grant No. NIE-G-74-0014 to Teachers and Writers Collaborative). Requests for reprints should be sent to first author at The Rockefeller University.

REFERENCES

Chomsky, C. 1969. *The acquisition of syntax in children from 5 to 10.* Cambridge, Mass.: The MIT Press.

Clark, H. H. and Haviland, S. E. 1977. Comprehension and the given-new contract. In R. O. Freedle (Ed.), *Discourse production and comprehension* (Vol. 1). Norwood, N.J.: Ablex Publishing Co.

de Villiers, P. A. and de Villiers, J. G. 1974. On this, that and the other. Nonegocentrism in very young children. *Journal of Experimental Child Psychology,* 1974, *18,* 438–447.

Educational Testing Service. 1976. How the essay in the CEEB English composition test is scored. Mimeo.

Glucksberg, S., Krauss, R. and Higgins, E. T. 1975. The development of referential communication skills. In F. D. Horowitz (Ed.), *Review of child development research.* (Vol. 4). Chicago: University of Chicago Press.

Halliday, M. A. K. and Hasan, R. 1976. *Cohesion in English.* London: Longman Group Ltd.

Loban, W. 1976. *Language development: kindergarten through grade twelve.* Urbana, Ill.: National Council of Teachers of English.

Maratsos, M. 1976. *The use of definite and indefinite reference in young children: an experimental study of semantic acquisition.* Cambridge: Cambridge University Press.

Palermo, D. and Molfese, D. 1972. Language acquisition from age five onward. *Psychological Bulletin,* 1972, *78,* 409–428.

11 Rhetorical Choices in Writing

Richard Lloyd-Jones
University of Iowa

Rhetoric is the study of effective choices among linguistic and discursive alternatives. I stipulate *study* instead of Aristotle's *art* because I want to emphasize theoretical knowledge as opposed to practical craft, but the issue is one of degree. I merely point out that an excellent writer is not necessarily a competent rhetorician, and at least some good rhetoricians write badly.

By choosing *linguistic and discursive alternatives* I imply that although linguists describe the features of the language as scientifically as they possibly can, writers' decisions about which form to use generally lie outside of linguistic analysis. The range of choice includes decisions about the large structures of discourse which are not usually treated by linguists. My objective is to identify the options in verbal language as broadly as possible and to put aside questions of *correctness*. Doctrines of correctness tend to allow little room for choice because they treat variant forms as falling away from excellence. I want to talk about describing the alternatives separately from valuing the alternatives, because different forms serve various intellectual and social functions.

Language, then, includes all of the available forms—dialects, idiolects, jargon, slang, written, oral, formal, casual, intimate, fragment, tropes, epics, reports, personal essays, theme, whatever—as long as it can be seen in terms of patterns consistent with our language as we experience it. Dealing with variant vocabulary is almost no issue for we have long recognized that English is a greater absorber of words from other languages and from inventors of words. Some purists occasionally grumble about neologisms, as well as words associated with social sub-groups. To be sure, all of us occasionally use words we don't mean, but inept choice in one instance does not imply that real choices are not available in other situations. Indeed, the situation itself is defined in part by the choices.

Phonology need not be a major problem for writers (people who pronounce differently at least claim to spell in the same way). The oral patterns of Massachusetts, or Texas, or Georgia are for some people sufficient reason to vote against a presidential candidate; regional and social differences correlated with phonological differences seem to some an adequate guide to character, but even the radio and TV networks have begun to employ people with regional phonologies.

The apologists for uniform spelling have far larger armies, but they have to explain away Donald Emery's booklet listing variant spellings in the five most common desk dictionaries. We do not really all spell the same way, but the differences are minor. Although once the variations were greater than they are now, and little seems to be gained by making a virtue of odd spelling, still the American obsession with the values of the spelling bee wastes school time and energy as we pretend to develop finicky similarity which we don't need. When misspellings (or unusual pronunciations) defy interpretation, they cease to be English. Forms which delay interpretation may be unwise, but not un-English. The issue, however, is one of priorities, of how much time one gives to spelling in school in contrast to time allowed for larger issues.

Total breakdowns in syntax are not likely, despite the usual complaints about *poor grammar*. Confused syntax of the type described by Mina Shaughnessey in *Errors and Expectations* may result from not knowing the forms precisely, or not knowing how to handle them in a strange context, or from haste, fear, or other personal problems, or from genuine confusion about what has to be said. Still, the syntactical variants which receive the most popular condemnation are ones with social rather than intellectual implications—tense forms, plurals, pronoun case forms. "Two book" is plural: "I goes tomorrow" is future; "between you and I" is objective. Statistically, though, these are probably not the most favored English forms, and they offend many users of English. Whether one wants to offend such users is a question of policy for a rhetorician.

Although most people assume that choices exist among the forms of discourse—in part because the discourse forms themselves are less clearly defined and taught than are sentence forms—still discourse forms exist as arbitrary patterns in language which thus must be related to something in external experience. Formulaic systems of organization or the traditional modes of discourse presume inevitability in relating language to the world. The preoccupation with the correct form of a letter or of a business report, or even of a three paragraph classroom theme reminds one that the larger features of language do not entirely escape the view of language as one correct machine willfully and constantly damaged by ignorant users. A rhetorician tries to relate the desirable forms to intended outcomes or policy and thus to recommend choice.

I have risked belaboring the obvious because so much of our standard advice to writers and teachers is based on assumptions that variations are symptoms of failure rather than of the complexity of human motives. Although I don't think most linguists or philosophers would object to my description of language in terms of alternatives—except to hesitate about my lumping the features of discourse into the same category as features of sentences and smaller units—still the attitudes associated with finding the absolutely correct form persist and undermine our thinking about rhetoric.

The crucial term in my definition of rhetoric is *effective choice,* and it invites problems analogous to those implied in thinking about *free will* and *sin.* The one right way of freely choosing to do God's will leaves one merely to determine the facts of what God wills. To sin is to exercise the will in disobedience. In contrast, rhetoric deals with the genuine contingency of multiple wills. One might choose any of several options because one wills different purposes. *Effective* implies the existence of person to be affected, and *choice* implies a chooser with a general policy for guidance and a specific purpose to be carried out. Both policy and purpose inevitably operate on something or someone existing in the external world. (If one writes to oneself, the same creator is both writer and reader but in different moments plays different roles.)

The triad of *chooser, reality* to be represented in the code, and *recipient* is a traditional formulation in discourse theory. The *reality* in fact contains the writer, the reader, and the writing, as well as what is written about. Since this reality is more complex than either writer or reader can fully comprehend, their separate perceptions of it are unique, even if the words they use are the same. We have ample evidence that the perceptions represented by words differ from person to person, (color blindness, hearing loss of high sounds) although our needs for precision are so specific to a situation and so capable of satisfaction in gross terms that these differences need not be practically objectionable. (In a choice between two buttons, one pink and blue, it is sufficient to speak of the *red* button.) The issue is not how we can represent in language the truth of reality, but rather how we understand the specific need of the moment within the framework of our ordinary sense of what is important.

Meaningful choice begins with a policy (or guiding principle)—tacit or overt—and is refined in a purpose. Most policies are tacit—vague yearnings, habits, unarticulated motives, unconscious or subconscious pressures which enable the organism to survive. The sensitive or self-conscious person may try to bring the policies to the surface in order to deal with them rationally. But the rapidity with which we confront decisions on possible actions required for survival may mean that most decisions are automatic. A person who tried to rationalize each word choice in a conversation would be paralyzed. Some people claim to know where each sentence will end before they begin it, but most of us start a sentence secure in the hope that we will figure out where it is to go as it goes. Still, our habits are directed by a sense of goal, and in purely social conversations the *purpose* is likely to be a part of our social context. We are clearly engaged with the other participants in the conversation, or at least we are so conscious of our anomalous irrelevance that we babble.

Writing presents a different issue than conversation because the forces of context are less distinct; yet they are more insistent by virtue of the solidity and permanence of a document. In the classroom or even in the novice manager's quarterly report we often find that bad writing results from the writer's not being able to imagine the specific purpose of the writing. Merely satisfying an assignment which does not present a goal within the student's own sense of context is not sufficient to provide structure to random data. The new employee who is just following orders cannot always be expected to have internalized institutional policy well enough to understand how assigned purpose grows out of the context. In schools we often substitute the formula paper—we give the *form of the report* or set paragraph-by-paragraph specifications—a form in place of a purpose. So also the government may contract for an instruction manual to go with complex equipment and give specifications for the content of each paragraph and voice of each verb. The actual writer, in this case, has no policy, but the narrowly prescribed function of the prose in reference to purpose makes it adequate if not memorable.

I have been trying to suggest differences between policy and purpose when, in fact, the terms represent overlapping notions. The purpose of a particular discourse is more conscious and situation specific than the general policy which determines a writer's usual stance or self with respect to the listener or reader. Policy may be represented in idiolect and style—habitual language choices among lexical and syntactic options. In this sense policy represents the writer's entire value system. A commonly used term to represent how policies and purposes are reflected in discourse is *voice*. *Voice* represents the *person* or *personality* or *character* made explicit. Efforts of writing teachers to make students aware of *voice* in writing are likely to focus on self-realization, a kind of modernization of Buffon's dictim, "Style is the man." The slightly Victorian among them might think more of F. L. Lucas' *character*. The *voice* is all one hears, and (even more) it is a voice filtered in transmission so that what is perceived by a reader is different from what is intended, sometimes because of the inadequacy of language, but most often because the reader is humanly limited. In any particular situation less than all of one's policy can be transmitted. In fact, then, the voice is not the *realization* of the writer; it is the creation of a sub-set of the writer's qualities so as to be consistent with a general policy and to serve *a* particular purpose. It is *character* in the sense of *role* rather than of *ethos*. A totally consistent person—say a saint whose simplicity of value admits no contradiction—can depend upon habitual choices, that is policy, to create in discourse, a unity which is related to a purpose. The rest of us have to find consistency by defining a role appropriate to our purpose and then in creating the language to support the role. In the process we may discover something about the self and about our policy, but our procedure is more nearly that of the playwright trying to approximate the ego-risks of actual communication.

The implication of this definition of voice is that the dramatic self is in part defined by its purposes in relation to the other person, the non-self, and to the whole physical situation within which the discourse takes place. For example, much of the effort in any discourse is to imply the degree of social intimacy with reader. Generally, in highly structured situations, the writer uses devices such as tabulation, predictive statements of the topic, explicit transitions, and analytic lists to imply formal distance. Writer and reader relate intellectually; the mortal selves are irrelevant. In more casual situations, contradictions, jargons, assumption of common background, and affective leaps hint at personal, epistolary relationships. In discourse, formal distance implies dialectic or logical proofs; intimacy suggests ethical proof. The scholar tends to prefer distance, but the teacher moves closer. Formal distance generally requires conventionally bland choices, but expressive purposes allow greater range. Whatever self is chosen (a formal *self* can also be existentially persuasive) the voice-role is established by language which implies the social relationship and the purpose.

If the purpose of the writer is to lay open a personal position by suggesting a unique self, for example, then it may be appropriate to choose language forms not generally approved, that is, forms outside of those statistically most favored by local authority. To express *black power* in certain situations one must use *black vernacular*. The expressive stance requires verbal forms associated with the group which holds the position; the expression may be written by one person, but it becomes the expression of the group, or at least it persuades by implying an identity of interest with the target audience. Such may also be said the for the usual speech at a political convention, which rallies the faithful by being an expression of their policies. The banalities of convention oratory do little to convince anyone who does not already feel a compulsion to identify with the speaker. One speaks the language (and values) of the group as required by the immediate purpose, even though one's complete policy could include far more. In contrast, to relate to a large hostile audience the *voice* may search for the statistical security of *standard English* in order not to insist upon separateness from the audience. One cannot, perhaps, speak the language of the sub-group without presumption or condescension, so one's purpose calls for language which is least committed to the *voices* of any group. This blandness may seem merely to be the same as the shared policy language of party politics.

Yet, blandness is different from coded language. When one compares Democratic support of *all people* and Republican praise of *liberty* with votes cast by party members, one can hardly escape the feeling that they are evoking emotions without content. They allege common party positions they don't have, but the code evokes applause and the appearance of a common purpose. It claims identity rather than non-hostility. If persuasion is really an effort to reveal that writer and reader have common interests, and not just an attempt to get readers to change their minds, then the appropriate voice is found in the shared code, and if their interests are really opposed, the bland speaker lies by implication. One can find exceptions. Eldredge Cleaver, for example, has been known to play on dialect differences to shame an audience of white liberals into espousing a cause, perhaps contrary to their interests, because they did not want to be identified with those who spoke standard English as a form of bland lying.

Most of our position-taking is not likely to be so aggressive, and propriety usually dictates social reserve—or a kind of conventional heartiness which no experienced person mistakes for intimacy. It is rather the language of non-hostility or even social indifference as it pretends fellowship. As a result, most of our language choices are bland; one can almost say that the objective of the schools is to acquaint all students with the blandest forms of English, the forms of least commitment, the forms of superficial order. Still, even the formulations of academic division and classification assert a view of the world. The bland language of science, for example, is fully committed to a view of reality. What Plato saw as *natural joints* are, after all, categories of the mind and are subject to the limits of human perception and to the language which derives from perceptions. Plato could see these forms as representing essential reality more significant than sensible surfaces, but we are caught in a nominalism informed by human policy. We say that the division of Gaul into three parts is an act of Caesar's to represent his sense of what was worth analyzing; he was a western politician, not an eastern mystic. Still, one suspects that Gauls and Gaul existed, and, given Caesar's purposes, they existed as he said. He did not lie, but he could not tell the whole truth. His analytic blandness passes for truth-telling even if it is partial. Moreover, his decision represents both policy and purpose.

That is where rhetoric and contingency come back to effective choice. Since we do not represent anything wholly, we choose language which will represent a part of us perceiving a part of the world, or which will exhibit facets of our perception to that part of another person which is important to us at the moment in order to accomplish our goals. My paraphrase of the original definition get longer and longer as I try to shade the meaning. Strictly, revision (a *reseeing*,) changes the meaning by altering the voice of the self, the tone toward the audience, or the attitude toward the material. People of different temperaments react differently to such efforts. A classical dualist might assume that once the truth is discovered and the available means of addressing a reader are selected, then the language is adjusted superficially to create a decorous style. Revision sometimes prettifies. On the other hand, stylistic monists sometimes become upset about requiring revision from students because revision forces the writer to say *something else*. Precisely. A reviser reconsiders the complex interrelationships of purposes so as to make better choices and thus must report a different segment of a total reality. As we re-view, we see in combination with memory the fuller reality.

In short, we can represent purposes in language within three rather broad but distinct categories: *explanatory, persuasive* or *expressive*. Every sample of discourse is driven by a mixture of all three purposes. These three basic purposes in writing can be related to three variables of the traditional formula for describing a rhetorical situation. Explanation is oriented to a posited, external reality; persuasion is oriented to the relationship with people; and expression is self forming and is a function of the writer's attempts to discover and organize particular levels of meaning. In addition, verbal play for its own sake overlays these three purposes, and, in general, is a function of what is called literature. This suggests that a piece of fiction, for example, is not literature until the language itself is deliberately colored or made translucent in order to heighten the reader's sense of verbal construct. The code itself is the chief part of the reality of fiction. On the other hand, surely one of the purposes of a novel is to supply information; verse satire is persuasive; the personal essay is expressive. A Darwin may blend tropes and oratorical twists into his *Origin* so that literary scholars turn to the book long after biologists lose interest. I want to emphasize here the importance of literature and the justifications for requiring elaborate study of literature in higher education; an experimental concern for the nuances of the language code ought to make it clear why literature is more than just another area to be treated in general education. Literature, by its preoccupation with the limits and possibilities of language, is the most self-aware representation of basic human purposes. (Probably the enormity of my assertion explains why the New Critics wanted a more modest and manageable methodology implied by a restrictive definition of literature).

I have hinted that different features of language can be expected to serve one kind of purpose more effectively than other kinds, but I can easily be persuaded to back away from any particular citation of relationships, for I am aware of how quaint seem the expressed decorum of subjects to Greek poetic forms. At least, nowadays we'll use iambs for all sorts of purposes. Still, we instruct writers of the need for exemplary *evidence* in some kinds of persuasion, for evocativeness in expression, and for certain structures in explanation (comparison, temporality, spatiality). We clearly need more elaborate schema for systematic instruction. Our present practice of depending upon the experienced taste of teachers is limited by the available taste, and it makes programmed learning rather problematical.

We observe that different people perform better with some purposes than with others. For example, a trained engineer usually explains well, but often relates to audiences badly and is too *inhibited* to reveal a self. That should warn us that a test of writing skill which does not account for purpose is probably limited in validity, and tests of features of language—say, of usage—are even more severely limited. What one gets of standardized tests is a measure of knowledge of conventional choices of features at the sub-sentence level.

12 Writing Ability As a Function of the Appreciation of Differences Between Oral and Written Communication

Georgia M. Green
Jerry L. Morgan
University of Illinois

Our purpose here is to consider writing ability from the point of view of an emerging pragmatic theory of communicative competence, and to focus on ways in which awareness of the differences between oral and written communication affects the ability to write well and the ability to make accurate assessments of writing ability. We restrict our remarks to writing ability as competence in the craft necessary to produce clear utilitarian prose, on the assumption that this craft is separable from the art of writing elegant, eloquent, or lyrical prose. Our concern is with characterizing what a language user knows who has mastered this aspect of written communication. This involves being able to choose language appropriate to the task, and, more important, being aware that communication is not a necessary consequence of expression (Reddy 1979), so that the writer must take care to anticipate and forestall possible confusion at every step, because the reader is in no position to ask for explications. Assessment of writing, therefore, must take into account not only the writer's choice of linguistic forms, but also how well the writer has managed to compensate for the reader's disadvantage in being unable to interact with him or her.

An adequate pragmatic theory of communicative competence (cf. Morgan 1978b) will, among other things, provide an account of how a language user tailors the phrasing of what she wants to communicate, according to her estimate of her audiences's ability to make particular inferences which depend on knowledge of both the language and the real world. Such a theory also provides a way of relating intentions (both expressive and affective), assumptions, and expectations to communicative forms (presumably both linguistic and gestural) in production, and in comprehension, relating forms to speakers' expectations, assumptions, and intentions.

But what is to be gained for writing assessment, by focussing on these differences? Two things, we hope. First, it is difficult to make an accurate assessment of writing ability unless conflicts of language choice (dialect and register) are distinguished from the ability to express thoughts in a clearly organized way. When such distinctions are not made, it is easy for misunderstanding to arise which may result in gross underassessments (Labov 1969), and/or misleading assessments. If only the inappropriate diction in a poorly written essay is remarked upon, for example, a student may falsely believe that the organization is clear and logical. Second, we expect that an understanding of the inherent differences between oral and written communication by assessors of writing will lead to an increased awareness of the challenges posed by communication without the possibility of feedback, and what the writer can do to meet them. Section 1 of this paper deals with the issue of language mastery, and section 2, with inherent differences between conversation and writing.

LANGUAGE MASTERY

There are two areas of potential importance for writing assessment that involve not so much the ability to write as the language of writing. Obviously the writer's dialect, if different from that of the written standard, or from that of the evaluator, can have a strong influence on the evaluator's assessment. An evaluator may assume that an expository essay written in a non-standard dialect of English is badly written. But the ability to write must not be confused with the ability to sound like a distinguished writer; or at least if dialect is to be a factor in writing evaluation, it should not influence the evaluator's rating of the other aspects of the piece, like clarity and organization.

A less obvious kind of language problem is a matter of *register* (Quirk et al., 1972). When Moliere's M. Jourdain observed that he had been speaking prose all his life, he was probably wrong. There are pervasive differences between the language of conversation and the language of expository prose. The most obvious are lexical differences, for example the use of *kids, can,* and *have to* in informal conversation, but *children, may,* and *must* for the same meanings in certain kinds of prose, and the inadmissibility in expository prose of conversationally important interjections like *well, you know, why,* and so on. There are also syntactic differences; many inverted structures like that in *"Sit down," said the teacher,* and *unextraposed* sentences like *That he's wrong is obvious* occur mainly in relatively formal written prose, and sound quite strange in conversation. Finally, there are higher-level semantic and pragmatic differences like the inadmissibility of first-person reference in some kinds of academic and bureaucratic prose, and the different kinds of hedges employed in the two modes (*I guess, I suppose, I think* etc., in conversation; *it seems, it may be, apparently,* in prose, for example). These differences are more or less arbitrary, a matter of implicit (occasionally explicit) convention, and do not stem from inherent differences between conversation and writing.

These differences are of minor importance in prose clarity, aesthetic judgments aside; but it is likely that they are important in giving the impression of clarity (or lack of it). One of the authors who has some proficiency in Albanian was once told by a native speaker of the language that he speaks Albanian *elegantly, like a professor.* This evaluation stemmed not from genuine fluency in the language, but from the fact that his experience with the language had been predominantly with the written register, rather than conversation. In other words, he sounded like a book. We have often had the experience of being impressed at first by the written work of a linguistics graduate student, only to decide on second reading that the work was poorly argued, or badly organized, or in fact without content. The student had merely acquired a few tricks of register than enabled him to sound like Chomsky. We have also had the opposite experience, perhaps more often than we realize, of underestimating the quality of a student's paper, and revising our opinion when we realized that we were reacting unreasonably to the register of a paper that was in fact clear and well-organized. That is, the student didn't sound like a linguist. This is apparently a natural and frequent kind of misevaluation, and must be controlled in the assessment process. It would also be useful to know at what age children become aware that there is a difference between conversational and written language, how much being read to contributes to this awareness, and at what age they can reasonable be expected to have mastered the written register, if indeed this difference is to be perpetuated in the educational system.

We suspect that there are other, less obvious differences of some importance that sociolinguists who specialize in conversational analysis may be able to tell us about. For example, some speakers have conversational politeness strategies that lead them to be somewhat circumspect, to avoid being too direct, to lead up to the point gradually. But often the clearest expository prose is that which gets right to the point. So the best conversation will make flaccid prose, and the best prose will sound harsh and abrupt as conversation.

MASTERY OF DIFFERENCES BETWEEN ORAL AND WRITTEN COMMUNICATION

Most important for coherence and clarity is the writer's ability to deal with the inherent communicative differences between conversation and writing (cf. Rubin 1978 for some discussion of these). There are, first of all, important channel differences, especially the information carried in speech by stress and intonation, and by non-verbal means like gesture and facial expressions.

For instance, although punctuation can differentiate the reportive or directive sense of *You're leaving tomorrow* from the question senses, it cannot distinguish the sincere information-seeking questions

$$\text{You're} \overline{\rvert \text{ leaving tomorrow}}$$
$$\&$$
$$\text{You're leaving to} \overline{\rvert \text{morrow}}$$

from the incredulity *echo* question (Liberman & Sag 1975)

$$\text{You're leaving to} \overline{\lceil \text{morrow}}$$

Even choice of a contrasting type face can only hint at what the intonation would more clearly express. Neither orthography nor punctuation can indicate the frequency (pitch) and nasality shifts that can be used in speech to indicate sarcasm or assumed role.

But we suspect that one of the major determinants of an individual's ability to write coherent expository prose is his or her appreciation of the communicative differences between written and oral communication. These differences follow from the fact that in typical conversations the speaker has some idea of what the hearer does and doesn't know, and has access to immediate feedback on whether he is making his point, losing his audience, being misunderstood, and so on. This is characteristic of oral communication in small groups, especially dyads; oral communication to large groups typically has all of the characteristics (linguistic and pragmatic) of written communication (except that oral delivery entails non-permanence and permits prosodic cues), precisely because in addressing a large group a speaker is less able to tell how his message is being received.

To put the differences between oral and written communication in relief, let us examine in detail some of the aspects of typical oral dyadic communication which are absent from written communication of all sorts, but occur in conversations like the following.

Joan: Hey, Bob? Got a minute? I've got a neat idea for our costume for Evelyn's party.
Bob: Yeah?
Joan: We can go as a paradox. I'll put on my lab coat and we can make a stethescope or something for you.
Bob: I don't get it.
Joan: Paradox. Pair-of-docs.... Doctors. White coats, stethescopes. You know.

Bob: (Groans). All right. . . . I suppose it's better than going as Peter Pan and Tinker Bell.

To begin with, an oral expositor in a one-to-one interaction generally does not plunge right into this argument. He first broaches the topic, and makes sure his addressee is willing to listen. This holds even (perhaps especially) for conversations which are not face-to-face, such as telephone conversations. Next, and very soon after approaching the addressee, a speaker will express his claim, proposal, hypothesis, or whatever, about the topic he has brought up. This holds for every kind of conversation from spur-of-the-moment invitations to go to the movies, to phone calls from political workers canvassing for candidates. One of the few situations where the speaker might not introduce his topic according to the conventional strategy is in certain kinds of solicitation, by magazine or encyclopedia salesmen, for example. And such situations stand out in two ways. First, it is clear that it is for deceptive purposes that the salespeople avoid saying *that* they are selling, and sometimes even *what* they are selling. Second, busy people tend to be quite annoyed by such tactics; they want to know the point of the conversation they have been drawn into.

After the speaker has broached her subject, and indicated her proposal, claim, etc,. she presents whatever rationale she may have for it. The exposition of reasons may range from simple to very complex. If at any point the addressee does not perceive the relevance of the speaker's discussion, he is free to interrupt and say so. Indeed he is expected to, for a speaker will be frustrated and annoyed to find out after presenting a complex rationale that the addressee did not follow the last 70% of it, and was aware of not following it. Any sane speaker, even a relatively inarticulate one, will be able to make clear the relevance of questioned remarks, at least to the extent that she has understood them. If necessary, she will ask questions herself of the addressee, until she finds out at which point the addressee failed to follow her exposition.

Finally, when the addressee has understood the substance of the expositor's remarks (and in fact, even if he has misunderstood them, as long as he thinks he has understood), he may be expected to indicate his agreement or disagreement with the speaker's proposal. (If it is disagreement, the whole process may be begun again, by either participant.)

Now, many of these characteristics are absent from the typical cases of written exposition, precisely because the intended audience is not at hand to interact with the expositor. The writer has no way of determining whether his audience wishes to hear him out. If he is a student, writing anything from an assigned paragraph to a doctoral dissertation, he assumes that his intended audience is willing to listen. If the writing is self-motivated, depending on the writer's skill, he will make an attempt to ensure interest, by any of several rhetorical techniques.

Obviously the audience cannot interrupt the expositor and say, "Hold on. I don't see the connection," or "So what?" The writer must assume her audience will follow her argument, but it takes a good deal of training and/or practice to be able to write in such a way that this is a reasonable assumption. She has to learn to make explicit all crucial assumptions which there is a reasonable chance her intended audience will not share, and to state explicitly the connections between assumptions and their consequences, and between intermediate conclusions and the main thesis.

Unpracticed writers often fail to state their purpose at the beginning of the paper; rather, they lead up to the point in a roundabout way, so that the point is like a punch line for the paper—to state it earlier would, they seem to think, spoil the effect. Since the audience cannot interrupt in puzzlement and ask what the point is of some very complex, and even logically presented argument, the writer must write so that the reader can anticipate what is going to come next, and how it relates to what has gone before and what will come after. This usually means sprinkling the paper with summaries and previews, and at the very least, providing an abstract or summary, and an outline at the beginning of the paper.

Finally, the audience cannot let the writer know immediately if she has been persuasive. A naive writer will assume she has, and stop when she has finished the substance of her argument. A writer with more foresight might end with a restatement of her point and a summary of the reasons for accepting it.

As a consequence of these differences, clear writing is far more demanding than speaking. Assuming that the writer knows what he wants to say, he must be able to anticipate where the reader is likely to have trouble comprehending, and then must be able to edit accordingly, in the hope of ensuring that the text will be understood as intended. There are a number of factors involved in this ability. At the sentence level, there are the obvious matters of lexical choice and syntactic ambiguity. It would be self-defeating, of course, to choose words that are unlikely to be familiar to the intended reader. One must also try to avoid potentially misleading syntactic ambiguity and those occasional syntactic monsters that are impossible to parse without pencil and paper. But these lexical and syntactic properties of sentences are probably of minor importance compared to higher-level discourse properties.

Research by philosophers, linguistics, and psychologists in the past several years has made it very clear that even in the most straightforward and colorless prose, far more is conveyed than just the literal meanings of the sentences that make up the text (e.g., Grice 1975, Horn 1972, Keenan and Kintsch 1974). Full comprehension of the text often requires of the reader a considerable amount of inferential reasoning, at several levels. Some of these inferences can be made only if the reader has the knowledge of the world necessary for making the inference.

In sentence processing, interpretation of various anaphoric devices, such as pronouns, demonstratives, and ellipsis, requires the reader to infer who or what the intended referent is (cf. e.g., Kantor 1977, Webber, 1978, for some discussion of the dimensions of this task). For example, the pronouns in the following sentences will most likely be interpreted differently, influenced by knowledge-based inferences about what is being described.

1. The thief broke John's arm, so he was taken to the emergency room.
2. The thief broke John's arm, so he was charged with assault.

Likewise, deleted material in the following is likely to be interpreted in different ways.

3. I asked my son to take out the garbage, because my husband didn't have time to. [take out the garbage, or ask my son to take out the garbage]
4. I asked the neighbors to be quiet, because my husband didn't have the nerve to. [be quiet, or ask the neighbors to be quiet]

All of these sentences are, strictly speaking, ambiguous. They have two possible literal interpretations, so the writer must be able to estimate whether the reader will be able to make the inferences necessary for the intended interpretation of the anaphoric device, or whether it should be replaced by a non-anaphoric element.

It is our impression, from informal direct observation, that the language of children contains proportionally more (and more uninterpretable) anaphoric devices than that of adults. Whether or not this is true, it is a potential place to look for evidence that the child has not mastered the task of putting himself in his audience's place.

Similar problems arise for the use of definite descriptions and other referring expressions that depend on knowledge of the world and inference to succeed. Many of us, no doubt, have been faced with a lost child asking, "Where's my mommy?", apparently assuming that the whole world knows who his mommy is. It is obvious that this kind of knowledge-based inference is necessary for the interpretation of referring expressions in adult literature, as in the use of *the* in (5).

5. I was doing a barrel roll at 30,000 feet when suddenly the left wing fell off.

But perhaps less obviously, even the most elementary children's literature makes this same kind of demand on the reader, as in the following passage from a book designed for beginning readers, *Are You My Mother?*, by P. D. Eastman:

> The egg jumped. It jumped, and jumped, and jumped! Out came the baby bird!
> (pp. 8–9)

It appears from the author's use of *the baby bird* rather than *a baby bird* that he expects the reader to know where baby birds come from.

Inference is also involved in higher-level aspects of comprehension, in ways that can be crucial to the clarity of the text. Grice's (1975) notion of *conversational implicature* and the associated notion of *indirect speech act* (Green 1975, Morgan 1978a) have been shown to be very important to comprehension of adult language use. The essence of Grice's idea is that the speaker conveys much information through inferences which the listener makes about the speaker's intentions in saying what he says. These inferences are based on the assumption that both speaker and listener are assuming that rational discourse is governed by adherence to what Grice termed *maxims of conversation*. These include injunctions such as: *be brief, be relevant,* and so on. This framework allows, among other things, a reasonable account of how it is that (6) can be used to convey (7), (8) can be used to convey (9), and (10) can be used as a refusal by someone who has just been offered a cookie.

6. Can you reach the salt?
7. Pass me the salt.
8. Who would believe such a man?
9. Nobody would believe such a man.
10. I'm on a diet.

Again we find that this kind of inference-based process is not confined to adult language use. Thus the following from *Are You My Mother?* (pp 31–33):

> So the baby bird went on. Now he came to a cow.
> "Are you my mother?" he said to the cow.
> "How could I be your mother?" said the cow. "I am a cow."

In this passage the cow has not said she is not the baby bird's mother, but she has certainly tried to convey that she is not. To understand this point, the reader must be able to infer that the cow is giving premises, more or less, from which the baby bird must conclude that the cow cannot be his mother. But the reader can make this inference only if he or she knows that an animal of one species cannot be the mother of an animal of another species. This same inferential ploy occurs in another place, but more subtly, when a dog replies (p. 29) to the same question, "I am not your mother. I am a dog." Unless the reader is able to make the same inference here, the second sentence will seem a total *non-sequitur.*

This is a case of another important kind of inference that is demanded of the reader: inferences about the logical and pragmatic relations between the sentences that make up the text. In this case, the connection is that the second sentence provides justification for the first. Unless the reader makes these inferred connections between the sentences (and larger units) of the text, the reader cannot be considered to have understood the text at all. Another example from Eastman's book:

> Now he looked way, way down. He saw a boat.
> "There she is!" said the baby bird.

Here the reader must infer that there is a causal connection between the second and third sentences—that it was seeing the boat, and concluding that it was his mother, that led the baby bird to say, "There she is!" Lacking these inferences, the reader cannot make sense of the passage.

The point of this example is that, if the words of chilren's writers are any indication, the problem of inference is not an exotic complication of sophisticated prose, but faces the reader/writer from an early age. Many of these inferences are so inevitable that we are not conscious of making them. And to make explicit *all* the inferences that we intend be made would result in a text that was not just tedious, but downright silly, and in fact unreadable. Not only aesthetics but intelligibility requires that some of the work be left to the reader.

Although the ability to deal with inferences in the more or less passive process of comprehension apparently develops early, it does not seem to transfer easily into the active process of writing. The good writer must be able to anticipate at least subconsciously which inferences will be difficult for the reader. Placing too many inferential demands on the reader can make a passage nearly unintelligible, even though the sentences are well-constructed and logically argued.

We turn now to the consideration of two areas of writing assessment which we believe may benefit directly from an appreciation of the challenges writing poses in comparison to communication in conversation. First of all, it is obvious that overly demanding inferences, missing premises, and tangled text structure can only be detected in the process of trying to *understand* the text. But certain kinds of intended inferences are signalled linguistically, and when they are thus flagged, can be examined for reasonableness. As a trivial example, the word *so* is a signal of a causal inference, and the evaluator will be alerted to consider whether it is a reasonable one, and whether readers can reasonably be expected to make it. An evaluator may be similarly alerted to look specifically at the clarity of organization, since it is gradually becoming clear from linguistic research that many syntactic constructions function to signal aspects of text structure. Rules like inversion transformations (Green 1980), re-ordering rules (Hermon 1978, 1979), and copying rules (Prince 1978a, b) turn out to be signals of things like scene-setting, important event, topic change, gap in the narrative, and so on. For example, sentence (11), which begins a children's book (Bruna 1975), sets the scene for the events which constitute the story by first implying the existence of a little white house, and then *introducing* two protagonists of the story onto the scene in terms of their relation to the house.

11. In a little white house lived two rabbits.

Its uninverted counterpart (12) is more abrupt and does not serve this purpose as well.

12. Two rabbits lived in a little white house.

We suspect that good writers develop the ability to fully exploit these devices, most probably subconsciously, in the hope of leading the reader to infer the correct connections among the parts of the text. At any rate, this is a promising area of research, which may eventually yield a further understanding of how particular syntactic choices may be used to direct the reader's attention as well as inferences.

Second, there is the by now well-recognized question of the match between the writer's intention, purpose, and goal in writing, and the evaluator's perception of them. These notions are central to a pragmatic theory of communicative competence, and their importance cannot be underestimated. If evaluation of a student's writing is to be of any use at all, it must be clearly established whether the student understood the nature of the task assigned; or if it is self-assigned, it must be clear what the student is trying to do in her writing. To obtain any useful measure of a student's writing proficiency, it must be possible to compare what the student has written with what she was trying to write.

Clearly an evaluator cannot take the writer's communicative purpose for granted, unless the writing assignment is certifiably free of vagueness, and equally clearly, writers should likewise learn not to take it for granted. It would seem to be worthwhile to investigate the possibility, both as a means of assessment and as a means of skill training, of requiring the writer to state the purpose of what he has written, and to describe the structure of the piece he writes, either as part of the piece, or written separately, or even done orally in an interview. However this is done, it should *not* be merely an outline of the usual sort, showing merely the hierarchical structure of the text, but should state also the purpose and function of each of the sub-units, and their relation to one another. Given this kind of information, it should be possible to get an accurate view of how well the student accomplished what he set out to do. And any difficulties the student has in doing this summary of this own intentions may be useful as diagnostic of specific weaknesses in the student's training.

Alternatively, one might explore the possibility of zeroing in on specific strengths and weaknesses in an individual's writing by controlling tightly the format and purpose of the writing to be assessed. (We are not suggesting this as a general strategy for regular writing assignments, since it might prove to have a largely stultifying effect, but only for those infrequent occasions when detailed assessment of writing proficiency is needed). Restricting the student's freedom in this fashion will decrease the likelihood that the student's interpretation of the task will be different from the evaluator's.

It has other potential advantages as well. Different genres have different text structures, and place different demands on the writer. For example, in simple narrative, the unmarked order of sentences follows the order of events; whereas, in expository prose the order of sentences is a more complicated problem, for the relations are often not temporal, but logical, and there is not always an obvious place to begin. Narrative is consequently easier to write, at least in this respect, than expository prose. It may be possible, by choosing the right succession of genres and formats, to hold some aspects constant, making some decisions by fiat for the student, so that other aspects can be isolated and studied—and practiced—separately.

We have been developing a view that both the ability to write well, and the ability to assess writing accurately derive in part from being able to appreciate differences between oral and written communication. From this point of view, a good writer will be characterized as one who is aware of the reader's disadvantage in not being able to interrupt and let the writer know that the exposition isn't being followed, and who is able to make compensating adjustments in presentation. He will be considerate of his readership, taxing the reader's reconstructive and inferential capacities as little as possible, without, of course, talking down to him. This means he will have to be a good judge of what his audience knows, and to the extent that this is impossible, to be able to write in such a way that the more ignorant will be able to follow, but the less ignorant will not feel they are being talked down to. Speaking to a small group, he would most likely get immediate feedback if he went too far in either direction. In writing, he must know how to avoid going too far. Thus, to be a good writer means, in part at least, to be sensitive to the differences between spoken and written communication situations, and to be able to compensate for the unavailability of feedback in the latter by being explicit about intended purposes, implications, assumptions, and logical relations among parts of the exposition. Assessment, in this context, means evaluating the appropriateness and sufficiency of the steps the writer has taken to meet these challenges.

ACKNOWLEDGMENTS

The preparation and presentation of this material was supported by the National Institute of Education under Contract No. US-NIE-C-400-76-0116, through the Center for the Study of Reading at the University of Illinois, and by grants furnished by the National Endowment for the Humanities (Grant FC262628-76-1030), the Rockefeller Foundation, and the Andrew W. Mellon Foundation to the Center for Advanced Study in the Behavioral Sciences for support during 1978-70. We are grateful to all these agencies for their support, and to the Center for its hospitality.

REFERENCES

Bruna, D. 1975. Miffy. New York: Two Continents.

Eastman, P. D. 1960. Are you my mother? A Beginner Book. Random House.

Green, G. 1975. How to get people to do things with words. In Cole, P., and Morgan, J., eds. Syntax and semantics, vol. 3: Speech acts. Academic Press, 107-142.

Green, G. 1980 in press. Some wherefores of English inversion language, Vol. 56.

Grice, H. P. 1975. Logic and conversation. In Cole, P., and Morgan, J., eds. Syntax and semantics, vol. 3: Speech acts. Academic Press. 41-48.

Hermon, G. 1978. Unpublished ms. on a function of adverb preposing. University of Illinois, Urbana, Illinois.

Hermon, G. 1979. On the discourse structure of direct quotation. Technical Report 143, Center for the Study of Reading, University of Illinois, Champaign, Illinois.

Horn, L. 1972. On the semantic properties of logical operators in English. UCLA dissertation. Available from Indiana University Linguistics Club.

Kantor, R. 1977. The management and comprehension of discourse connection by pronouns in English. Ohio State University dissertation.

Keenan, J. M., and Kintsch, W. 1974. The identification of explicitly and implicitly presented information. In The representation of meaning in memory. W. Kintsch, ed. Hillsdale, N.J.: Lawrence Erlbaum.

Labov, W. 1969. The logic of nonstandard English. Report of the Twentieth Annual Round Table Meeting on Linguistics and Language Studies. James Alatis, ed. School of Language and Linguistics. Georgetown University, Washington, D. C.

Morgan, J. 1978a. Two types of convention in indirect speech acts. In Cole, P. Syntax and semantics, vol. 9: Pragmatics. Academic Press, 261-280.

Morgan, J. 1978b. Toward a rational model of discourse comprehension. In Waltz, D., ed. Theoretical issues in natural language processing-2. Association for Computing Machinery. New York. 109-114.

Prince, E. 1978a. A comprehension of WH-clefts and it-clefts in discourse. To appear in Language, vol. 54, no. 4.

Prince, E. 1978b. Left-dislocation, it makes life simpler. Paper presented at winter meeting of the Linguistic Society of America.

Quirk, R., Greenbaum, S., Svartvik, I., and Leech, G. 1972. A grammar of contemporary English. New York: Seminar Press.

Reddy, M. 1979. The conduit metaphor. In A. Ortony, ed. Metaphor and thought. Cambridge University Press, 284-324.

Rubin, A. 1978. A theoretical taxonomy of the differences between oral and written language. Technical Report 35, Center for the Study of Reading. University of Illinois, Champaign, Ill. (A version will appear in R. J. Spiro, B. C. Bruce, and W. F. Brewer, eds., Theoretical issues in reading comprehension, Hillsdale, N.J.: Lawrence Erlbaum Associates.)

Webber, B. L. 1978. A formal approach to discourse anaphora. Technical Report 3761. Bolt Beranek and Newman, Inc., Cambridge, Mass.

13 Measuring the Communicative Effectiveness of Prose

E. D. Hirsch, Jr.
David P. Harrington
University of Virginia

INTRODUCTION: NATURE OF THE MEASUREMENT

In this preliminary report we describe the theoretical basis for a new method of measuring the quality of prose. We also report on some results from our early experiments. The primary aim of the work is to develop a method of measuring prose effectiveness on a single appropriate scale—to design, in effect, a weighing instrument that gives a certain value to a piece of prose in the way that a scale gives a weight for a piece of matter. This method, even if successful in all respects, will not necessarily be appropriate for all forms of writing assessment. On the other hand, it can claim to be the only method of writing assessment devised so far which exhibits a direct correlation between the assessment of prose and its actual effects upon its target audience. We hope that the method (if it does prove itself to be duplicable and scientifically valid) will also have application to instruction and research in writing. Moreover, because of the connection in our experiments between writing and reading, we hope that the work may also shed light on some aspects of reading.

The name we have given our measurement is *intrinsic communicative effectiveness*. It is a measure derived from the actual effects of a piece of prose as compared to its potential optimal effects on a competent audience. One way of imagining this intrinsic method is to assume that an inexpert writer had written a piece which was then rewritten by a very good professional writer in such a way that the new piece had the very same meaning as the original inexpert piece. We would then have two synonymous texts, one not very well written, the other nearly optimal in its effectiveness. If we assume that the optimal version is 100 percent effective in achieving its communicative purpose, then the inexpert version will achieve that same purpose with less effectiveness, say in the proportion of 70/100. On the other hand, a very different original text might have an intrinsic effectiveness of 85/100 with respect to its optimal form. Because both inexpert texts will have been scored with respect to their own best versions, their scores would be comparable with each other. On this principle, we could determine a rank order of several heterogeneous texts according to their intrinsic communicative effectiveness.

From this schematic description it may be seen that our measurement depends on two theoretical concepts: an optimal synonymous version of a text, and a competent audience by whose performance we can accurately compare the effects of the two versions. These are in fact the distinctive features of the research which we have been conducting. A technique of writing assessment based on synonymous texts and screened subjects does not appear in the literature of writing assessment or psycholinguistics. Hence, the relevant literature could be conceived as immensely large or almost non-existent.

The concept of synonymous texts has been dealt with in philosophy, theoretical linguistics, and cognitive psychology, but we lack an authoritative discussion which brings together this theoretical and empirical work from the three fields. In the 1950's there was an intense discussion of synonymy among analytical philosophers, largely because of the implications of the subject for logic and philosophy of science. The important documents in this debate are Mates, (1952); Quine (1952, 1953); Church (1954); Putnam (1954); Goodman (1952); and Shwayder (1954). In a review of this literature, Hirsch (1975) argues that some key elements of the debate are irrelevant to the empirical question of whether synonymous texts exist in natural languages. The argument hinges on whether synonymy shall be understood as universal substitutability or occasional substitutability, that is, whether two texts must mean the same thing all the time or just some of the time. In the empirical domain, the possibility of occasional substitutability is sufficient to justify the synonymy concept, since it is a matter for empirical verification whether one text means the same as another in a given case.

A similar view is taken by Harris (1973) from the standpoint of theoretical linguistics. After an exhaustive, booklength account of the linguistic arguments that have been put forward on both sides of the question, Harris concludes that there is no empirical or theoretical bar to perfect synonymy in natural languages. In fact, he concludes that synonymous utterances occur with great frequency. Since the appearance of Harris's book, no new linguistic arguments have been brought forward which modify or falsify his arguments and conclusions.

In psychological studies the evidence for synonymous texts is indirect. Even since the work of Fillenbaum and Sachs (1966, 1967), the evidence has grown that memory of linguistic meaning is to some degree independent of a definite, unique word sequence. Even if it is true, as shown by Kintsch and Vipond (1977), that some surface features tend to be remembered as constitutive of meaning, it is also true, as they concede, that some surface features are *not* constitutive of meaning, and could be replaced by other words and syntax. This same position was reached independently on theoretical grounds by Hirsch (1978). He argues that the binding of a meaning to a particular word sequence is a variable which depends upon the character of the discourse in question. In poetry, for instance, the possibilities of synonymy will be less than in technical prose.

In none of these studies, however, has there been a systematic attempt to produce synonymous texts, and then to test whether the attempt was successful. This is precisely what we do in our present work. To make our test we use an operational definition of synonymy under which we apply the following rigorous requirement: Can any question be devised, no matter how subtle or probing, which would be answered differently with regard to the meaning of the two texts? If anyone is able to devise such a question, we adjust the rewritten text to meet the rigorous criterion. It has been pointed out to us in meetings that this method depends upon *interpretation* of a text's meaning, and that under a different interpretation the synonymy test might not be passed. Our answer is that *all* discussions of synonymy are necessarily *post interpretationem*—both arguments for synonymy and arguments against. An additional answer is that nearly all the psychological effects of texts are *post interpretationem,* which is a very important reason for bringing the variable of meaning under control. In summary then, while there is widespread skepticism with regard to the existence of synonymous texts, this skepticism is fully met and disposed of in the literature. Moreover, since we use a clear operational definition of synonymy, and a clear operational test of it, our claim to synonymy in actual practice is open to verification.

While the careful screening of subjects for experimental purposes is hardly a novelty in science, it is a method little used in psycholinguistic research, possibly because of the well-grounded view that subject screening often amounts to the manipulation of conclusions. On the other hand, we believe that for certain kinds of psycholinguistic research, subject screening is a theoretical as well as a practical necessity. Our view is that so long as the procedures for screening are well-defined and duplicable, the problem of skewing the conclusions does not arise, and that screening in fact makes the conclusions more precise and reliable.

The screening process that is required is a cultural rather than a psychological screening. Reading and writing are learned, acculturated skills, and in reading and writing experiments we cannot assume that American College Sophomores are automatically appropriate subjects on the pattern of Norwegian White Rats. Some of the subjects who have participated in our work could not accurately read the directions for completing the experimental task. Indeed, the wide variations that are known to exist in reading acculturation caused some psychologists to suggest to us that our efforts were doomed from the start. For our part, we believe that the use of an unscreened random cross section of readers is an inappropriate way to measure the effectiveness of writing, and is more appropriate for measuring the characteristics of the readers.

Theorists of writing like Ong (1975) and many others have pointed out that any piece of writing assumes a definite range of cultural knowledge in its audience, including linguistic and translinguistic knowledge. A basic principle in gauging the intrinsic effectiveness of writing is therefore to observe its effects on the kind of audience for whom the writing was intended. This is altogether obvious in extreme cases such as a technical article in astrophysics, and extreme cases are useful in disclosing features of ordinary discourse which might otherwise be overlooked. Bransford, Barclay, and Franks (1972) have shown that extra-textual knowledge in a reader can become part of the meaning that the reader remembers as being in the text itself, so intimate is the interaction between a text and the acculturated knowledge of a reader. Similarly Marshall and Glock (1978) have shown that a distinct difference can exist in remembered text structure as between Ivy League students and community college students. We make no such sociological distinctions in screening our readers; we simply determine from their performance alone whether or not they are competent, acculturated readers for the task at hand. On that basis we exclude some readers at elite institutions, and include readers from community colleges and elsewhere. Ideological and social issues do not come into play here, or at least they should not, since the aim of education in literacy is to help as many people as possible become competent readers of several discourse types.

Our method of screening is at present based primarily on accuracy of remembered meaning, but we are still refining and testing our methods. In determining the best method of screening readers, we plan to test out methods which not only guage overall performance, but which also correlate all of our readers on the basis of equivalent control texts. Since such screening methods are entirely *ex post facto,* and can be used at any time on our stored data, advances in our techniques of screening can be applied at any time. What we are stressing here is not the validity of a particular screening method, but the validity of the screening principle in this kind of research.

In this general introductory description, we should explain, however briefly, the relationship of our work to the theory and practice of writing assessment.

The most widely used method of asssessment is of course the subjective judgment of the classroom teacher. Research has proved (McColly, 1970) what many students suspect, namely that classroom teachers differ greatly in their judgments. In a nine-class rank ordering, their correlation is about 40., which is only marginally better than the .31 correlation for the literate population at large (Diederich, 1961). To overcome this diversity of judgment is the aim of the method devised by The Educational Testing Service (ETS). This method could be called *socialized holistic scoring*. A *Chief Reader*, in consultation with experienced lieutenants called *Table Leaders* gives exemplary scores to papers written on a single assigned topic. The criteria for the scores are not explained; instead the group learns through examples what counts as a 1, 2, 3, or 4. In time the Table Leaders conform themselves to the implicit conventions that have governed the decisions of the Chief Reader, and after mastering these conventions, the Table Leaders go out to teach the conventions to numerous panels of sub-readers. By this means, the scoring of single-topic papers is kept reasonably consistent among the hundreds of readers who come together at a big ETS scoring session. The theoretical flaw in this eminently practical method is that everything hinges upon the unstated, ad hoc principles of the Chief Reader and his committee. Godschalk (1966) refers in passing to ETS evidence that papers from one year scored under one Chief Reader would get different scores in another year under another Chief Reader. The scoring principles rest on no stated criteria, and have never been correlated with the actual effects of writing.

This fault of inexplicitness is overcome in the *Primary Trait* method used by The National Assessment of Educational Progress (NAEP). Here the criteria are stated in detail for a paper written on an assigned topic, and *protocols* are provided to readers to help them decide which score category a paper belongs in. But these scoring traits are grounded only in a committee judgment which assumes that all student writers will have the same aim in their responses to the topic (Lloyd-Jones, 1977)—a fallacious assumption. Moreover, the committee's original judgment has no more independent validity than the committee judgment under the ETS systems. Again, the method is eminently practical, but it is also arbitrary to the extent that it can change as the committee changes, and bears no demonstrated relationship to the actual effects of writing.

Another method of rating papers, according to the average length and complexity of their *T-units,* while highly objective and duplicatable, has fallen into disfavor because it does not discriminate between papers which almost everyone would agree are bad and those which almost everyone would agree are good. A T-unit is *A single main clause plus whatever else goes with it* (Hunt, 1977). No doubt, a writer's ability to control a long, clause-ridden sentence is indeed evidence of syntactic maturity, but this ability could be tested very directly. The correlation between *T-units* and the quality of writing is an arbitrary and unsound correlation, in the view of most specialists.

WHAT QUALITIES CAN BE VALIDLY MEASURED?

The chief theoretical constraint on writing assessment is the impossibility of prior general agreement either about the important traits of writing, or about the weighting of those traits. In the real world, as Hume observed, we agree even less than we seem to agree (Hume, 1757). For example, we seem to agree, on the whole, that ideas are more important than diction in writing, but we do not finally agree on the value of a particular paper's ideas. We seem to agree initially that the persuasiveness of writing is more important than its mere lucidity, but in the end we are not uniformly persuaded by the same rhetorical arguments and strategies. In short, when we are left to ourselves, we will give very different holistic scores to individual pieces of writing—a fact that is well-documented in the assessment literature (Diederich, 1974; Diederich, French and Carlton, 1961).

This state of affairs imposes a serious theoretical constraint on the goal of valid assessment. Since we differ among ourselves in valuing writing, we cannot expect to achieve uniformity of judgment when we are rating the quality of writing. That is to say, we cannot expect uniformity *unless* we agree to adopt special criteria on the basis of their overwhelming rational appeal. The best theoretical candidate for that approach to assessment is Aristotle's principle of *intrinsic* evaluation as found in *The Poetics*. On that ancient principle, we judge a thing not according to our scheme of values, but to the values intrinsic to the thing itself—its entelechy. In simple terms, intrinsic evaluation means judging writing according to how well it does that which we believe it is *trying* to do. On this principle, each assessor temporarily foregoes his own values in a favor of the writer's. In that way, all assessors, though judging independently, could reach similar results by applying non-arbitrary standards that were *intrinsic* to the particular piece of writing (Hirsch, 1977).

The intrinsic approach to evaluation is the only one known to us which can overcome the practical problem of achieving uniform independent evaluations among judges who hold very different values. But this abstract Aristotelian principle would be of little practical use unless we could translate it into criteria that are directly applicable to writing. And this, in turn, would serve little purpose unless the criteria thus derived had an intuitive appeal to the literate public.

Another way of stating this practical problem is to say that valid assessment will depend, finally, on our being able to distinguish those significant qualities of writing about which people can agree, from those qualities about which people cannot possibly agree. That is, we need to discriminate the solvable problems of assessment from the unsolvable ones (Medawar, 1967). This means not only that we are theoretically constrained to use the Aristotelian principle of intrinsic evaluation, but also that we are practically constrained to judge only those traits of writing which can be judged similarly by independent groups of actual readers. Figure 1 distinguishes those traits which we can score with independent agreement from those traits which we cannot so score. It differs from traditional lists of *analytical* criteria in that its categories are determined by the logic of the assessment problem itself, and in particular by the need for independent rational agreement based on intrinsic principles.

The interpretation of this figure is straightforward. Independently valid assessments are limited necessarily to the domain where independent agreement is possible. Within that domain, we know that we can currently score aspects of correctness with independent validity. But, since we have no sound principle for *weighting* different aspects of correctness, we solve that problem by leaving these as separate unweighted categories. Their importance as factors will vary with different purposes and situations, and their weightings are left to *ad hoc* decisions. This means, therefore, that the full remaining weight of the assessment problem falls on the holistic domains of *intrinsic rhetorical effectiveness* and *intrinsic communicative effectiveness*.

At the present time we lack evidence to show that the rhetorical effectiveness of writing can be measured empirically, or judged with substantive accuracy. That is not surprising. Audiences are much more variable in what persuades them than they are in what communicates to them.

Type of Agreement	Traits
Consistent, Independent Agreement is Impossible	Intellectual Quality Aesthetic Quality
Consistent Independent Agreement may be impossible	Rhetorical Effectiveness
Consistent Independent Agreement is theoretically Possible	Communicative Effectiveness Correctness { Lexical Grammatical Orthographic

FIG. 1   Criteria for Writing Assessment

An identical grant proposal will persuade one panel but fail to persuade another, although its meaning is communicated clearly in both cases. We believe, therefore, that the category of *intrinsic communicative effectiveness* is the most promising topic for empirical assessment research. Successful empirical results in this area could later lead to subjective assessments that are strictly valid and independent.

WHAT IS INTRINSIC COMMUNICATIVE EFFECTIVENESS?

What does intrinsic communicative effectiveness mean? *Intrinsic,* as we have seen, means the kind and degree of effectiveness intended by the writer, rather than extrinsic criteria imposed by an assessor. An intrinsic measure is therefore governed entirely by the writer's intended meanings—whether they are muddy or clear, cogent or silly. If it appears that a writer intended to be vague and obscure,as some politicians do for good reason, then an intrinsic assessor will judge only the effectiveness with which that writer's vagueness and obscurity are conveyed. Intrinsicality, therefore, boils down to this: the writer is granted his meanings and purposes, and is judged only on the effectiveness with which those meanings and purposes are fulfilled. If intrinsic assessments are to be tested empirically, we must be able to create for experimental purposes, versions of writing samples which are nearly optimal in their communicative effectiveness and nearly identical in their meaning. This topic will be discussed in the following section.

The second aspect of Intrinsic Communicative Effectiveness, *communicative,* signifies those effects of discourse on readers which speech-act theorists have termed *locutionary* and *illocutionary* effects. (Austin 1962). It signifies that conveyance of *meaning* in the broadest sense of that term—i.e., implicit meaning as well as explicit meaning; attitudinal and stylistic as well as propositional meaning. It signifies, in short, the entire communicative dimension of writing, and excludes only its persuasive or *perlocutionary* effects. These latter effects are excluded not because they fall outside the writer's intrinsic purposes, but because (as we argued above) present evidence indicates that perlocutionary effects are too variable to be determined empirically for the heterogeneous audiences to which writing is normally directed.

The third aspect of Intrinsic Communicative Effectiveness, *effectiveness,* refers to actual or potential semantic effects on an audience. A piece of writing is said to be more effective if it produces the same intended semantic effects on the target audience with less effort and consequently in less time. That is the only criterion by which intrinsic effectiveness could be measured, since any semantic effect other than the intended one, would not be intrinsic to the

due to random fluctuation in factual, linguistic, and cultural knowledge of the sample readers. Such a broad general audience is, as we know, assumed in a great deal of published writing—quantitatively in most of the published writing that most of us read.

Because samples for a general audience are the easiest kind to assemble for experimental purposes, we have been restricting our experiments for Intrinsic Communicative Effectiveness to writing samples which assume just such a broad audience. Our rule of thumb is to use writing which posits a readership falling somewhere in the range between the *Reader's Digest* and *The Washington Post*. In an American context, that is precisely the kind of audience which most nearly approximates Dr. Johnson's common reader. As matters turn out, our preliminary statistical results have suggested the reality of that venerable theoretical construct.

A TYPICAL PRESENTATION DESCRIBED

A good way to convey the character of our experimental procedures would be to describe what happens in a typical audience presentation. At 7:30 p.m. a group of about 185 people assemble from the Charlottesville community— predominantly college students, but with some townspeople, professors, and graduate students. They assemble under the inducement of being paid for an hour's work, and also of being part of an experiment that is connected with the effort to improve the teaching of writing. The same arrangements are made at other colleges and with other groups. At the front of the large lecture room is a large digital timer made to order for us by a scoreboard manufacturing company. The timer, which can be seen easily from any part of the room, reads out in seconds, in four places. It runs continuously through the session, and enables the subjects to mark down their times as they complete tasks in the experimental booklets. For each session, two complementary booklets are distributed after having been shuffled in an ababababab pattern to assure good distribution of the readers for each booklet.

The instructions for reading the booklets may vary somewhat from session to session, depending upon the type of experiment we are conducting and the type of refinements in method we have evolved. In general the directions instruct the subjects to read at a comfortable pace for them, not to be disturbed by other reading at different paces (they are told that the booklets contain different materials) and to read as accurately as possible, since we only count the results for readers who score about 90 per cent right on the questionnaire for a given paper. The usual pattern for the two booklets is given in Table 1 with *a* representing the inexpert version, or the debased version, and *b* representing the expert version:

TABLE 1

Booklet A	Booklet B
1a	1b
2 (Control)	2 (Control)
3b	3a
4a	4b
5b	5a
6a	6b
7b	7a
8 (Filler)	8 (Filler)

After each paper there is a questionnaire on its content and meaning. The subjects are asked to answer this questionnaire only after they have marked down the time reading for the essay. They are also asked to mark down the timer reading when they have finished the questionnaire. So, for each paper we will have typically three timer readings, one at the start of reading, one at the end of reading, and one at the end of answering the questionnaire. Readers are told that the session will last 50 minutes once the instructions have been read and understood. In order to make sure that fast readers have something to occupy them during the whole 50 minutes, we put at the end a very long, very difficult filler essay, with a long, difficult questionnaire. Readers are told that they are not expected to finish, and that we will gratefully use whatever they complete. In the instructions, we try to eliminate some of the anxieties and competitiveness that might affect the validity of the reading data, and we assume that the two groups will exhibit about the same anxiety quotient. (In fact, the readers find the event an enjoyable one, and we notice that the number of participants goes up as the term progresses.) When the 50 minutes are up, readers are asked to stop and to fill out the reader profile sheet at the end of the booklet. So far, we have not had occasion to use the information on the profile sheet but we do, of course, record its data in the computer file in case the material will be of use to us or to others later on.

FORMING SYNONYMOUS VERSIONS

Our graduate program in English studies and creative writing, provides us with a large pool of talented and experienced writers. From this large group we have selected the ablest writers and editors to participate in our project. In order to produce a pair of synonymous versions for an inexpert original the rewriters are organized into teams of two members. Each team member independently writes a first-class synonymous version of an actual student paper. At that point the two writers confer to consider three issues: (1) whether each rewrite is strictly synonymous, (2) whether the questionnaire conforms to the agreed on principles detailed below and (3) whether the two rewrites could be improved in some ways. For the nonce, our writers restrict the word count of their versions to keep them within five per cent of the original word count. They have found that this is usually quite easy to do, since inexpert writers generally leave some of their meanings too inexplicit, and make other meanings unnecessarily explicit.

We are often asked under what principles our writers form their superior versions. Their overall principle is, of course, to convey the meanings of the original as effectively as possible. We do *not* prescribe the methods used to do this, and we believe that any attempt to do so at this point would be a serious mistake. There is so much variability in the effects of a particular writing technique, so much interaction between technique, meaning, and target audience, that any attempt to prescribe technique closely would be inadvisable. A practiced writer is constantly making delicate adjustments among all of these variables—adjustments which can be analyzed after the fact, but which cannot be prescribed before the fact without reference to the particular original.

The time for analysis, we believe, is after we have perfected an objective method of measurement, not before. Of course, our writers do follow certain well established general principles, documented in the handbooks, and followed by all good writers. Where a title is missing, we add one to orient the reader. We tend to write in extended paragraphs, because of the psychological necessity for the paragraph in writing (Hirsch 1977). Our sentences are varied and interconnected. Our organization is signposted, and so on. In short, the writing is the *kind* of writing that would be produced by an experienced professional, whereas the particularities of our techniques are inevitably highly variable. So far, our expert rewrites score close against each other, even when they are in very different styles.

Before a version is chosen for audience presentation, it is vetted by a second expert team which checks the papers again for synonymy, checks the questionnaire for appropriateness, and chooses what it guesses to be the better of the two rewrites. In checking for synonymy, our procedure is to play the part of the devil's advocate in order to discover some question about meaning which would be answered differently for the two versions. These questions, as we observed in Part I, are as subtle and probing as possible. Even if some small element of non-synonymy gets past this double screening, we believe that the procedure guarantees a sufficient degree of synonymy to make the results valid on that score. By having two expert synonymous versions, we are able to make calibration experiments to discover just how much variance in the results can be expected if another researcher attempted to duplicate our results.

FORMING QUESTIONNAIRES

At present our teams are using rules of thumb and common sense to make up the questionnaires. This is the only approach that has commended itself to us, since the appropriateness of a type of question will depend greatly on the type of essay being probed. Our method has been asked one question for every 75 words, to make the questions independent so that the answer to one does not automatically imply the answer to another; to vary the questions between explicit and implicit meaning where appropriate; to ask about small points only when an argument can be made that the point is not trivial in context; to cover several aspects of the meaning; to avoid distant implications in the meaning. While we are aware that following these rules of thumb may not generate duplicatable results, certain consistencies in our data indicate that they do. We hope that our future experiments will show that our methods do in fact lead to duplicatable results when we apply different questionnaires to previously presented papers. We are also designing methods which will compensate for any arbitrariness introduced by the questionnaires.

AN EXAMPLE

We think it will be instructive at this point to use some results we have observed for a specific pair of texts in order to illustrate the kind of data we have gathered and the kind of information contained in the data. Since more extensive descriptions and analyses of the data will be published elsewhere, we will keep technical descriptions of our statistical methods to a minimum here. However, the use of some statistical terminology is unavoidable.

The following data were generated from a student essay about the dilemma faced by an aspiring young journalist who was trying to decide whether to work on the staff of *Time* or of *Newsweek*. The original paper and a presumably superior rewritten version were given to a total of 239 readers in presentations at the University of Virginia and at the Sargeant Reynolds Community College. Both the original and the rewritten versions were placed in the fifth position in booklets which contained eleven essays each. After reading a particular version, readers were asked to answer seven multiple choice questions. The basic data gathered are summarized in Table 2.

In going from an original to a rewritten version, we have most often observed improvements in all three of the measurements summarized above. However, several rewritten versions have shown improvements in fewer than the three measures, as does the *Time* and *Newsweek* essay. This is to be expected, since it might not be possible to improve on some aspects of papers which were moderately well written to begin with.

TABLE 2

	Version	
	Original	Rewrite
Numbers of readers	118	121
Average reading rate	186.80 wpm	212.85 wpm
Average elapsed time answering questions	103.94 sec.	103.44 sec.
Average number correct answers	6.26	6.02

Observations for each of the above readers were taken on a common, control essay, so that adjustments could be made if the two groups of readers differed significantly on common measurements. In this case, the observed differences between the two groups on common measures was only slight, and any adjustments made with statistical techniques would be minimal.

The observed differences between the groups reading the two versions of the *Time* and *Newsweek* essay is a statistically significant difference. To be specific, a multivariate analysis of covariance, with the measures on the control used as covariates, produces a value of Hotelling's trace statistic which is significant at a level less than .001.

It is clear in this case (and statistical analyses support the observation) that the *most substantial* difference between the groups lies in the measured reading rates. The difference in average reading rates indicates roughly the difference in efficiency with which readers were able to assimilate the information contained in the two versions of the paper. The average reading rate on the original was only 87.8% of the average rate for the superior version. Of course, since our average rates are really estimates based on a total sample of 239, this ratio of average rates would vary from sample to sample. Calculations show that the standard error of the value 87.8% is approximately 3.1%.

A closer examination of the data for this essay sheds light on the following question: do the stylistic improvements in the superior version benefit fast and slow readers equally? Figure 2 presents the information in graphical form. We grouped the readers of each of the two versions into quintiles so that those readers whose rates fell in the lowest twentieth percentile would be placed in the first quintile, those whose rates fell between twentieth and fortieth would be placed in the second quintile, etc. The mean rates for each quintile on each version were then calculated. In Figure 2, mean rates for each of the quintiles were plotted above the appropriate quintile numbers. The values for the superior version were then connected with a solid line.

The implication of the figure is clear: its slight funnel shape demonstrates that the absolute gain in reading rate tends to increase for the faster readers of this piece. Several, but not all of the papers we have studied yield the same

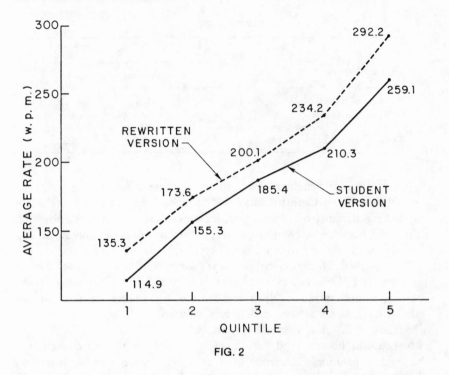

FIG. 2

pattern in a similar analysis. In some instances, the two lines are parallel, indicating that roughly the same absolute gain in rate is provided by the superior version for readers regardless of their reading rate. Some graphs show the smallest rate differentials for slow readers, while others show the largest rate differentials for slow readers. One of the aims of our further research will be to determine what characteristics of writing cause fast (or slow) readers to benefit disproportinatley from improvements in style.

Other analyses of our data show interesting variabilities in reader performance. Graphs similar to Figure 2 may be produced by forming quintiles that rank the readers according to rates observed on pieces of writing other than the one under study. We have, for instance, formed rankings of readers based on their average reading rate for all the writing in the booklet. If the booklet has writing that is heterogeneous enough, such a ranking will give a reasonably accurate ordering of the readers by their inherent reading speed. Graphs produced by this second method do not present as sharp a picture as Figure 2. The dotted and solid lines show various deviations from parallelism, and even cross with alarming regularity. The reason, however, seems clear. A high degree of familiarity with the topic addressed in a piece of writing can cause a usually slow reader to speed up, while readers unfamiliar with the topic will slow down. We have computed rank order correlations for reader rates on a given piece over against their rank order based on average rates for a booklet, and we find considerable fluctuation in these correlations. For a booklet such as that from which the *Time* and *Newsweek* essay was drawn, the correlations can vary from .64 to .84. Undoubtedly a strong influence on this variability was variation in topic familiarity. The implication is that topic familiarity is an important variable to control when assessing the communicative effectiveness of a text. We shall have to determine by further experiments whether our individual rank orderings, tailor-made to each pair of texts, is, as we believe, a sufficient control for topic familiarity.

Further presentations have shown consistent, duplicatable results when text pairs are presented to new audiences that are culturally similar to earlier ones. In addition, further analysis confirms that the most significant co-determinant of stylistic effects upon readers is topic familiarity. Thus, quite unexpectedly, our work is showing that the actual communicative effectiveness of writing depends crucially upon supra-linguistic (cultural) factors. Even with subject screening, these change with time, place, and subject population. We are planning new types of presentations to isolate this effect, and to analyze its implications for pedagogy.

Owing to the long interval between the writing and the printing of this essay, we are able to make the following additional comments about method and interpretation. *Method:* The best controlled way of forming synonymous text pairs is to degrade a good printed text according to definite rules, instead of rewriting a poor text. The pair thus formed will closely agree with another pair formed from the text under the same rules. *Interpretation:* A consistent result of our presentations is the counterintuitive one that an increase in topic familiarity causes an *increase* in the differential effects of a text pair upon an audience. Synonymous texts thus serve as sensitive indicators of certain supra-linguistic factors that affect reading.

CONCLUSION

Let us imagine for a moment that our work on intrinsic measurement has been successfully completed. Let us suppose that on the basis of our results any researcher could take the original *Time* and *Newsweek* essay, revise it according to explicit principles, present the versions to appropriate audiences under explicit ground rules, analyze the results in a standard way, and always come up with the same score for intrinsic effectiveness. This scoring would be based, let us say, on a scale of 1, 2, 3, 4, corresponding to D, C, B, A, with room between the scores for pluses and minuses. Under that system, the *Time* and *Newsweek* essay might get, say, a 3, and this result would be duplicated by any researcher. But obviously a classroom teacher is not going to run this elaborate and expensive test in order to score this trivial essay. In fact nobody is going to run such tests as a standard method of evaluation.

The practicality of our work, insofar as it concerns evaluation, depends, therefore, on its educative potential. Can a number of exemplary cases be analyzed in such a way that people could learn how to make subjective judgments which correspond to objective measurements? Present evidence suggests it will be possible.

For one thing, we know that a high degree of reliability is achieved by the socialized readers for an ETS scoring session on a single topic, even though the principles of scoring are largely implicit and arbitrary. The principles upon which our envisioned method would depend would be explicit and non-arbitrary. While the scoring would be a matter of subjective judgment, as in the ETS system, the scoring principles might be learned by anyone who could imagine how an appropriate reader would in fact read the piece of writing, and how a first-class version might affect such a reader. Any good writer must make just that kind of imaginative linguistic leap. If we discovered that people could duplicate objective scores with consistent accuracy, such people could be depended on to give scores that were both valid and reliable.

It is not yet clear whether this non-arbitrary approach to assessment will turn out to be appropriate or acceptable even if it works. But even if such a method were not widely accepted, the probability still remains that measurements of intrinsic effectiveness will yield interesting and perhaps surprising knowledge about writing. It may help uncover information about some significant factors not just in an effective style, but also in the revision process, and in the correlations between reading and writing.

ACKNOWLEDGMENTS

The research described in this chapter was supported in part by funds from the National Endowment for the Humanities, and in part by funds from the University of Virginia.

REFERENCES

Austin, J. L. 1962. *How to do things with words.* Oxford: Oxford University Press.

Bransford, J. D. Barclay, J. R., and Franks, J. J. Sentence memory: A constructive versus interpretative approach. *Cognitive Psychology,* 1972, *3,* 193–209.

Brewer, W. F. Memory for Ideas: Synonym Substitution. *Memory and Cognition,* 1975, *3,* 458–464.

Church, Alonzo, Intentional isomorphism and identity of belief, *Philosophical Studies,* 1954, *5,* 65–73.

Diederich, P. G., French, J. W, and Carlton, S. T. *Factors in judgments of writing ability,* Princeton, N.J.: Educational Testing Service, 1961.

Fillenbaum, S. Memory for gist: Some relevant variables. *Language and Speech,* 1966, *9,* 217–227.

Godschalk, F. I., Swineford, F., Coffman, W. E. *The measurement of writing ability,* New York, College Entrance Examination Board, 1966.

Goodman, N. On likeness of meaning. In Linsky, L., ed. *Semantics and the philosophy of language,* Cambridge, MA, 1952.

Harris, R. *Synonymy and linguistic analysis,* Oxford: Blackwell, 1973.

Hirsch, E. D. Stylistics and synonymity. *Critical Inquiry,* 1975, *1,* 559–579.

Hirsch, E. D. Reading and writing, *The Cornell Review,* 1978, *4,* 115–126.

Hume, D. *Of the Standard of taste.* Edinburgh, 1757.

Hunt, K. Early blooming and late blooming syntactic structures. *Evaluating writing,* Cooper, C. R. and Odell, L., Urbana: NCTE, 1977.

Johnson, S. *Lives of the english poets.* The Life of Gray. London, 1781.

Linsky, L. Synonymity. In P. Edwards (Ed.), *The Encyclopaedia of Philosophy.* New York: Macmillan, 1967.

Marshall, N. and Glock, M. Comprehension of connected discourse: A study into the structure of text and information recalled. *Reading Research Quarterly,* 14, 1978, 10–56.

Mates, B. Synonymity. In *Semantics and the philosophy of language,* ed. L. Linsky, Urbana: X 1952.

Medawar, P. B. *The art of the soluble.* London: Methuen, 1967.

Mellon, J. C. *National Assessment and the Teaching of English.* Urbana, Ill.: NCTE, 1975.

Meyer, B. *The organization of prose and its effects on memory,* Amsterdam: North Holland, 1975.

Kintsch, W. and Vipond, D. Reading comprehension and readability in educational practice and psychological theory, presented at conference on memory, Uppsala, 1977.

Lloyd-Jones, R. Primary trait scoring. In *Evaluating writing,* ed. Cooper, and Odell, Urbana: NCTE 1977.

Ong, W. J. *The Writer's Audience is Always a Fiction.* PMLA, 1975, *90,* 9–21.

Perelman, C. *Rhetorique et Philosophie.* Paris, 1952.

Putnam, H. Synonymity and the analysis of belief sentences. *Analysis,* 6, 1954, 114–122.

Quine, W. Two dogmas of empiricism, in *From a logical point of view,* Cambridge, MA, 1953.

Quine, W. Notes on existence and necessity, in *Semantics and the philosophy of language,* ed. Linsky, L., Urbana, 1952.

Sachs, J. Recognition memory for syntactic and semantic aspects of connected discourse. *Perception and Psychophysics,* 1967, *2,* 437–442.

Shwayder, D. Some remarks on synonymity and the language of semantics, *Philosophical Studies,* 5, 1954, 1–5.

14 Writing, Text, and the Reader

Lawrence T. Frase
Bell Laboratories

Prescriptive models of effective writing need formal empirical support. The use of a concept such as *coherence* to describe discourse, for example, suggests general properties of text, but there can be considerable variation in what the term means. One way of assigning more precise meaning to terms such as *coherence* is to begin by asking how such concepts might be measured. Having answered this question, one can then vary characteristics of written prose and determine whether they influence reading. An empirical orientation urges us, then, to look for evidence that certain aspects of written production affect readers in specific ways. While it is useful to study written products independent of readers, unless we can make clear distinctions about the characteristics of writing and predict their communicative effects, we may perpetuate unfounded assumptions about writing styles and how they communicate.

How the developing writer understands the needs of potential readers and how writing is varied to meet those needs are important questions for research. Therefore, there should be at least three goals of empirical research in writing:

1. Develop a better understanding of the elements of written discourse that control reading process.
2. Characterize the psychological processes that mediate discourse effects.
3. Develop methods for observing reading outcomes.

In this paper I describe several empirical studies which explored the communicative effects of technical documents. I also discuss some implications for research in writing and instructional practice. In these studies

(Schwartz, Fisher, & Frase, 1977; Frase & Schwartz, 1979) we began with a general question about the quality of writing. In order to understand the nature of writing problems, we were led to develop methods for testing reader response, to identify critical characteristics of written products, and to explore new text designs. Although these studies are limited in the features of written text that they explore, they raise a number of important issues concerning the processes and products of writing. The studies also illustrate how an empirical approach to understanding communicative effects of writing might be extended to investigating effects of other features of discourse structure and organization.

CONTEXTS FOR WRITING AND THE USE OF TECHNICAL DOCUMENTS

Reading researchers and text designers have been interested in understanding the features of documents that make them comprehensible to a variety of readers. In our work, we were especially interested in features of technical documents in the telecommunications area. While our background of experimental research on reading provided us with a context in which to view writing, we felt inadequate to make recommendations concerning the design of technical documents, based solely on research on reading, without first trying to understand the broad range of factors that constrain document writing and use. Since research on reading provides only one perspective on the problem, we wanted to explore the milieu in which document writing occurs in order to develop a realistic assessment of the origins of composition problems.

We began with a series of systematic interviews with writers of technical documents (consisting of a set of standard questions) to determine how and why documents were written (Schwartz, Fisher, & Frase, 1977). These interviews revealed a diversity of writing skills, tasks and activities. Some writers had authored textbooks, others had little experience and were working to develop better knowledge of the areas in which they had to write. For most of these writers, the act of putting ideas into words was not viewed as a major obstacle. Moreover, we observed very few writers who were sitting at a desk with pencil in hand. Rather, the planning and coordination of information appeared to constitute the bulk of their activities. This led us to interviews with administrative staff to determine how documents were planned and coordinated.

We also interviewed engineering and craft employees in the field and at their homes bases to study how documents were used, and we collected samples of documents and instances of problems in using documents. We asked employees to look up information and to solve other problems with a variety of documents. This descriptive work expanded our conception of the origins of documentation problems, taking us far beyond our initial interest in the psychological factors involved in document writing and use.

Our descriptive studies suggested seven points that might give rise to documentation problems and which could result in excess cost, absence of critical information or comprehensibility problems. The seven points were:

1. Training of writers.
2. Planning of documents.
3. Availability of preliminary information for document writers.
4. Design and writing of documents.
5. Evaluation of documents.
6. Distribution of documents.
7. Use of documents.

The documents that we reviewed were perceived by users and writers to be good documents. Yet instances of specific problems could be cited in each of these seven areas. The main point is that a variety of related factors contributed to the written products we examined. Thus, one might try to improve documents in a number of ways: by redesigning texts, training writers, or by approaching the problem as a management problem remote from the writer's or reader's task. For instance, equipment documents might lack important information on operating procedures. The origin of such problems is not necessarily in the writing, but may reflect that preliminary documents, available to a writer, do not contain sufficient information. In turn, this preliminary information depends upon early planning among management, technical and writing staff. Furthermore, the occurrence of such problems highlights the importance of evaluation procedures to detect and localize the details of missing information.

This brief sketch of the factors that constrain effective communication shows that a written product is much more than the act of putting words on paper. It is the result of a broad range of interconnected task and planning constraints that condition the content and form of the final product. Sixty to seventy percent of the communicative problems that we encountered stemmed from management or planning functions rather than design or editing functions. Our findings emphasize the importance, for composition, of developing in the writer (or otewise making available to the writer) an appropriate knowledge base for the support of writing activities. Research by others confirms the crucial role that planning plays in writing. For example, Matsuhashi and Cooper (1978) have found that high school students spend over 70% of their writing time in silence, presumably retrieving and organizing (thinking about) information. The amount of time that their subjects gave to what might be called the information management aspects of writing is magnified in the creation of the highly complex documents that have become a necessary support for the workings of our technological society.

Just as the composing process of individual writers is fruitful ground for the study of individual differences, so are the composing processes associated with publications in business and industry. To some extent, the processes engaged in by individual writers, for example, planning (see Flower & Hayes, in this volume), are mirrored in institutional documentation systems. In general, two important research areas in the study of writing are the role of writer knowledge, including the availability of source information in printed form, and the information planning and management activities of writers.

While our studies of the contexts in which writing occurs suggest specific recommendations, the descriptive nature of our work, although in some respects systematic, suffered from too much interpretation and too little empirical study of the effects that documents have on their users. We then decided to look more closely at the communicative characteristics of documents, and to identify critical features that could be manipulated experimentally to investigate their effects on readers. The following section describes a progressive narrowing of focus that culminated in hypotheses about psychological processes and the effects of the redesign of documents on reading performance.

ASSESSMENT OF COMMUNICATIVE EFFECTS
OF DOCUMENT CHARACTERISTICS

Our experimental approach to the effects that documents have on readers explored a variety of comprehension problems. Although we had broad samples of documents from which to draw, we felt that an intensive analysis of a few documents would be more provocative of further hypotheses than a broad analysis of a range of material (for instance, computer analysis of the readability of technical documents).

Effects of Sentence Design on Judgments of Sentence Effectiveness

Our first study employed technical documents for equipment that was currently being introduced into the field. These documents were judged by the technical staff to be *fairly good*. From an equipment manual we selected two chapters for analysis of the frequency and type of potential comprehensibility problems at the sentence level. The purpose of Study I was to identify in a preliminary way features of documents that could be modified to improve comprehensibility. The experiment involved three stages. In Stage 1 a psychologist reviewer went over each sentence in two chapters and rewrote the sentence where potential information processing difficulties were perceived. This was done by performing a task analysis for sentence comprehension and generating an alternative for each sentence which reduced the cognitive processing demands. For example, readability research suggests that very long sentences make heavy demands on a reader. Therefore, we reduced sentence length where appropriate. Not all of the changes that we made can be characterized this simply, but our purpose was to discover features of writing that inhibit comprehension, not to prove that the *a priori* rules that characterize our revisions are necessarily true. In this stage of our work, each original sentence was paired with its revised version. These pairs were compiled in booklets so that subjects could rate the sentences on a 7-point scale of communicative effectiveness (one end of the scale was *ineffective,* and other other end was *effective*). In Stage 2, all sentence changes were classified by agreement between two reviewers. In Stage 3, 20 college students (10 per chapter) read through the booklets of sentence pairs rating the original and revised versions of each sentence on a single scale.

We altered text sentences as follows: (1) shortening sentences, (2) listing sentence components, (3) clarifying referents, (4) clarifying wording, and (5) other (i.e., unclassifiable). Shortening sentences typically involved removing connectives and creating a list format for sentences with several distinct components, e.g.;

The XL-1 is installed as follows:
1. mount it on a wall
2. connect it to the circuit
3. test the circuit

Clarifying referents involved the replacement of pronouns with the nouns to which they referred. The *clarifying wording* category refers to sentences with jargon or redundant wording. For instance, "The X battery charger is available for charging up to 10 units simultaneously" was changed to, "The X battery charger can charge up to 10 units simultaneously". Of the 210 sentences analyzed, 26% appeared to violate limits of efficient processing. Fifteen percent of the sentences were shortened; 7% were put into a list format; 1% required clarifying a referent; 1% required clarificiation of wording, and 2% were changed in other ways.

How did readers respond to these changes? In Stage 3 of this study, we asked raters to judge how well the sentences conveyed their message (clarity and precision) by rating the sentences on a 7-point scale. Two versions of the same sentence, the original and revised, were compared on the same scale. The lowest rating possible for communicative effectiveness was 1; 4 was the midpoint (neither effective nor ineffective) and the highest possible was 7. Subjects rated the revised sentences as significantly (p. < .01) more effective than the original sentences. The mean rating for the original sentences was 4.8; for the revised sentences the ratings averaged 5.5. (It should be noted that even the original sentences were rated as fairly effective, that is, above the midpoint, or 4.0, of the scale). The rated improvement varied by category of change. The magnitude of change was .6 for shortened sentences, .8 for listing, .3 for clarifying referents, .7 for clarifying wording, and .6 for other types of change.

Our analysis and subjects' ratings revealed the frequency and effects on reader response of various changes. Although wording clarifications resulted in substantial improvements, this problem was infrequent, as were referential clarifications and *other* changes. Shortened sentences and listing sentences components were both frequent and judged to be effective changes. We therefore decided to pursue these latter two factors in greater depth. Before we did, however, we decided to investigate subjects' ratings more extensively. Human judgments are fallible, and there was much variability in ratings across sentences. In one case, a subject rated the revised version of sentences lower than the original version. Readers' criteria for rating the communicative effectiveness of sentences apparently varied widely. Subjects' overall consistency in detecting improved sentences could have resulted from the fact that they were presented with explicit comparisons of original and revised sentences, thus accentuating the critical dimensions for comparison.

To investigate this possibility, an additional study was undertaken. It was similar to the first except that the revised and original forms of sentences were separated and rated independently of one another. Our results indicated that the mean rating of the original sentences did not differ significantly from the mean rating of the revised verions (5.84 and 5.94, respectively). Presumably, the inability of subjects to discriminate between effective and less effective sentences was because there was no explicit standard of comparison available for judging each sentence, as in the first study in which revisions were presented along with the original sentences. Perhaps this finding has some implications for the way in which documents should be reviewed, but we have not explored this further.

The most frequent sentence changes that our subjects perceived as being effective involved clarifying sentence components. A common feature of these frequent changes may be characterized as *enumeration*. Enumeration entails segmenting a sentence or larger text into meaningful components , presumably allowing the reader to easily peruse a text and perhaps to store and retrieve information more effectively. Broadly, enumeration involves listing components of a sentence that correspond to components of propositions (such as subjects and objects). Psychologists (e.g., Kintsch, Kozmensky, Streby, McKoon & Keenan; 1975) have referred to these components as *arguments* and have demonstrated that reading time and recall are related to the number of different arguments in sentences. This kind of enumeration analysis provided one basis for the changes that we made in sentences. The work of Kintsch, *et al* (1975), along with the data from Study 1, have implications not only for designing more effective texts but also for writing instruction. For example, by arranging text so that its semantic components are visually segmented, the writer may facilitate a variety of cognitive operations.

We decided, in Study II, to explore the consequences of two stimulus changes that were related to the enumeration changes in Study I; (1) numbering components, and (2) listing components vertically. We wanted to determine the separate and combined effects of these changes.

Sentences were constructed to represent the following levels of the enumeration variable: 1) a base sentence in which components of the sentence are separated by commas (BS), 2) the same sentence content in which components of the sentence are numbered within the sentence (*CN*), and 3) the same sentence content in which components of the sentence are numbered and listed below the sentence stem (*CN,L*). Examples are shown below.

BS: The X1 consists of a battery powered subscriber unit with a portable plastic recharger, two small key units operating at 70 kHz in the COU-to SOU direction, and an integrated circuit derived line board for station interrupts.

CN: The X1 consists of: (1) a battery powered subscriber unit with a portable plastic recharger (2) two small key units operating at 70 kHz in the COU-to-SOU direction, and (3) an integrated circuit derived line board for station interrupts.
CN,L: The X1 consists of:

1. a battery powered subscriber unit with a portable plastic recharger
2. two small key units operating at 70 kHz in the COU-to-SOU direction
3. an integrated circuit derived line board for station interrupts

Eighteen college undergraduates participated in the study in which they were required to judge the communicative effectiveness of each of the three forms (given in various combinations) as in Study 1. Results are presented in Table 1.

In summary, Studies I and II demonstrate that subjective ratings of communicative effectiveness can be used to identify text variables that are potentially important to comprehension. Subjective judgments were discriminative to the extent that criteria for the judgments were clearly specified (by example) in the format of the rating task. On the basis of reader response to changed sentences, we predicted that enumerating the meaningful

TABLE 1
Sentence Ratings Resulting from Enumerating Components[a]

Comparison	Means[b]	F	Probability
BS-CN	4.56 – 5.83	5.24	<.05
BS-CN,L	4.89 – 6.17	9.15	<.01
CN-CN,L	5.22 – 6.06	9.62	<.01

[a]Df's = 1, 15 for all comparisons. BS = base sentence; CN = components numbered; CN,L = components numbered and listed vertically.
[b]The means are for the two conditions of the comparison.

components of a text would improve ratings of sentence effectiveness. This prediction was confirmed, and two components of enumeration were identified: identification of components and array in space.

Effects of Sentence Design on Comprehension and Document Use

While our findings based on subjective ratings of sentence effectiveness suggested how typographical formats might be used to facilitate sentence processing, we needed to establish that reading comprehension, not just reader opinion, is influenced by those designs. This section summarizes the results of several studies (Frase & Schwartz, 1979) that investigated effects of document design on the speed with which readers can use a document to verify complex information. The studies, concentrating as they do on visual design problems, may seem tangential to problems of writing. But one problem for the writer is to express, organize and arrange information in ways that are compatible with the comprehension process of readers. Visual features, such as typographical formats, are important for comprehension as illustrated in the following studies.

Previous research suggests that pauses mark effective segmentation points for the mature reader (Aaronson & Scarborough, 1976). The assumption is that these units represent points at which a reader must engage in special coding and storage activities. We decided to use phrase boundaries as a basis for spatial segmentation of text units, not only because there is evidence that such judgments can be reliably made (Johnson, 1970), but because this manipulation does not entail content changes or any changes in punctuation. The segmented format is derived from our judgments of where meaningful boundaries occur. We used no formal rules for deciding these boundaries. We know that accomplished readers have sufficient language competence to produce consensus about where meaningful segmentation can be made in a text. Johnson's work (1970), on the marking of pausal units, supports our assertion about segmentation competence. Johnson (1970) found a correlation of .98 between the judgments of the locations of pausal acceptability for two groups of college students.

Our goals in these studies were to determine if job-like activities (verifying complex information in a text) would be more efficient with segmented text than with standard text, to determine whether meaningful segmentation and indentation significantly support comprehension activities, and to explore these questions using documents that vary in length and difficulty. We compared performance on ordinary text with the following passage conditions: meaningfully segmented-indented; meaningfully segmented-not indented; non-meaningfully segmented-indented, and; non-meaningfully segmented-not indented. We attempted to facilitate segmentation by arranging texts so that each line of text ended at a meaningful boundary. This resulted in lines of unequal length and in ragged margins. Furthermore, subordination of units was indicated by indenting lines containing phrases that were subordinate to preceding lines. We systematically varied segmentation and indentation to explore the effect of non-meaningful segmentation (where lines of text ended within phrases) and lack of indentation. In short, these studies extended the findings and conjectures developed from the subjective ratings described in the previous section.

The experimental task required that subjects confirm or disconfirm statements by reading a text that appeared below the statement to be confirmed. The statement was exposed and, when the subject was ready, a clock started and the text appeared. The statements to be confirmed involved finding and integrating information from several sentences in the text. Subjects could not confirm a sentence merely by scanning the texts for relevant information. We used five technical passages and five different forms of text. Passages varied from 136 words to 279 words in length. Examples of the five text forms follow:

1. *Standard Text:*
   The carrier facility may be developed from single or mixed gauge, PIC or pulp (paper) insulated, copper or aluminum conductor cables with standard sheaths. The cable may be air-core or waterproof design; however, in the case of buried air-core PIC cables, the double sheath types are recommended.

2. *Meaningful Indented Text:*
   The carrier facility may be developed from
   single or mixed gauge,
   PIC or pulp (paper) insulated,
   copper or aluminum
           conductor cables with standard sheaths.

The cable may be
    air-core or
    waterproof design;
        however, in case of
        buried air-core PIC cables,
            the double-sheath types are recommended.

3. Meaningful Segmentation—Not Indented:
The carrier facility may be developed from
single or mixed gauge,
PIC or pulp (paper) insulated,
copper or aluminum
conductor cables with standard sheaths.
The cable may be
air-core or
waterproof design
however, in the case of
buried air-core PIC cables,
the double sheath types are recommended.

4. Non-Meaningful Segmentation—Indented:
The carrier facility may
    be developed from single
    or mixed PIC or
    pulp (paper) insulated, copper
        or aluminum conductor
cables with standard sheaths. The
    cable may be
    air-core or waterproof
        design; however, in the
        case of buried air-core PIC
            cables, the double-sheath types are recommended.

5. Non-Meaningful Segmentation—Not Indented:
The carrier facility may
be developed from single
or mixed PIC or
pulp (paper) insulated, copper
or aluminum conductor
cables with standard sheaths. The
cable may be
air-core or waterproof
design; however, in the
case of buried air-core PIC
cables, the double-sheath types are recommended.

TABLE 2
Consequences of Segmentation and Indentation

Experiment	Conditions		Consequence	Probability
	Segmentation	Indentation		
One	Meaningful	Present	18% faster than standard	<.001
Two	Meaningful	Absent	12% faster than standard	<.025
Three	Not Meaningful	Present	Not different	>.05
Four	Not Meaningful	Absent	16% slower	<.001

Four separate studies were conducted in which all subjects (college summer school students) verified sentences in the standard text format and in one of the experimental formats. The results may be summarized briefly. Subjects took from 20-30 seconds to verify each sentence. Table 2 shows how the formats affected reading speed relative to the standard text format. A number of analyses were performed on the data, which allowed us to look at the experiments separately and also in combination.

The most powerful comprehension factor was whether the information was meaningfully segmented or not, although indentation also had a significant effect. Table 2 demonstrates that by altering typographical characteristics it is possible to create designs which are either more or less efficient than standard text. These data shed light on persisting issues in document design, namely, whether there is an optimal length for lines and whether justified margins are desirable. Surface features appear to be of minor relevance to reading speed in the verification task. The critical variable appears to be whether the format results in a display of easily encoded units, regardless of the length of lines or neatness or margins. Because the length of words and size of meaningful chunks (in words) vary across texts, there can be no general rule for how long text lines should be. Nevertheless, if chunk size, word length, and other factors are known, it is possible to optimize the length of lines for a particular text.

SUMMARY AND CONCLUSIONS

In the early portion of this paper I referred to the need to support opinions about what constitutes *good* writing with empirical studies of the effects of features of written texts on readers. I have also tried to portray how such evidence can alter our ideas of "good writing," as well as some ways in which we might try to influence writing instruction.

We began with a general question about the comprehensibility of technical writing. Using interview techniques, we discovered that writing, *per se*, was a small part of the problem, although a significant one. A host of management, planning, and evaluation problems influence the words that are finally put on paper. These practical problems of logistics and monitoring of documents comprised a substantial portion of what we originally thought might be text design problems.

Subsequent to our interviews, we used subjective ratings of sentences to evaluate technical writing. Rating data are easily collected and they can be modified to reflect various factors. Ratings were informative because they revealed features of sentences that suggested hypotheses for further research. They also were sensitive to individual differences, revealing persons who do not discriminate well between efficient and less efficient modes of expression. Rating procedures may be a useful source of information about editorial competence, if properly used. Multidimensional scaling techniques, which reveal the dimensions used by individual raters, as well as the dimensions upon which stimuli are rated, may prove valuable in studying the editing component of composition (especially individual differences) and for the evaluation of writing. But our data also show that judgments are strongly dependent upon how the rating task is presented. Explicit criteria (sentence comparisons) were necessary to achieve usable results in our studies. From our results, a conjecture related to writing instruction is that to help students develop appropriate skills, instruction should provide explicit contrasts between effective and less effective forms of communication.

The rating data revealed writing problems that were both frequent and modifiable in important ways. The need to enumerate the major structural components of a text emerged as a dominant factor in our data, and it led us to further analyze the readers' cognitive processes to see how texts could be designed to facilitate these processes. In doing this we were able to achieve an 18% reduction in reading time for one class of functional reading tasks, namely, tasks that required the integration of complex sets of information in technical documents.

In summary, our work, starting with a general concern for the comprehensibility of technical writing, resulted in an expanded perspective on the constraints surrounding writing activities, suggestions for evaluation procedures, and procedures for exploring the characteristics of written products, as well as some evidence about effective document design. Our design work implies that cognition and the visual array of information on a page are closely related and that the content of writing and the visual design of written materials interact to control the reader's segmentation of inputs—an important component of reading comprehension. The results also suggest that, even though rules for design may not generalize to all texts, if critical discourse features are known it is possible to optimize the design of a particular text.

REFERENCES

Aaronson, D., & Scarborough, H. S. "Performance theories for sentence coding: some quantitative evidence." *Journal of Experimental Psychology: Human Perception and Performance,* 1976, *2,* 56–70.

Frase, L. T., & Schwartz, B. J. Typographical cues that facilitate comprehension. *Journal of Educational Psychology,* 1979, *71,* 197–206.

Johnson, R. E. Recall of prose as a functional of the structured importance of linguistic units. *Journal of Verbal Learning and Verbal Behavior,* 1970, *9,* 12–20.

Kintsch, W., Kozmensky, E., Streby, W. J., McKoon, G., & Keenan, J. M. Comprehension and recall of text as a function of content variables. *Journal of Verbal Learning and Verbal Behavior,* 1975, *14,* 196–214.

Matsuhashi, A., & Cooper, C. A video-monitored observation study: the transcribing behaviors and composing processes of four competent high school writers. Paper presented at the Annual Meeting of the American Educational Research Association, Toronto, March, 1978.

Schwartz, B. J., Fisher, D. L., & Frase, L. T. Psychological processes and document design. Paper presented at the Annual Meeting of the American Educational Research Association, New York, April, 1977.

15 Purpose in Learning to Write: An Approach to Writing in Three Curriculum Areas

Mary K. Healy
University of California, Berkeley

PURPOSE IN LEARNING TO WRITE

During the past fifteen years as a teacher of writing in junior and senior high school and during the past five years as a teacher/consultant for the University of California Bay Area Writing Project working with teachers interested in the teaching of writing at all grade levels, I have observed a wide variety of approaches to the teaching of writing and have experimented with many different methods myself. Throughout this observation and experimentation, I have been continually led back to one basic question: What is the main purpose for the writing demanded of students in school? The answer to this question that seems to emerge most often from my discussions with teachers is that the central purpose for the writing done in school is to evaluate what the writer has *already* learned, either through the mastery of a subject content which the writing is intended to reveal, or through the mastery of form and correctness which the writing is intended to demonstrate. In other words, written pieces seem to be most often treated as assessable end-products, used for evaluation, judgment, and grading.

Increasingly dissatisfied with the narrowness of this conception of the purpose for writing in school, I and two of my colleagues, Julie Askeland and Cathy Schengel, have been working with an approach to writing instruction with seventh grade students in a small (450 students) suburban junior high school. This approach is based on the proposition that if students were encouraged to see writing, in its initial stages, as the record of their first tangible connections with a subject, and as the changeable exploration of the field to be written about, then writing in school might lose some of its awful finality and gain in direct usefulness to the student writer. By describing our approach to the purposes for writing in school and presenting examples of students' writing that illustrate their responses to our approach, we hope to highlight the importance of purpose in writing development and to more effective writing instruction.

The impetus for our evolving writing program in English, social studies, and math classes came from the report of a research project on writing development conducted in England: *The Development of Writing Abilities (11-18)* (Britton, J.; Burgess, T.; Martin, N.; McLeod, A.; and Rosen, H., 1975). The researchers examined some 2000 pieces of school writing in various subject areas by 500 students from ages 11-18 in an attempt to describe the nature of writing development. From an analysis of these papers, the researchers described two dimensions of the writing process--the writer's *sense of audience* and the writer's *intended function.* The results of this investigation make quite clear that in the schools from which the papers were collected, student writers had a very narrow conception of the purpose for school writing and a narrow sense of the audience for whom they were writing. The majority of their papers fell into the *transactional* function category, in which one writes to report, inform, argue or persuade. Proportionally little of the writing fell into the *expressive* category wherein the writer explores new information and tries out new ideas before attempting more specialized forms of written expression.

With respect to audience, almost fifty percent of the papers revealed an audience of *teacher seen as examiner or assessor.* This finding has consequences for the development of expressive writing since, as the researchers point out, expressive writing rarely develops out of a student-audience relationship of *teacher seen as examiner or assessor.* Some of the other audience categories which the researchers identified—*adolescent to trusted adult, pupil to teacher seen as partner in dialogue* or *adolescent to peers* would seem to be more appropriate settings in which to encourage the use of expressive writing, and thus make students' initial attempts at getting something down less immediately intimidating.

WRITING IN DIFFERENT CURRICULUM CONTEXTS

How, then, could we, as teachers of different subjects in the school's curriculum, make use of the results of this research to aid the development of our students' writing skills? In exploring this question, we relied considerably on the work of the Writing Development Project, also at the University of London's Institute of Education, which, through a series of pamphlets about the role of talking and writing in different areas of the curriculum, has interpreted the results of the Writing Abilities research project for classroom teachers. Based on those booklets' anecdotal, classroom-based explorations, we decided how we were going to approach writing with our students--we would attempt to remove the act of writing from its traditional role as a final production coming at the end of a unit or series of lessons, the demonstrable end of a slice of learning. Instead, through a reliance on uses of writing at every step in the learning process in the classroom and through our *response* to, rather than *evaluation* of, this writing, we would gradually enable our students to view the act of writing as an aid to their learning, a tool to be used in acquiring mastery over new information, and a means of revealing, both to themselves and to a receptive audience, their present understanding of a given subject.

To accomplish this objective, we tried to alter the traditional role of the teacher as judge and evaluator and to demonstrate the important consultative roles possible for both teacher and peers. It was important, therefore, that both teachers and peers responded to writing at various stages of its production so that students could realize the ways in which different purposes for writing produce different types of discourse.

Mathematics

In the mathematics class, we introduced journal writing as a means of helping students learn mathematics. Students were first asked to write their reactions to the activities of the class. Some representative examples follow:

Example 1
The last unit (fractions) has been ok, I guess. I liked having math fourth period. This arrangement has been ok too. The work could have been a little bit harder, even though I worked fast and made stupid mistakes. I would have finished, but the homework was piled up skyhigh. I will give it to you on Monday morning in the big group. I love to divide and multiply fractions best. Will we get to divide fractions? Some people called this class and the kids in it stupid kids. That doesn't bother me that much, but a little.

11-year-old girl

Example 2
I think 77-78 is the best math year I've had, sure, I sit next to real goof-offs but I still get my work done. Math is my favorite academic course so far this year.

Although I like what we've been doing, I think we, as a class, should spend more time on real life situations. This checking unit is the idea I'm referring to, but we should also do income tax forms and other such materials.

We should try to put math to a practical use, (no offense intended) I would guess 80% of the class does not know how to apply math to real life problems. Instead we know $9 \times 9 = 81$, when what we ought to know is how to apply math concepts to real life situations.

12-year-old boy

Example 3

The one thing I have been doing in math for the last 7 years is making careless mistakes. Thats why I might get a bad grade on an easy test. I have been trying to work slower, hopeing that would stop my carelessness. Do you have any other suggestions?

Math is usually one of my better subjects. I really like the unit we are doing now. It is lots of fun. I am really getting tired of multeplication.

11-year-old girl

The teacher (Mrs. Askeland) responded encouragingly to these entries and as a guide for future personal attention in class began to keep track of how the individual students saw themselves as math students. She also compared what the students wrote about their work with what she had seen of their math performance on exercises and tests. From this fuller picture of the student as a learner of mathematics, she was able to plan lessons and activities more suited to individual students than a straightforward progression through a set curriculum might allow.

After these initial entries, the students were asked to write often in their journals. Frequently the journal was used as a means of having the students state their understanding of a process they were currently studying, *while* they were studying it, so that the students, by attempting to translate a mathematical concept into words, could come to grips with the current state of their understanding. The teacher typically made the following kind of request: "Write to a third grader explaining what prime numbers are. Use any examples which will make the idea clearer for the student." Some examples follow:

Example 4

I would tell him that a prime number is when it can only be divided by 1 and its self

example

say we have the numbers 3, 5, 7 and 8 See how many different numbers can divide into it

1. $3 = 1 \times 3$, $3 = 3 \times 1$, anything else? NO
2. $5 = 1 \times 5$, $5 = 5 \times 1$, anything else? NO
3. $7 = 1 \times 7$, $7 = 7 \times 1$, anything else? NO
4. $8 = 1 \times 8$, $8 = 8 \times 1$, anything else? yes

2×4, 4×2, thats all so then it's *composite*. anything that can be divided more than 1 and itself is called composite. Like number 4 is composite.

12-year-old boy

Example 5

First I would ask him or her there times tibles and then I would make a list of all the numbers (up to 200) then I would tell him to cross out all numbers that are multiples of 2, 5, 7, 11, 3 but not these numbers. Then I would tell him what a prime number is & then everything would be Hunnce Dorry!

11-year-old girl

Example 6

First I would give him/she two examples like, 7. "What are the factors of 7?" He/she would probably say 1 and 7 and 7 if he/she was smart. Then I would say "What are the factors of 3?" He/she would say (or I would help) He/she would say there are two numbers in each. I would say that is a prime because there are only *two* factors. Other numbers with *more than two* factors are called composite numbers.

11-year-old girl

Example 7

So, you want to know about primes, do you? Well, lets just only work on the primes between 1-12. A prime is a number in which no other numbers can be multiplied to make that number besides 1 and itself.

Here is the number 8. 8 is *not* prime.

You know the factors of 8.

1, 2, 4, 8 2×4 and 4×2

1×8 and 8×1

You see that 2×4 and 4×2 goes into eight.

But 11 is a prime number. No other factors besides 1 and 11 can make 11.

$1 \times 11 = 11$ $11 \times 1 = 11$

So, you see that eleven is prime because only itself times 1 equals it.

11-year-old boy

The entries demonstrated both a wide range of student understanding of the topic and a wide range of writing ability. After this writing had been completed, and before the teacher read the entries, the students shared what they had written in small groups, commenting on the accuracy of each other's explanation of the process. For those who had mastered the process and had succeeded in making this process clear in writing, there came the immediate positive recognition of the group members. For those who were still struggling with understanding the mathematical process, there were opportunities to hear a variety of clearer versions, and thereby, to adjust their own explanations where those were unclear or incomplete. They could then make judgments about their own writing and thinking before handing the journal in to the teacher.

The teacher in turn identified features in the students' writing which indicated how each had understood the task and responded to its demands. Thus she began to develop some understanding of the cognitive processes of individual students. She then wrote a comment for each child which attempted to either encourage the learning which was taking place or clarify a confusion or misunderstanding which was inhibiting the learning. By deciding to offer students opportunities of this kind, we believed they would come to rely on writing as a way of discovering what they knew and what they didn't know. In addition, we believed that the students would gradually learn how to shape what they wanted to say for a specific audience, a crucial writing skill applicable in all areas of the curriculum.

Social Studies

In the social studies classes the teacher (Cathy Schengel) also used journals for a variety of purposes. In addition to providing students opportunities to react to lessons in progress, these journals also became repositories for the students' recollections of information given in lectures, demonstrations, films. These brief expressive pieces were then used as data for the longer papers the students wrote. It appeared to us to be quite different to have students rely on their own reconstructions of what they had heard or seen than to have them rely on information they had recorded on the teacher-constructed worksheets we had used in the past. Most worksheets of this sort seemed to encourage rote learning because they set the boundaries within which the students were to record specific data. Writing in an expressive mode, on the other hand, allowed the students to make connections between what they had seen or heard and their previous body of knowledge.

As an example of the context for this type of writing in social studies, the class had begun a unit on global problems. During the first few days, the students worked in groups examining maps to compare the relationships in several major countries, between Gross National Product, life expectancy, infant mortality, and literacy. Once students had examined the maps, the teacher asked them to decide whether there was any connection between the various statistics. These group reports then formed the basis of a class discussion, which was followed by a journal-writing activity about the discussion.

Examples of complete journal entries follow:

Example 2

"I'm a little mixed on what to write....Literacy is "interconnected with" infant mortality because you have to read to understand health etc. It shows how population is high in some countries and in other countries not so populated. The facts show that many subjects, such as infant mortality, life expectancy, literacy, G.N.P., and population, can fit together in the world as global problems.

This, I'm pretty sure, doesn't make that much sence to you. It's hard for me to explain it. I think I really have to get into our subject more for this quarter to explain my answer(s) better.

such information about students writing in varied classroom contexts, it will offer a more adequate account of writing development, and one that is more useful to teachers.

As teachers, we recognize that the expressive writing students do gives us new information about the ways they understand what is going on in the classroom. And with that information we have been able to adjust our teaching methods to meet many of the needs revealed in students' writing. Thus, the analysis of writing done by students in instructional situations such as I have described can contribute not only to our understanding of writing development, but also to adaptive interaction in the classroom. We are encouraged by the response to our broader conception of the purpose for writing in school. We have a strong sense that we are on the right track when we observe the expanded role writing is playing in the daily events of our classes.

REFERENCES

Britton, J.; Burgess, T.; Martin, N.; McLeod, A.; & Rosen, H. *The development of writing abilities* (11–18). London: Macmillan Education, 1975.

Martin, Nancy, et al., *Writing and learning across the curriculum.* London: Ward Lock Educational, 1976.

16 Learning to Meet the Requirements of Written Text: Language Development in the School Years

David R. Olson and Nancy Torrance
The Ontario Institute for Studies in Education

Our concern in this paper is with some of the ways that the child's competence with an oral language becomes specialized to serve the intellectual functions of the school. Educators generally assume that the child brings to school a degree of mastery of a *mother tongue* sufficient to cope with a wide range of social situations. But how are we to describe the transformation through which that mother tongue passes in becoming a suitable instrument for schooling—for both reading and writing?

We shall develop two of these factors which appear to be particularly important in understanding and accounting for this transformation from oral to literate competence. The first is the realignment of functions. The plurifunctionality of oral language—the conflation of interpersonal and ideational functions in speech may be contrasted with the differentiation and specialization of those functions in writing.

The second is the relation between what was said *The sentence meaning* and what was meant or intended *The speaker's meaning*. Whereas in oral language the former is one among several transparent clues to the latter, in writing it comes to be an autonomous and explicit and opaque meaning in its own right which may or may not be an adequate representation of an intention. The growing ability to operate upon this sentence meaning whether in reading—learning to confine interpretation to the information in the text—or in writing—learning to make the sentence meaning an adequate and autonomous representation of one's intentions—is a primary form of language development during the school years. Let us discuss these themes in turn in the light of some of the current evidence we have collected on *schooled* language.

235

THE FUNCTIONS OF LANGUAGE

An analysis of language in terms of functions, as opposed to the simple acquisition of semantic systems or syntactic devices, appears to offer a promising approach both to the nature and development of language and to the analysis of the specialization of *schooled* language. Any one of a number of theories (Buhler, 1934; Austin, 1962; Searle, 1969) could set the stage for this discussion of the functions of language. The two classes of functions of primary concern to us are (1) the functions of maintaining social relations within and between participants and (2) the functions of maintaining logical relations within and between sentences. Extending the work of Buhler (1934), Popper (1972) argues that there is an evolution from animal languages to human languages, from the *lower* interpersonal signalling functions shared by animals and humans which are useful for constructing social relations and for controlling the behaviour of others, to the *higher* semantic functions which are found only in human language and which are useful for constructing true and valid descriptions. This dichotomy also reflects Austin's (1962) distinction between performative utterances and constative utterances or between illocutionary and locutionary acts. A similar theory has been independently developed by Grice (1975) who argues that an analysis requires that we recognize, and if necessary, distinguish, what the sentences means literally and semantically (the sentence meaning), from what the speaker means, intends, hopes to achieve, or achieves by uttering that sentence (the speaker's meaning). For a discussion of the relation between Austin's and Grice's theories of meaning see Strawson (1964).

Our suggestion is that in ordinary conversational language what is said provides only some cues to what the speaker *intends*. The shared prior knowledge, the shared perceptual context, preceeding utterances in the conversation, the assumed biases of the listener plus prosody, intonation and stress cues all share in the expression and recovery of the speaker's intention. What is said or lexicalized is only a fragmentary representation of what was meant. In schooled language, as we shall see, the relation between what is said and what is meant is much more direct. Meanwhile, it is important to notice that what a sentence *means* and what one means by a sentence may be quite different.

An interesting analysis of the structure of language in terms of its functions has been advanced by Halliday (1970). More recently he has used this analysis of functions to account for the acquisition of language in children (1974, 1975). At an early age, prior to one year, Halliday found evidence of six functions served by the child's distinctive expressions which he describes as the instrumental, regulatory, interactional, personal, heuristic and imaginative functions. By about one and a half years of age, the child has integrated these functions into two primary functions, the pragmatic (or intruder) function, largely from an integration of the instrumental and regulatory, and the mathetic (or observer) function, arising largely from an integration of the personal and heuristic. With development, the child's utterances become plurifunctional such that every utterance simultaneously serves ideational and interpersonal functions as well as a third function; the textual, an enabling function which provides the conditions for serving the other two. What in Stage 1 were considered functions, in the adult system become the social uses to which language is put. Other studies of child language acquisition have tended to support this kind of analysis. Nelson (1973) found that some children appeared to be primarily oriented towards the interpersonal functions of language while others were oriented towards the ideational functions of language. "One is learning an object language, one a social interaction language" (p. 22). Others have suggested that the interpersonal function is primary over the ideational function. Buhler (1934) claimed that "the first sensible words are either such affective expressions, or the signs of some wish" (p. 55). Bates, Camaioni and Volterra (1975) suggest that children pass through an illocutionary or interpersonal stage before they reach a locutionary stage. Consider now how these functions are organized in oral conversational language and how they may be reorganized under the influence of writing.

The Alignment of Functions in Ordinary Oral Language

Not only are the interpersonal functions prior to the ideational functions in language acquisition, they continue to be primary, we suggest, in ordinary oral language (see also Olson, 1977). Although adult language simultaneously serves a number of functions including that of regulating social interaction and making true descriptions, ordinary oral language is directed to a particular individual, usually with some intended effect, whether influencing his views, establishing or maintaining a certain social relationship or controlling his actions. Furthermore, the availability of immediate feedback permits the continuous monitoring of the listener's reactions to determine if the utterance needs to be modified, expanded, tempered or the like to achieve that effect. Hence the rhetorical function is predominant over the logical function: if you fail to maintain an appropriate interpersonal relationship, the conversation simply terminates. The predominance of the interpersonal function over the truth or logical function may be illustrated by noting that in ordinary conversation, topics are chosen for which the participants already share most of the relevant knowledge. These topics frequently include a common ancestry, a common geographic origin, a common contextual event ("Chilly, isn't it?") or failing that, a recently seen movie, read book or the like.

The primacy of the interpersonal functions over the logical functions in oral language is clearly shown in a recent study by Esther Goody (1975) of the use of questions among the Gonja of Ghana. After differentiating the locutionary (information) functions from the illocutionary (interpersonal or control) functions, she shows that the majority of questions among the Gonja are used not for the purpose of obtaining or sharing information, but for purposes of control over lower social status individuals, generally children. Thus, a teacher can question a child but a child cannot *ask* a question of a teacher. She concludes that, "The securing of information becomes secondary to considerations of status relations" (1975, p. 42).

Goody suggests that this subordination of the semantic and logical functions to the interpersonal, control functions in the use of questions may contrast substantially with the use of questions in our own society. The discrepancy may be less marked than she expected. Recent studies by Mitchell-Kernan and Kernan (1977) and Erin-Tripp (1977) show that for young children in a conventional setting, a proportion of utterances are directed toward the social ends of regulating the actions of others, testing status relations and the like. Mitchell-Kernan found that 7 to 12 year old children occasionally uttered commands to adults—"Give me the crayon", not because they could not reach it themselves but simply because they wanted to test their authority—to see if the listener would obey. In our own somewhat limited observations we have found that over 80% of utterances spoken by 4 year olds in a play situation served a primary social function. Thus it appears to be the case that the interpersonal functions are predominant over the logical functions for much of *oral* conversational language whether among non-literates, like the Gonja or among literates, like ourselves.

The Realignment of Functions in "Schooled" Language

The formal language of instruction appears to be quite different from conversational language; it is perhaps half-way between *utterances* and *texts*. The essence of schooled language is that it reflects the formal language of written text books. It is what Greenfield (1972) and Scribner (ref. note 2) have described as *speaking a written language*. More important the relationship between the interpersonal and the logical functions of language begin to reverse. Written language has the effect of distancing the speaker from the listener with the effect that the rhetorical or interpersonal functions may become somewhat secondary to the ideational functions of language. Precisely how this occurs is not clear but it may be the case that writing permits greater specialization of the logical function, at the expense of the interpersonal, or simply that writing may become more specialized for any purpose because those specialized forms are preserved in the culture (in poems, stories, encyclopedia, dictionaries and the like) and systematically taught to children.

However that specialization occurs, text books, the most representative of that form of schooled language, are particularly striking for their anonymity. It is not clear who is speaking or to whom the information is addressed. It is an attempt at a simple, impersonal, autonomous, true description. A text book, traditionally, is not merely the author's opinion of a state of affairs but rather of what society generally, takes as *known*.

Illustrative of this specialized form of language that is predominant in schools is the analysis of teacher-speech reported by Feldman and Wertsch (preprint). They found some important differences between the speech of teachers when they were teaching in the classroom and when they were engaged in ordinary lunch-room conversations. Specifically, some of the markers of the interpersonal functions common in conversations, what the authors call *stance indicators*, were absent in the classroom speech. Thus in the lunchroom, teachers use such expressions as "It seems to me,...", "I certainly expect (hope)...", and the like to qualify their statements, while in the classroom these qualifiers are absent. To some extent teachers talk as if they are representatives of the authorized view presented in text books!

However, even if the context expressed in teachers' language suspends the rhetorical stances of ordinary communication, the exhaustive analysis of *teacher talk* reported by Bellack, Kliebard, Hyman and Smith (1966) indicates that teachers continue to utilize the control functions of ordinary language in their use of questions in the classroom. Although their data were not analysed precisely according to the functions discussed above, they showed that in a High School teaching session, almost 50% of teacher's utterances were *soliciting* moves—questions and commands—to which a student response was obligatory. As a result 65% of students' utterances were responses to teachers soliciting moves. Questions and commands were, therefore, used less to provide information (the logical or ideational function) than they were to hold children responsible (the control function) for the information they had, presumably, acquired from the text. Further Bellack et al reported the same absence of stance indicators reported by Feldman and Wertsch. In spite of the fact that teachers are teaching highly controversial material, only 2% of teachers' utterances in the classroom conveyed or justified personal opinions. Interestingly, this suggests that by the time the child reaches High School classroom language has become highly specialized. The teacher, then, retains many of the more interpersonal, control functions of oral language but gives up others, such as stance indicators. So, while, minimizing the interpersonal aspects of statements in order to make them seem true descriptions of states of affairs, similar to textbook statements, the interpersonal aspects of questions are maximized, thus allowing the teacher to hold students responsible for information. The teacher, then, becomes primarily a *mediator* of texts. This gradual transition to the language of text during the school years is an important but relatively uncharted territory.

The primary difference, we suggest, between the oral conversational language of the child and the written texts of the school, is in the realignment of the interpersonal and the ideational functions of language. Some of our recent observations bear on this realignment of function. If we apply our analysis of functions to samples of children's speech obtained in school-like tasks, we find a reversal in the uses of language reported above for conversational speech. In these tasks, in which the experimenter asks for descriptions and explanations, utterances with a direct interpersonal purpose tend to disappear and are replaced by those with a primarily informational purpose. In fact, in this context about 80% of the utterances directly served the informational or logical functions of language. Indeed, this shift is sometimes obvious in the manner and intonation of the speech itself. In response to the teacher's/experimenter's questions some children will adopt a completely different speech register; they pause, take a deep breath, and without looking at the interlocutor, provide the required description, e.g., "The star is under the large, black square."

Other indications of this shift are visible in the studies mentioned above. Teachers in classrooms, as representatives of the official text view, rarely express their own feelings, beliefs, interpretations or opinions while in the staff rooms they are quite willing to relinquish that official stance. Yet even in the classroom, they do not relinquish that other aspect of the interpersonal function, the use of language to control the activities of the child through the use of the questions and commands. Presumably, a more detailed study of the language of the school would show a predominance of interpersonally biased oral language in the early grades with an increasing reliance on written text and text-like language in the later grades. Through the school years, the child is becoming more reliant upon text books for the acquisition of information. Indeed through the school years, authority passes from teacher to printed text. That is, the realignment of functions of language corresponds to a transition from oral to written forms of language.

There are good reasons why the ideational functions of language are progressively turned over to written language and why writing is such an optimal instrument for the specialization of the ideational or logical function of language. As we mentioned above, writing distances the speaker from the audience in a way that decreases the urgency of the interpersonal component. Further, the social relations holding between speaker and listener need not hold between writer and audience. But there is a second important reason why writing can serve to specialize the ideational functions of language. It is the presence of a permanent artifact, the written record, which permits the differentiation of what was said from what was *meant*. Once differentiated, the writer can edit and revise to make sure that the sentence meaning is an adequate representation of what the speaker intended. It is that attempt which makes language explicit and *prosaic*. The repeated scrutiny of what was actually *said* makes it much easier to check the truth and validity of the statements than would be the case in ordinary oral language.

Written language by virtue of the fact that it is explicit, is substantially different from typical oral speech; it is relatively free of the effects of context and stands as a permanent artifact with meanings that endure through time. Part of this explicitness is required because of the loss of certain types of information that would normally be carried by expression, intonation, gestures and ostensive factors which must therefore be made explicit in the text. An illustration of the relative explicitness of written language is taken from Lyons (1969) who pointed out that a large number of homophones in spoken language are disambiguated by spelling. There are, for example, many sentences which are ambiguous when spoken, that are perfectly clear when written ("cf., il vient toujours a sept heurs; il vient toujours a cette heure; he always comes at seven o'clock; he always comes at this time," p. 41). Moreover, text must be written in such a way that the *meaning* is unchanged if read in a different context than that in which it was written. That is, written materials are ordinarily portable and preserved over time, hence the writer must use language in such a way as to permit the text to preserve its meaning across space and time.

This is precisely the point made by such scholars as Goody and Watt (1968), McLuhan (1962) and Havelock (1973) in regard to the consequences of the invention and diffusion of alphabetic literacy. We have already suggested that by suppressing the rhetorical functions of language, statements become the specialized instruments of description and explanation—of the logical functions of language. But to better serve this specialized function, language has to be brought up to a much higher level of formal and explicit conventionalization. And the extent to which a writing system can be tailored to suit the requirement of explicitness depends on the nature of the script as scholars such as Havelock (1976) have shown. Havelock's monograph is the most recent of the books which insist both upon the peculiar nature of written as opposed to oral language and upon attributing those effects to the presence of an alphabetic writing system. The claim is that our familiarity with Roman and Greek culture is

grounded in one small technological fact. The civilization created by the Greeks and Romans was the first on the earth's surface which was founded upon the activity of the common reader; the first to be able to place the inscribed word in general circulation; the first, in short to become literate in the full meaning of that term, and to transmit its literacy to us" (p. 2).

The small technological fact Havelock argues, was the invention of the alphabetic script which permitted the making of statements which could be interpreted, to an unprecedented degree, independently of the context of the sentence and the prior knowledge and expectancies of the reader and hence independent of the intentions of the speaker/writer. The alphabet is therefore the tool of unambiguous, univocal, prosaic meaning. To serve this function the alphabet should be completely explicit, formal and mechanically interpreted. As Havelock says: "A successful or developed writing system is one which does not think at all"(p. 17) and again, "Ideally, there should be no exceptions to be supplied by guesswork from context"(p. 23). The alphabetic script achieved this explicitness by "atomizing linguistic sound into theoretic components" (p. 29). The alphabet was to writing what phonemes were to speech, the minimal set of distinguishable units capable of giving full expression to the precise articulated meanings of the language. The magnitude of the discovery was such that it occurred only once in the history of man.

We have argued, and supported by historical and anthropological evidence, the view that in writing what is said and what is meant stand in a somewhat different relation than in speech. That difference, we have suggested, is that in written language what is said (written) must be an adequate and lexicalized representation of what is meant or intended. The concern then, legitimately, falls upon what in fact is said, on the *literal* meanings of the sentences per se. Let us consider how this bias affects reading comprehension and subsequently affects the process of writing.

COMPREHENSION OF TEXT: LEARNING TO CONFINE INTERPRETATION TO THE INFORMATION EXPLICITLY CONVENTIONALIZED IN THE TEXT

Let us consider, then, some of the ways that the realignment of functions in written text influences the comprehension process of the children who deal with text. Our interest is in the changes in the comprehension processes of children through the school years as they progressively learn to deal with autonomous, printed texts. We shall describe this development in terms of the children's ability to confine interpretation to the information explicitly represented in the text. This is a complex skill with a long educational history and our intention is simply to chart some of the milestones in its development.

The argument we present is, in some ways, merely an extension and elaboration of one presented earlier (Olson, 1972) in which two higher order semantic functions were differentiated. In that paper a contrast was drawn between the processes of mapping sentences onto a perceived world and the processes of mapping sentences onto other sentences. In the early stages of language development it was suggested that children learn how sentences relate to situations. Once those extensional properties had been mastered children came to see how sentences related to each other. This learning was said to occur by virtue of the fact that two descriptions mapped onto a common state of affairs and it was this common extension that gave them their common meaning. One illustration was drawn from the relation between active and passive sentences. It was suggested that children first learned how to map sentences whether active or passive to a state of affairs. Only subsequently did they come to see that if one was true, then necessarily, the other was true as well. The same point was made of lexical meanings. A child may know the events that take particular lexical items as correct descriptions but fail to see that if one was true the other was necessarily true. For example, the child may describe a particular object as a *cat* and on another occasion as an *animal* and yet fail to see the defining relation between those two lexical items. Again, it was suggested that it was the common compliance class (Goodman, 1968, p. 144) of the two descriptions that was instrumental in the child's coming to see that the terms could be transformed or translated into one another. Finally, the argument was raised that these developments were, at least in part, the consequences of the reliance upon written language in the course of schooling. The former, the mapping of sentences onto situations, was described as the language of communication and instruction, while the latter, the mapping of sentences and lexemes onto each other was described as the language of explicit argument and of logical thinking. It is this latter process that we now describe as the specialization of the ideational function of language that occurs during the school years.

We shall describe this development in terms of the child's growing ability to handle the meanings of texts. This ability develops as the child passes through at least two stages from learning to match descriptions to known states of affairs (assimilation), to learning to imagine states of affairs of which the presented sentence is a true description (accommodation). This latter involves learning to confine interpretation to the statements *per se* and to the conventionalized relations between those statements. Let us consider them in turn.

Mapping Sentences to Known Events: Sentences as Descriptions

One way we have examined the development of the literate use of language is by specifically examining children's competence with the relationship between active and passive sentences and sentences involving the comparative more/less and bigger/smaller. Logically, these three relations may be described as possessing two variable elements linked by a relation term such that $A(R)B \rightarrow B(R^-)A$. A transformation applied to the variable elements or to the relation term produces a sentence that is false while the application of both yields a true sentence. Symmetrically, in comparing sentences, a mismatch in the order of the elements or a mismatch in the relation term makes one of the sentences false while a mismatch in both makes them equivalent.

A (R) B John hit Mary T
A (R⁻) B John was hit by Mary F
B (R) A Mary hit John F
B (R⁻) A Mary was hit by John T

The question of concern here is what does the child know about these relationships and how does that knowledge change with schooling.

We have known for some time that if you tell a child of, say, 5 years of age "John has more than Mary" he is unable to answer the question "Does Mary have less than John?" Similarly, if you tell him "John hit Mary" he is unable to answer the question "Was Mary hit by John?". We interpret this finding as a demonstration that young children fail to see the implications of statements. We were disturbed by the finding, however, that if you showed children a picture of the event portrayed by the first sentence they were able to answer the question. It seemed odd to claim that children could not draw implications from sentences if on some occasions they did appear to draw such implications.

In children's speech productions, too, Feider (1970) found that children 3 to 5 years of age were unable to apply both of these transformations to a sentence to form the complementary sentence. Two examples are given below with the adult form in brackets beneath:

1. Was I a baby, when I was standing on my head?
(Was I standing on my head when I was a baby?)
2. I am strong. I can beat Jackie up. That's why I'm strong.
(I am strong. I can beat Jackie up. That's why I can beat Jackie up. That's because I'm strong.)

The child in the above cases has carried out one of the transformations but not the other, hence the statements appear odd. To illustrate in 2., the child says "That's why I'm strong" when he meant "That's why I can beat Jackie up" or alternatively, "That's because I'm strong". The child's response fell neatly between these alternatives.

We recently conducted some experiments that cast a new light on this particular competence. In one of these experiments (Olson & Nickerson, 1977) we simply varied the degree to which the characters of the sentence were known to the children. In the pilot studies we used names of siblings and classmates. In the experiment we used the familiar Peanuts comic-strip characters, Snoopy, Lucy and Charlie Brown. There were four conditions. In the first we used the arbitrary names John and Mary that we had used in earlier studies, in the second, we used the familiar Peanuts names, in the third, we used the Peanuts names embedded in a meaningful story and in the fourth we used our pictures.

Two findings emerged. The more well-known the characters the better able were children to draw the correct implications. In terms of the theory we have been developing here, the more readily sentences could be assimilated to the child's commonsense knowledge of the world, the more successful was he in handling the grammatical-logical relations between sentences.

The second finding is more surprising. By performing an analysis on the number of correct responses to the sentence-question pairs we were able to show that children, when successful, proceed in a manner somewhat different from that of adults: for adults True Passives are most difficult; for children False Passives are most difficult. To account for these differences, we have postulated different processing models for children and adults. Adults, in these experiments, operate directly on the logical implications of the statements: If x hit y, then y was hit by x. Adults simply compare sequentially the constituents of the representations of the sentences keeping track of the mismatches by means of some truth index. Their reaction times reflect the number of these operations. For adults, we may say that the meaning operated on is in the text, or alternatively that sentences are treated as logical forms.

Children on the other hand, cannot calculate the logical implications of the statements *per se*. How, then, do they handle the equivalence relation between transformed versions of the same proposition? Both children and adults, at least when the contextual knowledge was adequate were able to assimilate the various forms of sentences described in these kinds of experiments. The children also, at least in some contexts, were able to come up with the same answers as adults. But they came to their conclusions in quite a different way. Adults, knowing the logical relations between the sentences, were able to retrieve and compare the critical constituents and make a judgement. Children, not knowing the logical or formal relations between the sentence meanings, had to assimilate what they heard to what they already knew using some context or background knowledge and then redescribe what they knew to fit the requirements of the questions. They achieved by assimilation and redescription what adults did by the comparison of constituents related by formal transformations. While children operate upon their more general knowledge representations, adults operate upon the more specific sentence representations.

Confining Interpretation to the Text

All of the children we studied had mastered the grammar and the semantics of the language; they could assimilate both active and passive sentences to their knowledge of the world (if there was a context to which it could be assimilated). In other words, they knew how to map language onto knowledge. However, that grammatical competence, was no assurance that the child knew the implicational relations that hold between the sentences *per se* or that he can transform one statement into another. A young child's judgment that two sentences are both true would be made on the basis of paraphrase—they are both true descriptions of some known event—not on the basis of formal logical entailment or of formal grammatical transformation of the sentence meaning. Another way to say this is that children treat these sentences as empirically related, that is, they are both true descriptions of a state of affairs, while adults treat them as formally or logically related—if one is true, necessarily the other is true.

And this we suggest is what children are acquiring in their early school years. They are learning to treat sentence meaning formally; to entertain sentences not merely as a transparent description of an underlying reality, but rather as a reality. They operate on this reality to create a meaning. We have called this *sentence accommodation*. Rather than merely assimilate a sentence (sometimes with some violence to the sentence per se) as a fragmentary clue to the intended or speaker's meaning, the child begins to accommodate himself to the sentence—*to imagine a state of affairs of which that sentence is a true description*. To do this, of course, the child must have both a highly conventionalized linguistic system and a willingness to entertain the reality specified by the statements that he encounters. It is the growing competence with these formalized meaning constituents that we have seen emerging in these studies.

This is not an achievement that is independent of other aspects of the child's development; there are, presumably several stages involved in the mastery of the logically related statements we have examined herein. There is first of all, as mentioned above, the development of sentence accommodation—the ability to create or imagine a state of affairs of which that sentence is a true description. This is a process that presumably begins with story telling and story reading and ends with studying expository text.

We believe the effect of writing then is to turn utterances as descriptions into formal propositions with implications. And the comprehension processes have to reflect this transformation. Sentences may be treated in either way; and while our children treat them as descriptions of known events, our adults treat them as logical propositions. This jump is fundamental to cognitive development in a literate culture but it is achieved, we suggest, primarily through the reflection on statements made possible by writing systems. And the children here are doing what we literate adults frequently do even in ordinary conversational language.

A recent experiment in our Laboratory by Michael Davis (1978) suggests much the same conclusion. He presented to 4th and 6th Graders (10 and 12 year olds) a series of 96 premises each of which was followed by a proposition which was either logically or pragmatically related to the initial premise. Subjects were asked to divide the propositions into two categories—those that were necessarily valid (the logically related ones) and those which were only probable but not necessarily valid (the pragmatically related ones). To illustrate, if given the premise:

The apples are in a container.
it follows logically that
The fruit is in a container.
but only pragmatically that
The apples are in a basket.

Davis hypothesized that this differentiation would develop with age (i.e., with schooling) and with increasing literacy (i.e., skill in reading). This was in fact the case. A signal detection analysis showed that d', the differentiation of the two classes of inference, increased from Grade 4 to Grade 6, and within each grade, d' increased with reading competence. An additional hypothesis that the differentiation could be made more accurately in reading than in listening was not supported—perhaps because the task called for immediate rather than delayed verification.

This study is important because the primary difference between logical and pragmatic inference is that the former relies exclusively on the sentence meaning, what the sentence in fact says, while the latter relies on an *interpreted* or elaborated meaning. It is this differentiation, we have suggested, that is facilitated by the use of written language and as this study shows, children become increasingly sensitive to this difference with developing literacy skills.

Other studies in our Laboratory which ave been reported elsewhere have been interpreted in the same way. Pike and Olson (1977) suggested that the concepts of *more* and *less* come to be used logically in a contrastive sense when the child begins to treat the descriptions as opaque and to operate on those descriptions rather than on the concrete displays. Ford (1976) made a similar suggestion regarding how young children perform on Piaget's class inclusion task. To the Experimenter's question, "There are two ducks and four rabbits: Are there more rabbits or animals?", the young child replies, "More rabbits, because there are only two ducks." Ford argued that in ordinary language, the disjunctive *or* relates alternatives of the same structural level (e.g., salt or pepper, tea or coffee). To succeed on the class-inclusion task the child must operate upon the meaning of the sentence even when that sentence calls for a reorganization of the conceptual world. He must operate upon the literal meaning of the sentence per se, or as we have said, he must *accommodate* to the sentence rather than simply assimilate the sentence to what he already knew and expected. Interestingly it is a task that children come to master in the early years of schooling.

To summarize to this point: Written language facilitates the differentiation of what was said from what was meant whereas speech simply uses that sentence meaning as a transparent cue to the speaker's intention. That is the beginning, we suggest, of the analysis of the *literal* meaning of the sentences and the origins of the process of sentence accommodation, the reworking of experience to suit the requirement of the sentence. The sensitivity to what in fact was said, and its growing autonomy from what was meant, is, as we shall see a primary task for writing.

THE WRITING OF TEXT: LEARNING TO MAKE SENTENCE MEANING AN ADEQUATE REPRESENTATION OF SPEAKER'S MEANING

Our suggestions regarding writing are straightforward implications of the issues we raised in regard to reading. The problem in writing, as we suggested earlier, is to make the sentence meaning, what was said, an adequate and autonomous reflection of what was meant. We shall review very briefly some of the cultural-historical evidence on the evolution of writing which supports this view and then we shall suggest some of the ways that a child's oral conversational language must be transformed in the process of learning to cope with the requirements of written text.

Returning to the historical evidence cited earlier, we find that Havelock (1973) contrasts the use of the alphabetic script with its advantages of explicitness and unambiguity with that of the less efficient syllabaries that preceeded it:

The syllabic system . . . provided techniques for the recall of what was already familiar, not instruments for the formulating of novel statements which could further the exploration of new experiences (p. 238).

Indeed, the explicitness and unambiguity of the alphabetic writing system allowed the formation of explicit sentence meanings, meanings which were minimally open to interpretation. Perhaps we should clarify what we mean by *open to interpretation*. It is a concept which applies primarily to written texts. In conversation one may ask "What do you mean?" as a request for clarification of intentions, but one cannot do an exegetical analysis of a statement per se unless it is preserved. Rycroft (1975) goes so far as to claim that some statements like "Paris is the capital of France" have only one meaning, while other expressions as in poetry, novels and dreams have either no meaning or several meanings. This somewhat overstates the claim we wish to make. It may be that any statement can be assigned alternative representations. For instance the meaning of "John hit Mary" will vary somewhat depending on whether John is in a car, holding a bat or standing next to Mary. Statements themselves, then, are never completely autonomous (The idealized speaker/hearer postulated in linguistic theory may be the closest that one comes to a completely autonomous representation of meaning.) and the reader must use context as a guide to the correct interpretation.

The object in prose writing, however, is to make the contextualizing presuppositions explicit so that the reader derives the intended meaning from the statement. While sentences themselves cannot be treated as autonomous expressions of meaning, a single sentence meaning may be derived for a statement within a given context provided that context is explicit enough. Any particular statement then may have several alternative representations, but that statement in context may have only one. Whether a passage of prose can be an autonomous expression of meaning may also be open to debate. It may be possible that statements within a text can be so conventionalized and explicit as to make the text autonomous; more often however the meaning of a whole text will depend to a large degree on the context in which *it* is embedded; for example, the author's collected works, other works on the same topic and so on.

Once the possibility develops that text can specify its meanings, it is not simply that the reader must learn to *confine interpretation to the information in the text* as we have argued above. The converse responsibility falls upon the writer. His task becomes that of attempting to create autonomous text—to write in such a manner that the sentence meaning is an adequate representation of the intended meaning and therefore relies solely on conventionalized or explicit premises and is not open to personal interpretation. Moreover, the sentence has to withstand analysis and scrutiny of its presuppositions and implications. This fostered the use of prose as a form of extended statement called the essay in which both presuppositions and implications were explicitly drawn. This form of extended statement is produced by what may be called the essayist technique.

The essayist technique is a means for formulating abstract general statements from which a set of implications can be drawn—a development that has had important consequences for scientific and philosophical thought. Innis (1951) in examining the *bias of communication* noted that the rise of modern science was accompanied by a fundamental alteration in the use of language. The Royal Society founded in 1662, he says, "was concerned with the advancement of science and the improvement of the English language as a medium of prose. It demanded a 'mathematical plainness of language' and rejection of 'all amplifications, digression and swellings of style'" (p. 56). This reliance upon prose as the instrument of certain knowledge, was the central distinguishing feature of the British empiricist and associationist tradition. John Locke (1632–1704), whose *An essay concerning human understanding* was an early attempt at extended prose statement, represents the intellectual bias which originated at that time and that, to a large extent, characterizes our present use of schooled language. Knowledge was taken to be the product of an extended logical essay—the technique of examining and reexamining an assertion to determine all of its implications in a single coherent text.

It is interesting to note that when Locke began his criticism of human understanding he thought that he could write it on one sheet of paper in an evening—by the time he had exhausted the possibilities of the subject utilizing the new technology, the essay had taken twenty years and two volumes. Locke's *essayist* technique differed notably from the predominant writing style of the time. Ellul (1964) says: "An uninitiated reader who opens a scientific treatise on law, economy, medicine or history published between the sixteenth and eighteenth centuries is struck most forcibly by the complete absence of logical order (p. 39)...it was more a question of personal exchange than of taking an objective position" (p. 41). Locke made similar criticisms of the essays of Montaigne (Locke's Journal). The essay came to serve as an "exploratory device" for examining an old problem and in the course of that examination, producing new knowledge. While oral discussion as Havelock and Ong have suggested biased statements in the direction of proverbs, metaphors and witty sayings, written statements are uniquely adapted to an analysis of the implications of those statements. Havelock has suggested that if one's mental resources are utilized to remember the statement, there are no residual resources to reflect on the logical implications of those statements; writing the statement down released mental resources for other activities. Descartes (1911/1968) had earlier made the same point in a different context. In his "Rules for the direction of mind" he claimed that a written enumeration of logical steps of a proof was required for any complete science, since the memory alone often could not by itself, pass to true and certain judgments (pp. 19–20, 63–65). This hypothesis has somewhat obvious empirical implications. But the use of writing not only had the consequence of making the logical implications of statements more detectable, but also had the effect of altering the statement themselves. The tendency to look at statements to see what could be deduced from them, what they entailed, yielded implications—implications which were often out of phase with experience. The detection of such false implications could serve as an occasion for reformulating the original statement. If one considers the sort of statements that would survive the analysis of presuppositions and implications, one arrives at the criteria of sentences which had (1) great generality and which are (2) not easily falsifiable. These criteria are in fact those of general theories. The use of the essay method, therefore, was the occasion for the creation of such theories; that is, the essay is a machine to think with as I. A. Richards suggested (1925/1968).

The process of formulating statements and deriving their implications, testing or examining the truth of those implications and using the results to revise or generalize the original assertion is not only a characterization of the philosophical methods of the empiricist philosophers (it is perhaps less relevant that they were empiricists than that they were essayists), but also a characterization of the methods of deductive empirical science. In science, one can see most clearly the process of making assertions, deriving implications and verifying or falsifying these implications by empirical means. The result is not an *ordinary language,* it is the language refined and biased under the impact of literacy. It is the specialized tool of analytic thinking and explicit argument and it is the tool that has been adopted by science and philosophy and consequently by the schools. Standard English is not a *mother tongue* but rather the language of literate explicit logical prose; and more important, it is the language that the child learns not as a "mother tongue" in childhood but in the process of schooling—particularly in learning to read and write.

What then, would be uniquely required of children learning to write? From a commonsensical point of view the only requirement would be that the child learn to do with writing what he can already do in speech: writing is *canned* speech. Indeed, the simplest forms of writing may be little more than the recording of particular utterances which may occur in a dialogue. But the moment it is written down, its status changes in the direction we have suggested above—towards the creation of text. It's recipient may change; it may fall into the hands of others or the writer may read it himself. Secondly, the code for representing meaning is *stripped down* to the lexical and syntactic features shared within a group of speakers. Those other cues to meaning such as the context of the utterance and the prior, or presupposed knowledge shared by the speaker and listener is lost. So too are the prosodic cues which are so important in specifying the speech act which the sentence represents. For example, in print, the accusative "Did you spill your milk?' and the interrogative "Did you spill your milk?" come out looking equivalent.

What then are the transformations which utterances undergo in the process of becoming text? Following the suggestion above we shall discuss two of these, the transformation from listener to audience and listener to self and the transformation from intended meaning to expressed or sentence meaning.

First, as we suggested above, writing separates the speaker from the listener, frequently both in space and in time. One effect, already mentioned, is to weaken the interpersonal aspect of meaning. The other, of greater interest here is the transformation of the recipient of language from listener to audience. In conversation the participants are active and responsive, turn-taking in ways that are fully conventionalized (Schegloff, 1972). Writing turns the reader into an audience which may read (or listen) but not participate in the formulation or the production of the discourse. With the larger audience created by both oratory and writing (the audience is again dramatically increased in size by the invention of print and publishing as Watt (1957) has pointed out) the text has to be formulated in a way that is appropriate not only for a present participant (as in conversations) but also for the audience that may encounter that text. As such it cannot draw upon shared prior knowledge or on immediate supporting context but must be derived from shared myths, shared "first" principles or shared rules of argument. Further, the primary role of turn-taking in conversations when suspended results in the extended monologue speech. We have observed children at the early stage of such monologue speech in the *show-and-tell* sessions of kindergarten and in some of our attempts to elicit explanations and definitions of common objects or words from them. Many children have difficulty in shedding the familiar turn-taking rules appropriate for conversation. Thus, for example, the Experimenter frequently has to interject such dummy utterances as "Can you tell me anything else?" or "Yes?" in order to get the young child to continue in his monologue. When they do begin to detect the requirements of monologue speech it is frequently signalled by obvious changes in eye contact and intonation. The child comes to know that he is speaking *for the record*. Gumperz makes a similar observation about the obvious shift in language as a stewardess switches from an announcement to a conversation.

A second aspect of the transformation from listener to audience is that of the child coming to read what he himself has written. This we suggest is the beginning of reflective language. At first, and the weakness continues into adulthood, we repeatedly discover that the child on reading his writing believes that the sentence has said exactly what he had intended it to say. With practice, the child comes to be aware that the sentence, once it is written in a text, has its own *sentence meaning* which is specified by the lexical and syntactic properties of the sentence per se and by presuppositions made explicit in the preceding text. Moreover, this sentence meaning may or may not be an adequate representation of his intended meaning. Once he learns to handle these two layers of meaning, he is in the position to learn to progressively shape the former to meet the requirements of the latter just as in comprehension he has learned to rework his expectations or intentions to fit the requirements of the sentence meaning. It is the playing off of these two aspects of meaning, one more or less objective, the sentence meaning, and one more or less subjective, the speaker's meaning, that provides the greatest opportunity for the radical reworking of both language and meanings by means of writing.

The second major transformation of speech into writing is directly related to the first. The attempt to make *sentence meaning* an adequate representation of intended meaning or *speaker's meaning* requires a radical expansion of powers of lexical and syntactic meaning, an increase in the conventionalization of lexical and syntactic symbols. Since so much of the meaning in oral conversational meaning is carried by intonation and by context and by the continuous interaction with other participants and since these are all lost in a system that preserves only lexicon and syntax, the lexicon and syntax must be both expanded and formalized to meet the requirements of writing. We may illustrate this point in two ways. First, in conversation, the particular speech act being carried out is signalled by intonation or gesture. In writing, the speech act must be lexicalized via verbs and adverbs of manner, thus "... he demanded, accused, asserted, insisted, promised, persuaded" or "he said sternly, demandingly, loudly, softly, accusingly, obsequeously" etc.

Secondly, the lexicalized meaning comes to be predominant in written language and the conventionalized lexical meaning must be given its due. To illustrate in ordinary oral language, a double-negative may be treated as simply redundant; "She didn't have no sense" will be treated as an ungrammatical paraphrase of "She didn't have any sense". In written language, however, each negative is given its due lexical meaning such that "It isn't nothing" is paraphrased as "It is something". Similarly, to return to our earlier example, the disjunctive *or* has to be treated as differentiating mutually exclusive classes even if those distinct classes have to be purely conceptual to properly answer the question "Are there more rabbits or animals?" Whether such differences can be detected experimentally remains to be seen.

The central problem then, in learning to read is the relation between the language that the child brings to school and the language of formal texts. Text is explicit while the child's speech is somewhat eliptical; speech occurs in the context of non-linguistic activity while text provides its own context; speech is primarily rhetorical or interpersonally biased while text is primarily truth-functionally biased; speech hesitates at every point to adjust itself to the requirements of the listener while text is fixed and the child is required to come around to the requirements of the text; speech is an elaboration of previously shared meanings, while text specifies a set of meanings which are somewhat foreign and often incongruent with the world-view of the child.

When the child comes to school, he brings with him a set of procedures for assigning meanings to language primarily in terms of the interpersonal functions that language is to serve, while assuming a shared commonsense picture of reality. In learning to deal with text, both through reading it and writing it, he begins to specialize his language to better serve their ideational or logical functions. This specialization occurs we have suggested by first becoming aware of and then by developing skill in the playing off of the meanings in the language; the sentence meanings against the intentions or the speaker's meanings. When texts per se become adequate autonomous expressions of the speaker's meanings the writer will have unlocked one of the powers of the literate technology.

REFERENCES

Austin, J. L. *How do things with words.* Edited by J. O. Urmson. New York: Oxford University Press, 1962.

Bates, E., Camaioni, L. and Volterra, V. The acquisition of performatives prior to speech. *Merrill-Palmer Quarterly, 1975, 21,* 205–226.

Bellack, A. A., Kliebard, H. M., Hyman, R. T. and Smith, F. L. *The language of the classroom.* New York: Teacher's College Press, 1966.

Buhler, K. *Sprachtheorie.* Jana: Verlag, 1934.

Davis, M. Verifying logical and pragmatic implications in reading and listening. Unpublished Masters dissertation. Toronto: University of Toronto, 1978.

Descartes. *The philosophical works of Descartes* (translated by E. S. Haldane and G. R. T. Ross). London: Cambridge University Press, 1911/1968.

Ellul, J. *The technological society.* New York: Vintage Books, 1964.

Ervin-Tripp, S. Wait for me, Roller Skate. In S. Ervin-Tripp and C. Mitchell-Kernan (Eds.), *Child Discourse.* New York: Academic Press, 1977.

Feider, H. The grammar of asymmetric relations in child language and cognition. *Glossa, 1970, 4,* 197–205.

Feldman, C. F. and Wertsch, J. V. Context dependent properties of teachers' speech. (preprint)

Ford, W. G. The language of disjunction. Unpublished Doctoral dissertation. Toronto: University of Toronto, 1976.

Goodman, N. *Language of art: An approach to a theory of symbols.* Indianapolis: Bobbs-Merrill, 1968.

Goody, E. Towards a theory of questions. Draft of the Malinowski lecture, London School of Economics, August, 1975.

Goody, J. and Watt, I. The consequences of literacy. In J. Goody (Ed.), *Literacy in Traditional Societies.* Cambridge: Cambridge University Press, 1968.

Greenfield, P. M. Oral and written language: The consequences for cognitive development in Africa, the United States and England. *Language and Speech, 1972, 15,* 169–178.

Grice, H. P. Logic and conversation. In P. Cole and J. Morgan (Eds.), *Syntax and Semantics: Speech Acts.* New York: Academic Press, 1975.

Gumperz, J. J. *Language, social knowledge and interpersonal relations.* Berkeley: University of California.

Halliday, M. A. K. Language structure and language function. In J. Lyons (Ed.), *New Horizons in Linguistics.* England: Penguin Books, 1970.

Halliday, M. A. K. *Explorations in the functions of language.* London: Edward Arnold Ltd., 1974.

Halliday, M. A. K. Learning how to mean. In E. Lenneberg and E. Lenneberg (Eds.), *Foundations of Language Development, Vol. 2: A Multidisciplinary Approach.* Unesco: Academic Press, 1975.

Havelock, E. Prologue to Greek literacy. *Lectures in memory of Louise Taft Semple, second series, 1966–1971.* Cincinatti: University of Oklahoma Press for the University of Cincinatti Press, 1973.

Havelock, E. *Origins of western literacy.* Toronto: O. I. S. E. Press, 1951.

Innis, E. *The bias of communication.* Toronto: University of Toronto Press, 1951.

Lyons, J. *Introduction to theoretical linguistics.* Cambridge: Cambridge University Press, 1969.

McLuhan, M. *The Gutenberg galaxy.* Toronto: University of Toronto Press, 1962.

Mitchell-Kernan, C. and Kernan, K. T. Pragmatics of directive choice among children. In S. Ervin-Tripp and C. Mitchell-Kernan (Eds.), *Child Discourse.* New York: Academic Press, 1977.

Nelson, K. Structure and strategy in learning to talk. *Monographs of the Society for Research in Child Development,* 1973, *38,* Serial #149, Nos. 1–2.

Olson, D. R. Language use for communicating, instructing and thinking. In R. Freedle and J. B. Carroll (Eds.), *Language Comprehension and the Acquisition of Knowledge.* New York: Winston/Wiley, 1972.

Olson, D. R. From utterance to text: The bias of language in speech and writing. *Harvard Educational Review,* 1977, *47*(3), 257–281.

Olson, D. R. and Nickerson, N. The contexts of comprehension: On children's understanding of the relations between active and passive sentences. *Journal of Experimental Child Psychology,* 1977, *23,* 402–414.

Pike, R. and Olson, R. A question of *more* or *less. Child Development,* 1977, *48,* 579–586.

Popper, K. *Objective knowledge: An evolutionary approach.* Oxford: Clarendon Press, 1972.

Richards, I. A. *Principles of literary criticism.* New York: Harcourt, Brace and World Inc., 1925/1968.

Rycroft, C. *New York Review of Books.* April 3, 1975.

Schegloff, E. Sequencing in conversational openings. In J. Gumperz and D. Hymes (Eds.), *Directions in Sociolinguistics.* New York: Holt, 1972.

Scribner, S. The cognitive consequences of literacy. Unpublished manuscript, 1968.

Searle, J. R. *Speech acts: An essay in the philosophy of language.* Cambridge: Cambridge University Press, 1969.

Strawson, P. F. Intention and convention in speech acts. *Philosophical Review,* 1964, *73*(4), 439–460.

Watt, I. *The rise of the novel: Studies in Defoe, Richardson and Fielding.* Berkeley: University of California Press, 1957.

Author Index

Numbers in *italics* indicate pages with complete bibliographic information.

Subject Index